North Carolina
Real Estate Law

North Carolina Real Estate Law

Second Edition

Neal R. Bevans

PROFESSOR
WESTERN PIEDMONT COMMUNITY COLLEGE

CAROLINA ACADEMIC PRESS
Durham, North Carolina

Library of Congress Cataloging-in-Publication Data

Bevans, Neal R., 1961-
  North Carolina real estate law / Neal R. Bevans. -- 2nd ed.
     p. cm.
  ISBN 978-1-59460-755-4 (alk. paper)
 1. Real property--North Carolina. 2. Real estate business--Law and legislation--North
Carolina. 3. Vendors and purchasers--North Carolina. I. Title.

   KFN7512.B48 2009
   346.75604'3--dc22

                    2009024432

Carolina Academic Press
700 Kent Street
Durham, North Carolina 27701
Telephone (919) 489-7486
Fax (919) 493-5668
www.cap-press.com

For my parents,
Robert and Patricia Bevans

Contents

Preface

This is a textbook designed to teach the basics of North Carolina real estate law. Designed with both the instructor and paralegal students in mind, this text seeks a balance between two competing interests: theory and practice. The theoretical underpinnings of real estate law are essential for anyone studying the topic, but a student must also have a solid grasp of the practical aspects, from liens to title searches. The text includes not only discussions of the theoretical basics of real estate law, but also places a premium on practical applications, which form the core of a real estate practice.

North Carolina
Real Estate Law

Chapter 1

Introduction to Real Estate

Chapter Objectives

At the conclusion of this chapter, you should be able to:

- Explain the differences between real and personal property
- Explain the economic characteristics of real property
- Describe the real estate market
- List and explain the various classifications of real property
- Explain air and mineral rights as they relate to real property

I. Real Property versus Personal Property

All property can be divided into two different classifications: real property or personal property. Although the original meanings of these terms had more to do with the types of damages associated with the civil actions on which they were brought, in modern times real property refers to land and personal property refers to all other types of property. Under this definition, real property refers to land and anything permanently attached to the land, such as houses, trees and any other permanent fixtures. Personal property refers to non-real estate items, including everything from apples to automobiles.

The reason that the law makes a distinction between these two types of property is that the classification affects many of the rights and legal remedies available to the owners. For one thing, the way that ownership is transferred in real estate is different from the way it is transferred in personal property. We will see, time and again, that there is a great deal of symbolism in real estate transactions that arises directly from the fact that real estate is stationary. Because it cannot be moved, unlike personal property, there must be a symbolic transfer of physical possession. For personal property, possession often equates to ownership. Bills of sale, receipts and other indicia of title are helpful in proving ownership in personal property, but possession is the best way. In fact, the old common law rule that "possession is 9/10ths of the law" is a maxim that applies to personal property, not real property. Real property ownership interests are transferred by deed. The deed serves both as a record of the transfer of ownership rights and as a symbol of those rights.

Taxes are assessed differently between personal property and real property. Taxes on personal property are assessed by sale price (usually), while taxes on real property are based on the assessed value. In addition, the transfer of real estate interests must be in writing before they can legally be effective. This is a requirement of the **Statute of Frauds**, which we will explore in greater detail in future chapters. Most contracts transferring ownership in personal property are not required to be in writing. We will explore these, and many other important aspects of real estate law in future chapters.

> **Statute of Frauds:** Originally enacted in England and later adopted in all American states; it is a statute that requires certain types of contracts to be in writing before they can be enforced. Typical contracts covered by the Statute of Frauds include contracts to answer for the debt of another and transactions involving real estate.

In the past, the difference in classification between real and personal property also had an effect on probate law. Real property interests were transferred to heirs in different ways than personal property. Although many of those probate rules have changed, there are still important differences in the way that title to real property and personal property is transferred through estate administration.

Figure 1-1. The Differences between Real Property and Personal Property

Personal property	Real property
Usually refers to mobile items	Always refers to land
Often taxed on sale price	Often taxed on assessed value
Ownership is evidenced by possession	Ownership is evidence by deed
Statute of Frauds usually does not apply	Statute of Frauds applies to almost all transactions

---

A. What Makes Real Property So Unique?

Real property is a unique and specialized area of law for several reasons. Some of these reasons involve the physical characteristics of real estate itself, while others have more to do with financial considerations in purchasing, using, and investing in real estate. For one thing, real estate occupies a fixed point on the globe. Rivers may change course, houses may be torn down, but the underlying land remains where it is. Land that is submerged under a lake is still there, even if inaccessible.

Real property has its own set of laws, statutes, cases and judicial interpretations that make it an entirely separate branch of law. Many attorneys focus on this area to the exclusion of other areas of practice. It is as specialized as criminal defense, trademark or labor law. Attorneys and paralegals can spend decades in the practice of real property law and still not learn all of its aspects. During the course of this book, we will be discussing many of these legal implications, from easements to encroachments, from mortgages to metes and bounds descriptions. Along the way, we will learn a great deal about North Carolina property law, but it is impossible to condense all of the law of this complicated and far-ranging subject into a single textbook.

> Sidebar: One of the best treatises on North Carolina real property law is *Webster's Real Estate Law in North Carolina*. Considered by many to be the 'bible' of real estate law in the state, almost every legal professional who practices real property law in this state has a copy.

Real property is also unique because of the financial arrangements that are made in order to purchase real property. Later, we will examine the issue of deeds of trust and mortgages, and the legal impact of these financing instruments on real estate ownership.

B. Physical Characteristics of Land

Real property has several distinctive characteristics that separate it from personal property. For instance, land occupies a specific point on the globe. Unlike personal property, land is fixed and immovable. It always remains where it is and cannot be relocated. For this reason, it is the perfect vehicle for assessing taxes. In chapter 13, we will explore how real estate taxes are assessed on real property. Another physical characteristic includes the fact no two pieces of land are identical. Each one is unique, with its own special characteristics and chain of ownership. Because land is also located within different jurisdictions, the rules governing real estate transactions and ownership, even the method for recording deeds, varies considerably. Land falls under the law of whatever state it happens to be located in. A single individual can own land in any of a number of different states and each parcel will fall under different rules and statutes. An owner cannot claim, for instance, that simply because he is the owner of all of the tracts, the tracts should all fall under one set of rules. Land is governed by the law of the jurisdiction where it is located.

This fact controls some of the rules regarding lawsuits with real estate issues. There is, in fact, a specific term for this type of jurisdiction. It is called **In rem jurisdiction**. This is a court's power to enter decisions and rulings simply because the land involved happens to be within the court's geographic limits. In most lawsuits, the court's jurisdiction is based on personal jurisdiction, that is, power over the people involved in the suit. We will explore many of these jurisdictional questions in a later chapter.

In rem jurisdiction: A court's power to render decisions based on the location of the land within the court's geographic boundaries.

Figure 1-2. Physical Characteristics of Land

Land is
- Permanently fixed and immovable
- Unique; no two pieces of land are exactly the same
- Often used by local governments for assessing taxes

C. Economic Characteristics of Land

In addition to the unique physical characteristics, land also has some interesting economic characteristics. For one thing, land is an excellent investment. In the past, a person's wealth was measured by the extent of his real estate holdings. Land ownership continues to be an important source of investment income for many individuals. Purchasing a home is still one of the largest financial commitments that most people will ever make.

Sidebar: There is at least one major movie star who earns more money every year from his real estate investments than the millions he makes on making action films.

Land also presents some economic benefits to persons who are not wealthy. In fact, one of the best economic benefits of land ownership concerns the tax consequences of home ownership. In a later chapter, we will explore how a homeowner earns a substantial tax benefit from being able to deduct mortgage interest payments from a yearly income tax return.

Real estate also has another interesting aspect. As a general rule, it steadily appreciates in value. Because there is a fixed supply of land, and an ever-growing population, the laws of supply and demand put upward pressure on real estate prices. In many areas of the country, the value of a person's home and land increases about 6% a year. This makes land an attractive investment even for those with a moderately sized bank account.

In recent years, falling interest rates have also encouraged people to refinance their homes. This has the advantage of allowing an owner to receive some of the **equity** value in a home as cash that can be spent on other projects, or used to finance college tuition, vacations or any of a number of projects.

> **Equity:** A person's value in property once she has subtracted the amount owed on the property from its current fair market value.

Equity itself is another economic characteristic of land ownership. When we say that a person has equity in his home, what we are actually saying is that there is a difference between what the person owes on the home and what the home (and land) are actually worth.

Example: John purchased his home ten years ago and has been making regular, monthly mortgage payments on it ever since. His original loan amount was for $100,000. In the past ten years, he has lowered the balance of the loan to $85,000. However, because John's house has steadily been appreciating in value for the past ten years, the house is now worth $120,000. How much equity does John have?

Answer: John has $35,000 in equity. How do we arrive at this amount? Subtract the amount that John owes on the house from the current value $120,000 − $85,000 = $35,000.

Although this appears to be a simple paper gain, John can actually borrow against his equity. He can apply for a second mortgage, and borrow against this 'paper value' for real money.

II. The Real Estate Market

There is a market for land, just as there is a market for commodities or goods. The real estate market has its own rules and regulations. It also has participants, such as brokers, agents, loan correspondents, attorneys and paralegals, to name just a few. We will explore the role played by all of these participants as we develop the concepts of real estate.

We will begin our discussion of the real estate market with a straightforward example.

Maria and John Seller have grown tired of their house and they want to put it up for sale. They contact Real & Ready Real Estate Agency to discuss their options. Alma Agent tells them that if they sign a listing agreement with the agency, Real & Ready will advertise their house for sale, put a sign in their yard, list the home in the Multiple Listing Service and do some other activities to give the house the best chance of being sold.

Maria and John decide to put their house up for sale and they list it with Real & Ready. Bill Buyer sees the house listed and decides that he wishes to purchase the home. He contacts Real & Ready and gets the price particulars. Then he goes to a bank, meets with a loan officer and arranges financing to purchase the home.

This is a scenario that happens every day across the United States. We will use it to explore some of the basic issues involved in real estate transactions.

In any market there must be buyers and sellers. Maria and John are sellers and Bill is a buyer. Real & Ready is acting for Maria and John to list the house for sale. In exchange for this service, Real & Ready will receive a percentage of the total sale price (called a commission). The Sellers could have put their house up for sale on their own. For instance, they could have paid for an ad in the local newspaper, put a sign in their yard, and printed up brochures to distribute to various places around the city, but they have decided that they would prefer to leave the job of marketing their home to professionals. Later, we will see that listing a home with a real estate agent brings with it certain advantages that are almost impossible for an individual to match.

When Bill Buyer decides to purchase the Sellers' home, he goes to a bank to borrow money. Most people who buy homes must apply for a mortgage because few people have that much ready cash on hand. The real estate market then also involves banks and other lending institutions. The banks, in turn, rely on others to review a borrower's application, assess the possible risk of the transaction and estimate the value of the home.

In this book we will demonstrate the activities carried out by all of these people and show how they play a vital role in the real estate market in North Carolina. However, before we can expand on any of these issues in depth, it is important to have a firm understanding of the various classifications of real estate.

III. Classifying Property by Use

One of the oldest, and most easily understood, methods of classifying property is by the use to which it is put. There are several different categories of property, including residential property, condominiums, mobile homes, manufactured housing, commercial property, industrial and farm property. In the next few paragraphs, we will examine these various types of property classifications as they are defined under North Carolina law.

However, before we set out these classifications, we should examine exactly how the term "land" is defined in North Carolina. First of all, land is often used interchangeably with other terms such as "Real property," "**Tenements**" and "**Hereditaments**." These terms are not actually synonymous. Each has a specific meaning. A tenement, for example, refers not only to the land, but rights associated with the land, such as the right to use crops grown on the land. Hereditaments, on the other hand, refer to the rights in land (including tenements) that can be passed through probate proceedings.

> **Tenement:** A right or interest in the profits, crops or profits from land
>
> **Hereditament:** Property, rights or interests that are capable of being transferred by testate or intestate succession.
>
> Sidebar: For many people, land also implicitly contains the rights associated with owning it, such as the right to use, possess, sell, transfer, mortgage, etc.

For our purposes, we will define land as including the grass, soil, trees and anything else permanently affixed to the ground, including the soil underneath and the structures above. It also includes the owner's air rights in the space above the property. With this working definition of land, we will now examine specific sub-categories of land.

A. Unimproved Land

When land contains improvements, it means that it contains structures. Unimproved land has no buildings or other structures on it, so it is often referred to as raw land. Such property can be developed into any number of uses: homes, businesses, farms or parks. Once land has been improved, it can be re-classified into residential, farm, commercial, industrial or recreational. The categories are all based on the way in which the land is used.

B. Residential Property

Property categorized as residential refers to land that contains a structure that is designed to be used for personal living, such as a home. There are numerous subcategories of residential properties, including single and multi-family units, apartments, condominiums, mobile homes and manufactured homes.

1. Single-Family Homes

The category of single-family homes consists of the typical family home, as well as some variations, including duplexes, two family units sharing a single roof, triplexes (three family units), condominiums and townhouses. Usually when a residence goes above four family units sharing one roof it is characterized as an apartment.

2. Apartments

An apartment is a type of residential real estate consisting of five or more living units per building. In many large urban areas, there may be hundreds of apartments in any given complex. Apartments are popular because the residents have far less responsibility for maintaining the building, generally no responsibility for keeping up the grounds and do not require a large initial investment in order to move in. On the other hand, people who rent apartments do not receive the kind of financial advantages that homeowners receive. Apartment buildings can be a great financial investment for the owners, even when they provide few, if any, financial incentives for the residents. Apartment residents, or tenants, pay rent to the apartment owners in exchange for the use of the premises. We examine Landlord-tenant law in much greater detail in chapter 4.

C. Condominiums and Townhouses

A condominium resembles an apartment, but is actually more like a hybrid between a home and an apartment. In an apartment, the tenant does not have any ownership interests in the dwelling. He must seek permission from the owner before making a change to the interior. He is not allowed to make any changes to the exterior. A condominium gives the resident an ownership interest in the interior of the dwelling, but no rights to the exterior. As far as the interior goes, the resident has the same legal rights as a homeowner. Condominiums can be sold just like homes, but the only thing that is being sold is what is inside the four walls of the condo. No actual land is transferred in the sale of a condominium. The owner of a condominium receives the same favorable tax treatment as a homeowner, but does not have the worries about exterior upkeep and maintenance. Condominium owners must pay yearly fees to condominium associations who contract with maintenance firms to take care of yard work and maintain the various facilities. Condominiums often have pool and work-out facilities and are often very attractive to people who do not wish to worry about home maintenance, yet wish to receive the financial benefits of home ownership.

Condominiums have common areas that are owned and maintained by a homeowner's association. These common areas consist of the sidewalks connecting the various units and the amenities, such as swimming pools, tennis courts and walking trails. A condominium owner usually pays mandatory, annual dues to the homeowner's association to help defray the cost of maintaining these public areas.

> Sidebar: Condominiums in North Carolina fall under two different statutes. For a condominium constructed and opened prior to October 1, 1986, the relevant statute is the "Unit Ownership Act," NCGS §47A-1. For condominiums established after that date, the relevant statute is the "North Carolina Condominium Act," NCGS §47C-1-101.

1. Townhouses

Where condominium owners own only the inside of their individual units, townhouse owners own the entire unit, both the inside walls and the exterior walls. They also actually own the land that the townhouse is situated upon. There are no specific statutes that govern the creation of townhouses. Instead, townhouses are controlled by the same rules and statutes that govern single-family homes. If a townhouse development contains more than 20 units and was created after January 1, 1999, however, it does fall under the Planned Community Act, NCGS §47F-1-101, and must abide by its restrictions. However, it does not apply to planned communities having no more than 20 units or for lots not designed for residential purposes.[1]

2. Cooperatives

Cooperatives, unlike condominiums and townhouses, are often large tracts of land, or working farms in which several persons have an ownership interest. Unlike condominiums, both interior and exterior portions of the property are owned jointly by all of the members of the cooperative.

D. Mobile Homes under North Carolina Law

Mobile homes are usually considered to be personal property and not real property. This classification carries with it some very important consequences. The owner of a mobile home does not receive the same kind of favorable tax treatment as does a homeowner. The mobile home owner cannot, for instance, "write off" his mortgage interest payments for the year on his annual income tax return. This limitation can sometimes be overcome by removing the wheels of a mobile home and permanently affixing it to the

---

1. NCGS§47F-1-102(b)(2).

ground. Because houses are by their very nature permanently attached to the real estate—thus becoming real estate—anything that a mobile home owner can do to duplicate this process will push the mobile home further from a personal property classification towards a real property classification.

Because a mobile home is considered to be personal property, not real property, it comes under the jurisdiction of the Uniform Commercial Code, not state real property laws. The Uniform Commercial Code governs transactions in personal property, and has very specific rules about the transfer of ownership, shipment of goods and other issues. These rules differ from real property rules in significant ways. Some decisions from the North Carolina Court of Appeals and Supreme Court have actually held that a mobile home is a form of motor vehicle, not real estate.[2]

> Sidebar: Under North Carolina law, a mobile home is personal property, an item that is "movable at the time of identification to the contract for sale" and thus governed by the Uniform Commercial Code, not real property law.[3]

In order for a mobile home to change from a classification of personal property to real property, several actions must take place. Among them are:

(1) Whether the structure must comply with the N.C. Regulations for Manufactured/Mobile Homes, which are consistent with Housing and Urban Development (HUD) national regulations, or with the Building Code

(2) Whether the structure is attached to a permanent foundation

(3) Whether, after constructed, the structure can easily be moved or has to be moved like a site-built home

(4) Whether title to the home is registered with the N.C. Department of Motor Vehicles or title must be conveyed by a real property deed

(5) How the structure is delivered to the homesite.[4]

E. Manufactured Housing and "Kit" Homes

In recent years there has been a huge upswing in the creation of manufactured housing. Manufactured homes are houses in which all or some of the fabrication occurs away from the actual home site. In prior decades, manufactured housing fell into the same category as mobile homes. However, because these houses are actually permanently affixed to the real estate, and are never intended to be movable, most states have abolished the distinction between manufactured homes and traditional homes that are constructed entirely on the scene.

F. Commercial Property

Commercial property consists of lots and buildings specifically designed for businesses. They include a wide range of activities, from doctors' offices to malls. They all share some common features, however. First of all, they are not designed as living spaces. People do

---

2. *Hughes v. Young*, 115 N.C.App. 325, 328, 444 S.E.2d 248, 250 (1994).
3. *Alberti v. Manufactured Homes, Inc.*, 329 N.C. 727, 407 S.E.2d 819 (1991).
4. *Briggs v. Rankin*, 127 N.C.App. 477, 480–481, 491 S.E.2d 234, 237 (N.C.App.,1997).

not reside in commercial properties; they work in them. Secondly, they have design features not commonly seen in residential properties. They have parking lots, elevators, trade and customer entrances. They must often abide by specific federal and state regulations, such as the Americans with Disabilities Act that dictates design features such as handicapped parking and ramps for wheelchair access.

1. Retail/Wholesale

Retail and wholesale properties are designed for what most of us would term normal business purposes. These properties contain stores and shops of an almost infinite variety. Generally speaking, retail properties consist of stores, while wholesale properties consist of warehouses and supply depots where the merchandise is stored. Wholesale establishments are also where business owners go to order the merchandise that they will later sell on a retail basis to members of the public.

2. Shopping Centers and Malls

Malls and shopping centers have become increasingly important to the American economy in the past several decades. Some shopping malls occupy hundreds of square acres and function very much like small cities. There are numerous legal issues that revolve around the selection, construction and maintenance of such a huge facility. The same concerns are found, to a lesser extent, in shopping centers and other areas specifically devoted to the business of providing merchandise to the public.

G. Industrial Property

Another classification of property is industrial property. This consists of factories, research facilities and other production facilities. These structures often involve loud, noxious and often dangerous manufacturing practices. Because of these drawbacks, industrial properties are located at a distance from residential areas, where their offensive qualities can be muted, at least to an extent.

1. Industrial Parks

In recognition of the important role of industry, some towns and cities have created industrial parks, allowing numerous industries to work in a central location, often close to major highways, electrical systems and other parts of the infrastructure that will assist the businesses in their tasks.

2. Light Industry/Heavy Industry

Industrial property can be further broken down into two sub-categories, light industry and heavy industry. Light industry could be any manufacturing plant or factory that does not emit excessive odors, heavy traffic or loud noises. Heavy industry, on the other hand, would meet all of the qualifications of noxious odors, heavy traffic coming and going from the plant and excessive noise. Heavy industry is usually located as far from residential properties as possible, not only for these reasons, but also because some factories also emit pollution and use dangerous chemicals in their manufacturing processes.

H. Farm and Rural Property

Farm and rural property is a designation reserved for those areas devoted to agriculture. These areas are devoted to the cultivation of crops or livestock. They may also consist of vast tracts of land that are usually not zoned and are often taxed at a low rate.

I. Recreational Property

Recreational property consists of federal, state, county or city-owned parks. These areas have been specifically set aside for the use of citizens and residents. They are usually centered around wooded areas, lakes or rivers, where people can congregate to enjoy the outdoors.

J. Government-Owned Land

The final classification of real estate consists of the vast acreage in the United States that is owned by federal or state governments. Government-owned land takes up almost one-third of the land in the United States. If this amount seems large, consider how much acreage is taken up with military bases, colleges, federal, state and county buildings.

IV. Air and Mineral Rights

In this final section, we discuss some of the rights that are associated with land ownership. Air and mineral rights are some of the most basic rights that landowners possess and therefore we will discuss them in this introductory chapter. Later, we will explore the other rights conferred by land ownership.

A. Air Rights

Before the advent of aviation, the issue of air rights was not considered to be a very important topic. The traditional approach to air rights, as well as rights in the soil, was that ownership in the land extended as far above the ground as the owner wished and as far below the surface as possible. However, the invention of the airplane threw this approach into disarray. If we imagine that an invisible wall rises up from the boundaries of the property all the way to the sky, then every time a plane flies overhead a trespass occurs. However, such a ruling would have seriously hampered the development of air flight and an entire industry would have been still-born if such an interpretation were allowed to stand. North Carolina addressed this issue by modifying the rights of landowners to the airspace above their property, specifically air flights over private property. Consider Figure 1-3.

Figure 1-3. Air Rights in North Carolina

§ 63-12. Ownership of space

The ownership of the space above the lands and waters of this State is declared to be vested in the several owners of the surface beneath, subject to the right of flight described in G.S. 63-13.

§ 63-13. Lawfulness of flight

Flight in aircraft over the lands and waters of this State is lawful, unless at such a low altitude as to interfere with the then existing use to which the land or water, or the space over the land or water, is put by the owner, or unless so conducted as to be injurious to the health and happiness, or imminently dangerous to persons or property lawfully on the land or water beneath. The landing of an aircraft on the lands or waters of another, without his consent, is unlawful, except in the case of a forced landing.

Under the common law of real property in North Carolina, the rights of the owner were stated in a Latin phrase, "cujus est solum, ejus usque ad coelum et ad inferos." (The rights of the owner extend all the way to heaven and all the way to hell."[5] However, in the modern era, the definition of air rights has changed. These days, ownership in the air space above the actual boundaries of the land extends only as far as is necessary for the owner's use.

B. Mineral Rights

Mineral rights consist of a landowner's right to remove minerals, ores and other substances from the soil itself. These rights are part and parcel of the rights conferred by real estate ownership. However, like many other types of rights, they are subject to certain restrictions. Simply because someone has the right to remove minerals from his soil does not necessarily mean that he has the right to dig a mine. Mineral rights, like many other rights, may also be conveyed separately from the title to the land. A previous landowner might have sold the property's mineral rights to another. Such issues often require a title search to pin down the details.

Chapter Summary

Property can be divided into two broad categories: real property and personal property. Personal property consists of moveable items that are not permanently attached to real estate. Real property, on the other hand, consists of land and anything permanently affixed to land. Real estate has specific and unique characteristics. Among its physical characteristics: land occupies a fixed point on the globe, no two parcels of real estate are identical, and it is immobile. Among its economic characteristics are such things as real estate generally appreciates in value over time and makes an excellent investment. There is a market for real estate, just as there is a market for any other product. The real estate market consists of buyers and sellers, as well as the professionals involved in facilitating the sale, funding the sale, and making sure that the legalities of the sale are observed.

---

5. *Jones v. Loan Association*, 252 N.C. 626, 637, 114 S.E.2d 638, 646 (1960).

One way of classifying real estate is by the way that it is used. Unimproved land consists of vacant land that has no structures placed upon it. Land can be further categorized by residential property, which is reserved for living space; commercial property, which is designed for businesses; and industrial property, which is reserved for manufacturing and warehousing products. In North Carolina, a landowner's right to the airspace above his property extends only so far as is reasonable for him to use it. A landowner also has the right to remove the minerals from his soil, commonly referred to as mineral rights but with certain restrictions.

Relevant Case

Hensley v. Ray's Motor Co. of Forest City, Inc.[6]

CALABRIA, Judge.

On 8 January 1994, Gary Hensley ("plaintiff") entered into a contract to purchase a mobile home from Ray's Motor Company of Forest City, Inc., d/b/a Applegate Mobile Homes ("Applegate"), a North Carolina corporation engaged in the sale and distribution of mobile homes. The mobile home was manufactured by Southern Energy Homes of North Carolina, Inc., d/b/a Imperial Homes ("Imperial"). On the back of the contract, under "Additional Terms and Conditions," a one-year period of limitation clause provided the following: "I [the purchaser] understand and agree that if either of us [the purchaser and seller] should breach this contract—the other of us shall have only one year after the occurrence of that breach in which to commence an action for a breach of this contract." The mobile home was delivered and set up in April 1994. Plaintiff immediately noticed problems and notified the Department of Insurance. Throughout the 1994 calendar year, plaintiff continued to observe and report defects in the mobile home to Imperial, and Imperial made certain repairs. On 2 December 1994, Imperial and Applegate were notified by the Department of Insurance to investigate and correct problems reported by plaintiff. Thereafter, the Department of Insurance notified plaintiff they had received further information, and it was their belief the problems had been resolved. More importantly, the Department of Insurance provided plaintiff a final opportunity to respond if the information was unsatisfactory. When plaintiff failed to respond, the Department of Insurance closed plaintiff's file.

On 23 and 27 March 1995, Imperial wrote to plaintiff in order to set up a time when representatives from Imperial and Applegate could inspect plaintiff's home to address his remaining items of concern. Imperial attempted to contact plaintiff on at least five occasions in order to either view the home and have a contractor make the necessary repairs or settle the continuing problems with a cash settlement. Correspondence with plaintiff's attorney indicated plaintiff wanted a new mobile home or a full refund, both of which Imperial was unwilling to provide. On 27 October 1997, over three years after delivery of the home and discovery of the defects, plaintiff filed suit in Cleveland County District Court against Imperial and Applegate. Imperial and Applegate answered the complaint and moved to dismiss plaintiff's claims, asserting as an affirmative defense that the claim was barred by the statute of limitations. On 15 September 2000, the trial court granted Applegate's motion to dismiss but denied Imperial's motion to dismiss. Plaintiff filed a

---

6. 158 N.C.App. 261, 580 S.E.2d 721 (2003).

notice of voluntary dismissal against Imperial, then appealed the trial court's granting of Applegate's motion.

On appeal, plaintiff asserts three arguments: (I) the mobile home was an improvement to property; therefore, the applicable standard of limitations is six years; (II) the contract for the mobile home was primarily a contract for services; and (III) even if the contract is governed by North Carolina's Uniform Commercial Code ("UCC") as a transaction in goods, Applegate is estopped from pleading the statute of limitations.

I. Nature of the Mobile Home

Plaintiff contends the purchase and setup of a mobile home is an improvement to real property, requiring a six-year statute of limitations as an action to "recover damages based upon or arising out of the defective or unsafe condition of an improvement to real property...." N.C. Gen.Stat. § 1-50(a)(5) (2001).(citing Peoples Sav. & Loan Ass'n v. Citicorp Acceptance Co., 103 N.C.App. 762, 407 S.E.2d 251 (1991); King Homes, Inc. v. Bryson, 273 N.C. 84, 159 S.E.2d 329 (1968)).

We have stated that under some circumstances, mobile homes can be considered realty and thereby could constitute an improvement to real property. Hughes, 115 N.C.App. at 328, 444 S.E.2d at 250. These circumstances include where a plaintiff shows either (1) annexation of the mobile home to land with the intent that it be permanent or (2) circumstances surrounding the association between the land and the mobile home or the relationship between the parties otherwise justifies treating the mobile home as realty which is to become or is part of the land. Id. In the instant case, plaintiff has made no allegations that the mobile home was permanently affixed to the property. Additionally, plaintiff failed to show any relationship between the parties or between the land and the mobile home which would otherwise justify treating the mobile home as an improvement to the land on which it has been placed. In light of our traditional treatment of mobile homes and absent allegations justifying the characterization of the mobile home as realty, we hold the plaintiff's mobile home does not constitute an improvement to land.

II. Mixed Contract

Alternatively, plaintiff argues the sales contract for the mobile home was primarily a contract for services because Applegate delivered and set up the mobile home. The contract in the instant case is a mixed contract in that it encompassed both the sale of a good (i.e. the mobile home) and the provision of services (i.e. the delivery and setup). Accordingly, this Court must determine whether the contract is controlled by the UCC as a sale of goods or is governed by the common law of contracts as a service contract. The scope of the UCC is limited to "transactions in goods" and does not apply to contracts for the provision of services. N.C. Gen.Stat. § 25-2-102 (2001). The leading case on the UCC's applicability to contracts which involve both goods and services is Bonebrake v. Cox, 499 F.2d 951 (8th Cir.1974). In Bonebrake, the Court determined a contract for both goods and services should be considered a "sale of goods" under the UCC because [the] test for inclusion or exclusion is not whether [the sale of goods and the provision of services] are mixed, but, granting that they are mixed, whether their predominant factor, their thrust, their purpose, reasonably stated, is the rendition of service, with goods incidentally involved ... or is a transaction of sale, with labor incidentally involved.... Bonebrake, 499 F.2d at 960. While North Carolina has yet to expressly adopt the so-called "predominant factor" test set out in Bonebrake, previous decisions by North Carolina courts accord with the test. See, e.g., Batiste v. Home Products Corp., 32 N.C.App. 1, 6, 231 S.E.2d 269, 272 (1977) (examining the "essence of the relationship" between a physician and a patient to determine whether the prescription of medication by the physician was the sale of goods or the provision of services); HPS, Inc. v. All Wood Turning Corp., 21 N.C.App. 321, 324, 204 S.E.2d 188, 189 (1974) (treating a contract to furnish and install a boiler conversion system as a sale of goods). Surveying the jurisdictions which have addressed mixed contracts reveals the Bonebrake test has been overwhelmingly adopted. David J. Marchitelli, Annotation, Causes of Action Governed by Limitations Period in UCC § 2-725, 49 A.L.R.5th 1, 102–06 (1997). We expressly adopt the test enunciated in Bonebrake as the appropriate test to determine whether the UCC controls the rights of the parties to a contract involving both the sale of goods and the provision of services.

Accordingly, where the predominant factor of a contract is the rendition of services with the sale of goods incidentally involved, the UCC is not applicable. However, where the predominant factor of the contract is the sale of goods with the provision of services incidentally involved, the UCC controls.

Factors which have been used in determining whether a mixed contract should be governed by the UCC include the following: "(1) the language of the contract, (2) the nature of the business of the supplier, and (3) the intrinsic worth of the materials." See, e.g., Princess Cruises, Inc. v. General Elec. Co., 143 F.3d 828, 833 (4th Cir.1998); Parks v. Alteon, Inc., 161 F.Supp.2d 645, 649 (M.D.N.C.2001). Applying these factors here, we note the language of the contract deals primarily with the terms of sale, including the price, warranties, description and model of the mobile home, and options and accessories. The nature of Applegate's business is the sale and distribution of mobile homes. Finally, the intrinsic worth of the mobile home is approximately its fair market value or the purchase price. Accordingly, we hold the contract is predominantly a contract for the sale of goods, and the provisions of the UCC control the rights of the parties.

Under the UCC, "[a]n action for breach of any contract for sale must be commenced within four years after the cause of action has accrued. By the original agreement the parties may reduce the period of limitation to not less than one year but may not extend it." N.C. Gen.Stat. § 25-2-725(1) (2001). In the instant case, the contract of sale limited the time to bring an action for breach of contract to one year. Applegate delivered the mobile home in April 1994. Plaintiff became aware of the breach no later than his notification to the Department of Insurance in November 1994. Plaintiff failed to file suit for breach of contract until 27 October 1997, over three years after Applegate tendered delivery. Accordingly, we conclude plaintiff's action is barred by the applicable statute of limitations.

We have carefully considered plaintiff's remaining claims and found them to be without merit.

Affirmed.

Review Questions

1. Explain five important distinctions between real property and personal property.
2. What are three economic characteristics of real estate?
3. What is the difference between an apartment and a single-family residence?
4. Under North Carolina law, what is the difference between a condominium and a townhouse?
5. What are some of the economic characteristics of real estate?
6. Explain the holding in the "Relevant Case" excerpt in this chapter. What does the court say about the classification of mobile homes as real property or personal property?
7. How have air rights changed since the 1800s?
8. What does the term "Tenement" mean in the context of real property law?
9. Characterize the following as either real property or personal property:
   a. Trees growing on the lot
   b. The house situated on the lot
   c. A built-in deck
   d. Potted plants and shrubs sitting on that same deck
   e. Kitchen cabinets permanently mounted inside the house
10. What is the difference between mineral rights and air rights?
11. What is the Statute of Frauds?
12. Explain the rules about in rem jurisdiction as they apply to real estate.
13. What is equity? How can a person borrow against her equity in her home?
14. List and explain the various classifications of real property.

Assignment

1. In local newspapers, real estate booklets, Internet sites or other sources, locate as many different types of real property discussed in this chapter. They may be for sale or lease. Classify these various types of property according to the categories listed in this chapter. How many such properties can you find? Is there one category that you find more often than any other? If so, why?

2. Using Google Earth, locate a parcel of land near where you live and then locate the same parcel in the online tax records for your county. What information can you learn from the two sites? Can you identify the following?

- Total acreage
- Whether a house exists on the property?
- If there is a house, what is the square footage? How many bedrooms and bathrooms?

- Who owns the property?
- When did the current owners acquire the property?
- What is the deed book reference for the transaction where they acquired the property?
- What is the assessed value of the property?
- What was the sale price of the house when it was sold to the current owners?

Terms and Phrases

Equity   Air rights
Tenement   Mineral rights
Hereditament   Statute of Frauds
In rem jurisdiction   Unimproved land
Condominium   Apartment
Townhouse

Chapter 2

Real Estate Professions

Chapter Objectives

At the conclusion of this chapter, you should be able to:

- Explain the law of principal and agency
- Explain how the law of agency applies to real estate agents
- Explain the legal and ethical rules that govern real-estate agents
- List and explain the various other professions involved in real estate
- Explain the difference between a real-estate broker and a real estate salesperson in North Carolina

I. Introduction to Real Estate Professions

There are many different types of professions closely associated with real estate. If you examine a typical real estate transaction, you will see that there are several professions that owe their livelihood to the real estate market. We mentioned, in chapter one, John and Maria Seller's intention to put their house up for sale. In that case, they contacted a real estate agent to list their house for sale. In the next few sections we will outline the steps that the Sellers are going to follow and the various professionals with whom they will come into contact.

The Seller's first step after deciding to sell their home will probably be to contact a local real-estate agent and discuss the possibility of listing their house for sale with that company. The real estate agent will probably come out to the house, meet with John and Maria to discuss the process of listing their house for sale. One of the very first items to be addressed between the Sellers and the real estate agent is the sale price of the home. The Sellers would obviously like to sell the house for as much money as possible, while still setting a realistic price that would attract potential buyers. Although a real estate agent can probably give a good rough estimate of the value of the property, the smartest move would be to bring in a real estate appraiser. Once a sale price is agreed upon, the next step would be for the Sellers and the real estate agent to sign a broker's agreement.

A broker's agreement is the contract between the house seller and the agent setting out the duties and responsibilities of each. The real estate agent agrees to make all reasonable efforts to sell the house and when the agent produces a buyer who is able to purchase the home, the agent is entitled to a commission based on the final sale price of the house.

Once a buyer appears and wishes to purchase John's house, we find that there are additional people involved in the transaction. We will explore each of these professions and the role that they play. For one thing, the buyer will undoubtedly seek to finance the purchase of the home and that will involve going to a bank or lending institution.

So far, we have listed numerous people who are directly or indirectly involved in a real estate transaction. In this chapter, we will concentrate on those professions who are directly involved with real estate in North Carolina. As such, we will ignore professions such as interior designers and others who make a living indirectly through real estate, but are not directly involved in a real estate transaction.

II. The Law of Agency

There are times when persons, or corporations, are unwilling or unable to conduct business on their own behalf. In those situations, they will often select an agent to work for them. The person who hires an agent is referred to as the principal. The Principal-Agent relationship has existed in one form or another for thousands of years. While we will not be exploring the extensive history of the law of **agency**, it is important to begin this chapter with a general introduction to the topic, if, for no other reason, than most of the real estate professions mentioned in this chapter involve some type of principal-agent relationship.

Agency: A voluntary, consensual business relationship between two persons or business entities.

A. What Is an Agency Relationship?

An agency is created when the principal engages an agent to act on his or her behalf. The agent works for the principal and is empowered, to a degree, to negotiate and enter into binding agreements in the name of the principal. An agent's authority flows directly from the principal. Given the nature of an agency relationship, and that an agent can legally bind a principal to any of a number of business relationships, most principals and agents spell out the parameters of their agreement with great specificity. One such example of a principal-agency agreement is the brokerage agreement entered into by a home seller and a real estate broker. Real estate brokers act as agents for the homeowner, who is, obviously, the principal.

Agents are considered to have a fiduciary relationship to a principal. A fiduciary is someone who owes a legal and ethical duty to act in the best interests of another person. This fiduciary status creates several legal obligations on the part of the agent, including the obligation to act ethically, to act in the best interests of the principal and to avoid conflicts of interest, among others.

B. Creating an Agency Relationship

The most common way to create an agency relationship is through the express agreement of the parties. Normally, this agreement is spelled out in writing, where the principal specifies the types of actions that the agent will carry out and the extent of the agent's responsibilities. The agent will also want his or her method of compensation spelled out in equally clear detail in the agreement.

C. Agent's Duty to the Principal

Once the principal-agency relationship has been created, the law imposes specific duties that the agent owes to the principal. These duties are summarized in Figure 2-1.

Figure 2-1. Agent's Duties to Principal

1. Obedience
2. Care
3. Loyalty
4. Accounting

---

1. Obedience

An agent's first duty is to obey the instructions of the principal. The agent acts as the principal's representative and the agent's obedience to the principal's directions is one of the core requirements of a principal-agency relationship. The principal's instructions may be spelled out in detail, or the principal may simply rely on the education, training and experience of the agent in bringing about the best possible result.

2. Care

While the agent is working for the principal, the agent has a duty of acting with diligence and due care in performing his or her duties. In fact, the agent will be held to the standard of what other reasonable and prudent agents in the same situation would have done. If the agent fails to exercise that degree of care, the principal may have an action against the agent for negligence.

3. Loyalty

Another core requirement of the agency relationship is the loyalty owed by the agent to the principal. An agent must always act in the best interests of the principal. This duty requires that when an agent is faced with a conflict of interest, such as when the interests of the agent and the interests of the principal are at cross-purposes, the agent should withdraw from representing the principal. The duty of loyalty also requires an agent to ensure that the interests of the principal are placed foremost in the business relationship. Later, when we discuss the specifics of a real estate broker's relationship with a homeowner, we will see that when a buyer confides relevant information to the broker, the broker is required to pass that information along to the homeowner/principal.

The duty of loyalty also requires that an agent avoid self-dealing. This is a term that refers to an agent using the principal-agency relationship to enrich himself at the expense of the principal.

Scenario #1. Avoiding Self Dealing

While Bill Broker is representing Sal Seller, Bill learns that Sal is planning on buying some tracts of land across town. Sal is desperate to acquire these tracts and will pay almost any price to get them. Bill secretly purchases these tracts for a modest sum and then offers them to Sal at twice the price that he paid. Bill is using the information that he gained from his agency relationship to enrich himself at the expense of his principal. Such an action is a violation of the agency relationship and would open Bill up to civil action by Sal (and possible sanction by the Real Estate Commission).

4. Accounting

Among the more mundane duties of the agent is the responsibility of keeping track of all financial arrangements between the agent and the principal. This duty of accounting extends to any financial arrangement, negotiation, earnest money or other financial exchange that occurs within the confines of the agent-principal relationship.

D. Ratification

In discussing agency relationships, what occurs when the agent exceeds his or her authority? Suppose, for example, that an agent is simply authorized to provide information to a particular buyer and then to relay any offers made by the buyer. However, when the buyer makes what the agent believes to be a particularly good offer, the agent accepts on behalf of the principal. The agent was not authorized to accept and when the principal learns of this action, the principal would be within his rights to take action against the agent for exceeding the agent's authority. However, suppose that the principal agrees with the agent's actions, even while he acknowledges that the agent had no authority to act? In such a situation, the legal doctrine of ratification becomes important.

> **Ratification:** Confirmation of a prior act that may not have been authorized, but to which the principal agrees to be bound.

When an agent lacks authority for an action, but the principal agrees to abide by those actions, the principal is said to have ratified the agent's behavior. Ratification is important because it confers the principal's agreement on the earlier, unapproved action, and results in a legally binding agreement. However, an agent should not exceed his or her authority in the belief that the principal will later ratify the actions. The principal might just as easily declare the agent's actions to be invalid under their arrangement and the result might well be catastrophic for the agent. In such a scenario, the agent could be liable to the principal and the buyer.

E. Agent's Duty to Third Parties

The rules change when the agent is dealing with a party other than the principal. An agent's duties to third parties include:

- The duty of honesty and fair dealing
- The duty not to commit fraud
- The duty to avoid negligent misrepresentation.

1. The Duty of Honesty and Fair Dealing

An agent has a responsibility to deal with third parties in an honest and fair way. On a practical level, an agent must avoid deceptive trade practices and other unfair (or illegal) practices. This duty is also strongly connected with the second and third duty to third parties, the duty to avoid fraud and misrepresentation.

2. Duty Not to Commit Fraud

Fraud is a legal action that can be brought when an agent commits any act or fails to act in such a way that conceals material facts. The act must cause injury to the third party or give the agent an unjustified or unconscionable advantage.

Figure 2-2. The Legal Elements of Fraud

Fraud involves proof of the following:
- The agent made a representation of a material fact or concealed a fact
- The representation was false
- The agent knew the representation was false
- The agent made the representation with the intent that the other party would rely on it
- The other party's reliance on the representation was reasonable under the circumstances
- The other party suffered injury from his reliance on the representation.

---

a. Material Facts

One of the most important elements in a fraud action is proof that the representation involved a **material fact**. A material fact is a fact that is a central point in the agreement, or a critical factor in the negotiations. When an agent states that he is representing a certain principal, when in fact he is not, this is a material fact and will leave the agent open to a claim of fraud.

i. Salesmanship and Puffing

The types of statements that salespersons make in discussing a sale usually do not qualify as fraud. It is not fraud to claim that, "this house is the best on the market," or "I don't know when I've seen a more beautiful yard." These statements are commonly referred to as "puffing" and no reasonable person would believe that they are statements of actual fact. On the other hand, it is fraud to claim that a house has never suffered from roof damage, when in fact it has, or that last year's floods "never touched this place," when in fact the basement and first floor were flooded.

> **Material fact:** A critical fact in the contract or negotiations, one that, if truthfully revealed, might abort the transaction.

> **Puffing:** Typical sales exaggerations about an item for sale; common sales statements that do not misrepresent material facts.

3. Duty to Avoid Negligent Misrepresentation

In many ways, negligent misrepresentation and fraud are quite similar, with one important exception. Fraud involves an intentional action. When an agent commits fraud, he or she is actively lying. In negligent misrepresentation, a statement is made without knowledge of its veracity, or with reckless disregard for the truth. The important distinction between negligent misrepresentation and fraud is that an agent can be liable under negligent misrepresentation for a statement that the agent actually believed was true, but one that the agent did not verify. The elements of negligent misrepresentation are presented in Figure 2-3.

Figure 2-3. The Legal Elements of Negligent Misrepresentation

- The agent made a false statement
- The agent believed that the statement was true
- But the agent had no reasonable grounds for this belief or made the statement in reckless disregard of the truth
- A third party suffered a financial loss because of reasonable reliance on this false statement

---

F. Principal's Duty to Agent

So far, we have discussed the wide range of duties owed by agents to principals. However, the principal also has some responsibilities to the agent, even if they are light when compared to the duties of the agent to the principal.

A principal has the following duties to an agent:

1. Duty to compensate the agent

2. Duty not to unfairly injure the agent's reputation

3. Duty to cooperate

1. Duty to Compensate the Agent

Among the more obvious duties owed by a principal to an agent is the duty to compensate the agent for services rendered. When the agent performs as agreed, the agent is due compensation for his or her services. A failure by the principal to pay the agent opens the principal up for a lawsuit to collect the agent's fees. (See the "Relevant Case" excerpt at the end of this chapter.) This obligation to compensate the agent involves not only payment for services rendered, but also for the agent's expenses in carrying about his duties.

2. Duty Not to Unfairly Injure the Agent's Reputation

The principal is also under an obligation not to unfairly injure the agent's reputation. A principal is liable to an agent when the principal claims that the agent failed to adequately complete an assignment, when the agent actually did complete it in satisfactory fashion. In many ways, an action under this duty resembles a suit for defamation.

3. Duty to Cooperate

Finally, the principal has a duty to cooperate with the agent as the agent attempts to carry out the principal's business. A principal is not permitted to throw obstructions in the agent's way in order to avoid paying the agent's compensation when he or she fails to complete the assignment. A direct corollary of this obligation is that a principal cannot terminate the relationship for unjust or frivolous reasons. (This chapter's "Relevant Case" explores this issue.)

G. Applying Agency Law to Real Estate Transactions

Up to this point, our discussion of agency law has been in general terms. Now it is time to apply this general law to the specific area of real estate agents. A real estate agent is a true agent, as that term is defined under the law. However, real estate agents not only owe all of the previously discussed duties to their clients, they also owe additional duties. Although we use the term "agent" to refer to real estate professionals such as brokers and salespersons, it is important to note that in a strict sense, the duties and obligations of these real estate professionals go beyond the dictates of agency law. There are additional duties imposed on these individuals by the North Carolina Real Estate Commission. A real estate professional has not only the typical duties imposed in an agency relationship, but also the requirements of disclosure, consumer protection and even federal law that make a licensed real estate broker or salesperson begin to resemble an attorney more so than a commissioned middleman. It is these additional duties that we will explore in this section.

1. A Real Estate Agent's Duty of Care

A real estate agent's duty of care is actually a broader legal obligation than set out for other types of agents. Real estate agents must use skill, care and diligence in the performance of their duties.

A homeowner hires an agent to take advantage of the agent's education, training and skill in real estate matters. In North Carolina, agents are licensed by the state. With that greater skill comes greater responsibility. Agents must show reasonable diligence in performing their duties. The North Carolina Supreme Court has weighed in on this issue by stating that a real estate broker "is bound to exercise reasonable care and skill, or the care and skill ordinarily possessed and used by other persons employed in a similar undertaking. He must exert himself with reasonable diligence on his principal's behalf, and is bound to obtain for the latter the most advantageous bargain possible under the circumstances of the particular situation. Thus, a broker employed to sell property has the specific duty of exercising reasonable care and diligence to effect a sale to the best advantage of the principal—that is, on the best terms and at the best price possible."[1]

2. An Agent's Responsibility to Disclose Information

An agent must make full and complete disclosure to the principal of any information that is or may become relevant to the real estate transaction. This includes information relayed to the agent from the buyer. In North Carolina, the appellate courts have established this duty as, "A broker has a duty not to conceal from the purchasers any material facts and to make full and open disclosure of all such information."[2] In fact, "A broker who

---

1. *Carver v. Lykes*, 262 N.C. 345, 355, 137 S.E.2d 139, 147 (1964).
2. *Hearne v. Statesville Lodge No. 687*, 143 N.C.App. 560, 561, 546 S.E.2d 414, 415 (2001).

makes a fraudulent misrepresentation or who conceals a material fact when there is a duty to speak to a prospective purchaser in connection with the sale of the principal's property is personally liable to the purchaser notwithstanding that the broker was acting in the capacity of agent for the seller."[3]

III. Real Estate Agents under North Carolina Law

Before a person can act as an agent in a real estate transaction, he or she must be licensed by the North Carolina Real Estate Commission. The commission recognizes only one type of real estate agent: broker. A broker can carry out the full range of activities normally associated with a real estate agent. Salespersons, a classification that existed prior to 2006, were eliminated by G.S. §93A-4.3.

The real estate agent usually does not work independently. The agent is often affiliated with a larger company that has other individuals, including secretaries, other real estate agents and support staff necessary to maintain a sizable office. Because of this, the North Carolina Real Estate Commission recognizes a third category of agent: the firm. The NCREC issues firm licenses to a business to act as a broker.

A. Real Estate Brokers

A broker, whether as an individual or a firm, is responsible for representing the interests of the principal in real estate transactions. These transactions can involve sale, lease and purchases. Principals can be buyers, sellers or, in some instances, both. Because brokers and salespersons can carry out the same activities (if the salesperson is acting under the supervision of a broker) we will refer to the brokers, salespersons and firms collectively as the real estate *agent*.

1. Different Types of Real Estate Agents

North Carolina recognizes three different types of real estate agents: seller's agents, buyer's agents and dual agents. Each of these agency relationships carry their own set of specific legal issues. We will address each one in turn.

a. Seller's Agent

The seller's agent is easily the most recognizable and the most traditional. A seller's agent is hired by a person who wishes to sell his or her home and the agent and the seller enter into a listing agreement (see chapter 8, Real Estate Contracts) where the seller agrees to use the agent's services to list the home for sale, make it available for potential buyers and to disclose legally necessary information. In exchange for this service, the agent will be reimbursed with a commission. In the straightforward language of the North Carolina Real Estate Commission, a seller's agent has specific duties:

The listing firm and its agents must

- promote your best interests

---

3. *Johnson v. Beverly-Hanks & Associates, Inc.*, 328 N.C. 202, 400 S.E.2d 38 (1991).

- be loyal to you
- follow your lawful instructions
- provide you with all material facts that could influence your decisions
- use reasonable skill, care and diligence, and
- account for all monies they handle for you.[4]

The seller's agent is the type of agency that we can easily recognize from the general description of principal-agency law discussed earlier in this chapter. Traditionally, this was the only agency relationship seen in real estate sales, but in recent years other types of agency relationships have been established and have been recognized by the North Carolina Real Estate Commission. One such innovation is the buyer's agent.

b. Buyer's Agent

As its name suggests, a buyer's agent is not employed by the seller but works for the buyer. A buyer's agent works with the principal to secure the best possible property at the best possible price for the buyer. A buyer's agent owes his or her duties to the buyer, not the seller and also earns a commission from the buyer. Because of the potential legal difficulties such an arrangement can create, the North Carolina Real Estate Commission requires all agents to disclose their legal status to their principals and also requires the principals to sign off on this arrangement in a brochure that agents must present to their principals. Again, the North Carolina Real Estate Commission has created a no-nonsense guide for those individuals seeking to hire a buyer's agent. See Figure 2-4.[5]

Figure 2-4. Duties of Buyer's Agents in North Carolina

BUYERS

When buying real estate, you may have several choices as to how you want a real estate firm and its agents to work with you. For example, you may want them to represent only you (as a **buyer's agent**). You may be willing for them to represent both you and the seller at the same time (as a **dual agent**). Or you may agree to let them represent only the seller (**seller's agent** or **subagent**). Some agents will offer you a choice of these services. Others may not.

Buyer's Agent

Duties to Buyer:

If the real estate firm and its agents represent you, they must
- promote your best interests
- be loyal to you
- follow your lawful instructions
- provide you with all material facts that could influence your decisions
- use reasonable skill, care and diligence, and
- account for all monies they handle for you.

Once you have agreed (either orally or in writing) for the firm and its agents to be your buyer's agent, they may not give any confidential information about you to sellers or their agents without your permission so long as they represent you. But until you make this agreement with your buyer's agent, you should avoid telling the agent anything you would not want a seller to know.

---

4. http://www.ncrec.state.nc.us/publications-bulletins/WorkingWith.html.
5. http://www.ncrec.state.nc.us/publications-bulletins/WorkingWith.html.

c. Dual Agents

North Carolina also recognizes that there are times when a single individual may represent both the buyer and seller in a transaction. The agent is strictly required to disclose all potential conflicts to both parties and is required to obtain written permission from both before being allowed to proceed in such a transaction. Agents are not relieved of their duties to represent the best interests of both parties in such a transaction, although the practical difficulties of this would seem obvious.

d. Rules and Regulations Governing Real Estate Agents

In addition to licensing new applicants, the Commission is also responsible for promulgating rules and regulations that govern the activities of agents. The Commission is specifically authorized to take disciplinary action against agents who break these rules. Some of the actions that will result in disciplinary action include:

- Negligent or willful misrepresentations about material facts
- Making false promises designed to influence or persuade a person
- Dual agency
- Failing to account for client money or absconding with client funds. For additional examples, see Figure 2-5.

B. The North Carolina Real Estate Commission

The government entity responsible for licensing and other matters related to real estate agents is the North Carolina Real Estate Commission. This agency not only governs practicing agents, but also provides educational programs and conducts licensure examinations for people seeking to become either brokers or agents. The North Carolina statute governing the Real Estate Commission is NCGS §93A-3.

C. Becoming a Broker in North Carolina

In order to become a real-estate agent in North Carolina a person must meet the following qualifications:

- Must be at least 18 years of age
- Must be a United States citizen
- Must have a valid Social Security number
- Must meet the Commission standard of good moral character
- Must successfully complete the real estate education requirements
- Must attain a passing score on the real estate license examination

In order to sit for the broker exam, an applicant must have completed a 67-hour Salesperson Pre-license Course and a 60-hour Broker Pre-license Course. Both courses must be offered at a Commission-approved school. Obviously, the applicant must successfully complete both courses.

Figure 2-5. NCGS§ 93A-2. Definitions and Exceptions

(a) A real estate broker within the meaning of this Chapter is any person, partnership, corporation, limited liability company, association, or other business entity who for a compensation or valuable consideration or promise thereof lists or offers to list, sells or offers to sell, buys or offers to buy, auctions or offers to auction (specifically not including a mere crier of sales), or negotiates the purchase or sale or exchange of real estate, or who leases or offers to lease, or who sells or offers to sell leases of whatever character, or rents or offers to rent any real estate or the improvement thereon, for others.

(1) The term broker in charge within the meaning of this Chapter means a real estate broker who has been designated as the broker having responsibility for the supervision of real estate salespersons engaged in real estate brokerage at a particular real estate office and for other administrative and supervisory duties as the Commission shall prescribe by rule.

(2) The term provisional broker within the meaning of this Chapter means a real estate broker who, pending acquisition and documentation to the Commission of the education or experience prescribed by either G.S. 93A 4(a1) or G.S. 93A 4.3, must be supervised by a broker in charge when performing any act for which a real estate license is required.

(b) The term real estate salesperson within the meaning of this Chapter shall mean and include any person who was formerly licensed by the Commission as a real estate salesperson before April 1, 2006.

(c) The provisions of this Chapter do not apply to and do not include:

(1) Any person, partnership, corporation, limited liability company, association, or other business entity who, as owner or lessor, shall perform any of the acts aforesaid with reference to property owned or leased by them, where the acts are performed in the regular course of or as incident to the management of that property and the investment therein.

(2) Any person acting as an attorney in fact under a duly executed power of attorney from the owner authorizing the final consummation of performance of any contract for the sale, lease or exchange of real estate.

(3) The acts or services of an attorney at law.

(4) Any person, while acting as a receiver, trustee in bankruptcy, guardian, administrator or executor or any person acting under order of any court.

(5) Any person, while acting as a trustee under a trust agreement, deed of trust or will, or that person's regular salaried employees.

(6) Any salaried person employed by a licensed real estate broker, for and on behalf of the owner of any real estate or the improvements thereon, which the licensed broker has contracted to manage for the owner, if the salaried employee's employment is limited to: exhibiting units on the real estate to prospective tenants; providing the prospective tenants with information about the lease of the units; accepting applications for lease of the units; completing and executing preprinted form leases; and accepting security deposits and rental payments for the units only when the deposits and rental payments are made payable to the owner or the broker employed by the owner. The salaried employee shall not negotiate the amount of security deposits or rental payments and shall not negotiate leases or any rental agreements on behalf of the owner or broker.

(7) Any owner who personally leases or sells the owner's own property.

(8) Any housing authority organized in accordance with the provisions of Chapter 157 of the General Statutes and any regular salaried employees of the housing authority when performing acts authorized in this Chapter as to any property owned or leased by the housing authority. This exception shall not apply to any person, partnership, corporation, limited liability company, association, or other business entity that contracts with a housing authority to sell or manage property owned or leased by the housing authority.

The licensing examination is four hours long. A passing score of 75% is required. That translates into correctly answering 82 out of 110 questions. The bulk of the test questions come from basic real estate law and brokerage practice. See Figure 2-6.

Figure 2-6. Numbers of Questions on the NC Real Estate Licensing Exam

Real Estate Law and Brokerage Practice	40–48 questions
Miscellaneous Topics	9–13
NC Real Estate licensing law, commission rules, trust account guidelines	9–13
Real estate finance	12–16
Real estate valuation	8–12
Real estate math problems	17–23
Total	110

D. Sanctioning Real Estate Brokers

If a real estate agent violates any of the rules and regulations governing real estate practice, there are several possible sanctions that could be brought to bear. For instance, the Commission could temporarily suspend the agent's license to practice. In particularly egregious cases, the agent's license may be permanently revoked. In addition to losing his or her livelihood, the offending agent may also be civilly liable to the client or other person injured by the agent's actions. Finally, an agent's actions might also rise to the level of a criminal action and therefore could be prosecuted for a crime.

1. Ethical Duties of Real Estate Agents

Among the legal duties owed by real estate agents to their clients, there are also ethical concerns. Real estate agents in North Carolina have a strict code of ethics that prevents real estate agents from working against a client's interests.

Figure 2-7. Summary of Possible Sanctions against Real Estate Agents

- Temporary or permanent suspension of license
- Civil liability to the client or third party
- Criminal liability

E. Continuing Education Requirements for Real Estate Brokers

In addition to the other rules already discussed, an agent is also required to periodically attend education and/or ethics courses as part of a continuing education program.

F. Services Provided by Real Estate Agents

In later chapters, we explore the basic contractual agreement between the agent and seller, but a word about the agent's services is also appropriate here. When a seller contracts with a real estate agent, the seller will benefit from several services offered by the agent. Among these services are:

- Advertising and marketing the property
- Listing the property in the Multiple Listing Service
- Locating buyers who are ready, willing and able to purchase the real estate

1. Multiple Listing Service

The Multiple Listing Service is an invaluable aid to real estate agents. The MLS is essentially a database of available properties. It both advertises the parcel and offers an incentive to other agents to help sell the property. The advertisement portion of the MLS is seen in the extensive descriptions (and accompanying photograph) of the parcel for sale. An MLS listing has information about lot size, internal and external features of the residence, information about total square footage, bathrooms, bedrooms and many other items. The incentive offered by the MLS entry is that other real estate agents in the area will see the listing and will share in the commission if they can produce a buyer for the property. These days, the MLS is not only in print form, but is also available on computer networks for licensed real estate agents. The MLS continues to be an extremely valuable resource for people buying or selling real estate.

> Sidebar: The term "hot sheet" is still used for newly listed properties on the Multiple Listing Service. The term originally referred to the hard copy of the MLS that came out at intervals between the publications of the entire MLS for a region. However, the "hot sheet" now refers to a recently posted property on the computer-network version of the MLS.

IV. Real Estate Professions

In the following sections, we will describe many of the different types of professionals involved at every phase of a real estate transaction. We will begin with real estate investors.

A. Real Estate Investors

We have said that real estate can be a good place to invest money. However, the real estate market has some important limitations. For one thing, there are tax consequences and many divergent financial issues to consider before launching a career as a real estate tycoon.

1. Small Investors and "Fixer-Uppers"

There are some individuals who earn their income exclusively from real estate. Whether they are in the business of acquiring properties to hold as rental units or to resell, these small investors have to do a lot of work to make a decent living. Later, when we discuss the tax consequences of real estate sales, we will see that although homeowners enjoy substantial tax benefits for their residences, real estate investors generally do not.

Some people are in the business of buying foreclosed properties. Pending foreclosures are advertised in local newspapers and anyone who has the money, and the time, can bid at one of these auctions and acquire full title to the property.

Other individuals acquire houses and lots with the idea of fixing them up to resell them. This can sometimes be lucrative, but more often than not involves a lot of work for a relatively small return on the investment. In order to make a decent living, these investors must turn over several homes year. There are also federal and state tax laws to consider. We will discuss capital gains in a future chapter.

2. Real Estate Investment Trusts

A real estate investment trust (REIT) resembles a mutual fund. Members of a real estate trust own shares or certificates that they can buy and sell. These shares represent the percentage of ownership in the real estate investment trust. The trust devotes itself to the business of purchasing, managing and selling tracts of real estate for profit.

B. Loan Officers

Loan officers play a critical role in the sale and purchase of real estate for the simple reason that most people do not have thousands of dollars of ready cash on hand to purchase real estate. Most buyers must go to a local banker or other lending institution and borrow funds for such a purchase. Although we use the term 'loan officer' in this section, there are actually several positions associated with mortgage lending. Lending institutions have individuals who act as customer service representatives who meet with potential borrowers, underwriters to evaluate the risk of loaning the money to the buyer, committees to review applications and make decisions about loans and a host of other individuals involved throughout the loan application and processing period.

C. Appraisers

A discussion of appraisers could easily fill an entire book of its own. Appraisers are in the business of evaluating properties and assessing fair market value of real estate. Among an appraiser's many duties is assessing the value of the real estate that a buyer intends to acquire. The bank will often bring in an appraiser to make sure the real estate is worth what the buyer is paying for it. After all, the bank is lending money based on the value of the property and it is only prudent to establish that value before loaning money.

In a typical residential sale, the real estate appraiser will come to the seller's house, inspect it inside and out and list the features available in the home. The appraiser uses several techniques to derive a final value on the real estate. Among these techniques is a comparison of this parcel with other, similar parcels. Appraisers often visit the Registrar of Deeds office and the Tax office in order to keep their information as up to date as possible.

This question of how to assess the value of real estate is an important question. Not only is it an important consideration for homeowners wishing to get as much profit as possible from the sale of their homes, but it is also important for several other aspects of real estate transactions. Mortgage lenders will also wish to have the house evaluated for value before loaning funds to purchase it. Because the home is essentially the collateral for the loan, lenders always want to know that the money they have lent is potentially recoverable from a foreclosure sale on the property should the borrower fail to pay.

Real estate valuation is also important for tax purposes. In chapter 13, when we discuss real estate taxation in North Carolina, we will see that real property taxes are assessed on property value. Putting a price on real estate is also important for other reasons. But to return to our first example, what are some of the ways that real estate agents, and others, put a value on real property?

1. Real Estate Valuation

In order to have any real merit, the process of putting a monetary value on property must be based on some type of objective criteria. It is not enough for an agent simply to say, "I think that you can get X for your home." Such an assessment runs the risk of grossly under- or over-estimating the value of the client's home and can contribute to serious problems later on. A house that is over-priced, for example, is unlikely to sell. A house that is under-priced will leave the homeowner dissatisfied with the resultant profit. One way of avoiding this problem is to have the home evaluated by a professional appraiser.

2. Real Estate Appraisal

A professional appraiser is in the business of assigning value to real estate. An appraiser must be licensed by the state. The North Carolina Appraisal Board governs all aspects of licensing and regulating appraisers. See Figure 2-8.

Figure 2-8. North Carolina Statutes Governing Appraisals

§93E-1-2.1. Registration, license, or certificate required of real estate appraisers

Beginning October 1, 1995, it shall be unlawful for any person in this State to act as a real estate appraiser, to directly or indirectly engage or assume to engage in the business of real estate appraisal, or to advertise or hold himself or herself out as engaging in or conducting the business of real estate appraisal without first obtaining a registration, license, or certificate issued by the Appraisal Board under the provisions of this Chapter. It shall also be unlawful, with regard to any real property where any portion of that property is located within this State, for any person to perform any of the acts listed above without first being registered, licensed, or certified by the Appraisal Board under the provisions of this Chapter.

An appraiser enters the picture when he or she is contacted by a mortgage lender and asked to prepare an appraisal of the property as part of the overall loan process. When a buyer wishes to borrow money to purchase a home, the lending institution will bring in an appraiser to ensure that the value of the real estate matches the value of the mortgage. Many lenders who are regulated by federal agencies are also required to engage a licensed appraiser. Although the homeowner eventually pays the appraisal fee, either directly to the appraiser or indirectly by reimbursing the lender's outlay, the appraiser is usually considered to be in a business relationship with the lender. As such, the homeowner may not receive a copy of the appraisal report unless the lender approves it. However, other federal provisions, such as the Equal Credit Opportunity Act, authorize giving a copy of the appraisal report to the homeowner when the request is made in writing.

Appraisers use several techniques to arrive at a final monetary value for a parcel of real estate. These methods can be complicated, but essentially boil down to an item-by-item analysis of the real estate and a comparison of the real estate to other similar parcels. Although this oversimplifies the appraisal process, the essential activities of the appraisal are to arrive at an accurate estimate of the real estate's value. Among the activities carried out by appraisers to reach this final estimate are:

- Reviewing tax records
- Examining Deeds and recent sales
- Measuring property boundaries
- Reviewing MLS listings

Sidebar: A "Drive-By Appraisal" is an appraisal based only on the exterior appearance of the home. Whether such an appraisal is sufficient depends not only on the client's request, but also the extent of appraisal requested.

Figure 2-9. There Are Several Different Methods Used to Appraise the Value of Property

- Cost of the property
- Comparison of sale prices
- Determining market value of the property

In order to arrive at the final estimate, an appraiser will often visit several different local governmental offices, including the Registrar of Deeds office, the Tax Office, and the Zoning Board, among others.

Sidebar: The appraiser's fee is usually paid as part of the other fees at the closing.

Appraisers are not the only professionals who estimate property value, although they are the only ones licensed to do so. In a typical real estate transaction, brokers often prepare a form of value estimation as a way to guide a client in setting a sale price. This is usually referred to as a Comparative Market Analysis.

3. Comparative Market Analysis

When a real estate broker or salesperson prepares a Comparative Market Analysis (CMA), this is not an appraisal. Such analyses do not violate North Carolina law regulating appraisers when the real estate broker clearly points out that the CMA is not prepared by a licensed appraiser, is not an actual appraisal and cannot be used for lending purposes.

Sidebar: A Comparative Market Analysis (CMA) is sometimes referred to as a 'broker price opinion.'

CMAs are usually prepared for real estate clients as a means of providing some guidance on sale (or purchase) price. A Comparative Market Analysis is a presentation of recent sales of similarly-situated properties. A CMA is based first on homes/properties with similar features, amenities and locations as the house currently up for sale. The CMA will provide information on the sale price of these properties and uses this as a means to estimate a value for the sale price of the client's home.

Sidebar: In some cases, the broker may receive a fee for preparing a CMA, but only when this fee is charged to an actual client, or as part of an employee relocation program.

Figure 2-10. Comparative Market Analysis under North Carolina Law

N.C.G.S. § 93E-1-3. When registration, license, or certificate not required
(c) Nothing in this Chapter shall preclude a real estate broker or salesman licensed under Chapter 93A of the General Statutes from performing a comparative market analysis as defined in G.S. 93E-1-4, provided the person does not represent himself or herself as being a registered trainee or a State-licensed or State-certified real estate appraiser. A real estate broker or salesperson may perform a comparative market analysis for compensation or other valuable consideration only for prospective or actual brokerage clients or for real property involved in an employee relocation program.

N.C.G.S. § 93E-1-4(7a)
"Comparative market analysis" means the analysis of sales of similar recently sold properties in order to derive an indication of the probable sales price of a particular property by a licensed real estate broker or salesperson.

In addition to appraisers and real estate brokers, there is another real estate professional closely involved in the real estate transaction. This is the surveyor.

D. Surveyors

Surveyors are responsible for double-checking the accuracy of property boundary lines. Surveying work involves careful attention to detail. A surveyor must go the actual property and measure off distances and directions and either compare these with an existing property description or create a property description from scratch. They use extremely precise measuring equipment to ensure the highest possible accuracy in property descriptions.

E. The Legal Team

Lawyers and paralegals play an important role in real estate transactions. Whether drafting deeds, conducting title searches or orchestrating the closing, lawyers are as critical to the process as real estate agents. Attorneys work closely with paralegals who carry out many of the daily activities, such as title searches, document preparation and coordinating the many documents that it takes to bring a real estate transaction to a conclusion. These professionals are so important to the process that their role is explored throughout this book, from preparing metes and bounds descriptions (Chapter 3) to their role in the closing process (Chapter 12).

F. Contractors

General contractors construct residential and commercial properties. A general contractor often hires sub-contractors to work on specific phases of a construction project.

In fact, one of the requirements of a successful closing is a release from a general contractor stating that all sub-contractors have been paid and that there are no outstanding claims on the property.

G. Property Managers

When a person works as a property manager, he or she supervises rental property for another. In a typical scenario, a property manager will be hired by a property owner to administer several different rental properties. The owner wishes to earn an income from renting out these properties, but does not wish to deal with the day-to-day frustrations of being a landlord. The owner will hire someone else to collect the rent, handle tenant complaints and the plethora of details involved in landlord-tenant arrangements. A property manager may be paid a percentage of the rent or a flat fee for this service. (See Chapter 10 for a complete overview of Landlord-Tenant Law.) There is statutory authority for the belief that a property manager who manages property owned by another must be a licensed real estate agent in North Carolina. See Figure 2-11.

Figure 2-11. NCGS§ 93A-2. Definitions and Exceptions

(a) A real estate broker within the meaning of this Chapter is any person, partnership, corporation, limited liability company, association, or other business entity who for a compensation or valuable consideration or promise thereof lists or offers to list, sells or offers to sell, buys or offers to buy, auctions or offers to auction (specifically not including a mere crier of sales), or negotiates the purchase or sale or exchange of real estate, or who leases or offers to lease, or who sells or offers to sell leases of whatever character, or rents or offers to rent any real estate or the improvement thereon, for others.

H. Inspectors

When a buyer and seller create an offer of purchase contract (Chapter 5), the buyer often inserts a clause making the offer conditional on an inspection of the premises. This means that the buyer's offer to purchase the home is conditional on an inspector's report that there are no major problems with the property.

1. Real Estate Inspections

A real estate inspector is responsible for examining the property in great detail to assess its various systems. A thorough real estate inspection ensures that the buyer will not discover any major problems with the home after taking possession and also protects the interests of the mortgage lender. In many ways, an inspection resembles an appraisal. However, where an appraiser is assessing the home for value, an inspector is examining the home for problems or damage. When we use the term 'inspector' in this context, we are not referring to government employees who inspect construction sites to ensure that they meet local building and electrical codes. We will examine this type of inspection in a later chapter. When we speak of inspectors in this section, we are referring to individuals who are privately employed and who are in the business of examining completed structures to search for structural or other damage.

2. Inspectors' Duties

An inspector usually enters the premises pursuant to a contract of sale between the homeowner and buyer. The buyer often includes a contract clause that stipulates an inspection within a set amount of time of the contract date. An inspection is often a requirement imposed by the lender as well. The inspector is paid by the buyer and makes a written report to the buyer. This report includes an in-depth analysis of all of the major home systems, including structural, electrical, heating and air conditioning, plumbing and others. See Figure 2-12 for an example of a typical inspection checklist.

Figure 2-12. Typical Inspection Checklist

			Condition		
Exterior Features	Good	Fair	Poor	Bad	Comments
Windows					
Doors					
Chimneys					
Roof Ventilation					
Interior Features					
Overall appearance					
Ceiling					
Walls					

The inspector's final report will often run to dozens of pages and provide an in-depth analysis of systems and structures in the house and the inspector's notes about any problems or repairs that are needed. An inspector is also familiar with building codes and can advise the client when plumbing, electrical or other systems are not in compliance with the applicable codes.

Relevant Case

Allman v. Charles, 111 N.C.App. 673, 433 S.E.2d 3 (1993)

McCRODDEN, Judge.

Plaintiff brought this action to recover a real estate commission fee of six percent of the $182,500.00 contract price defendant agreed to accept for the sale of her home. Defendant appeals from the judgment finding that plaintiff had found a buyer ready, willing and able to purchase defendant's house and ordering defendant to pay a real estate broker's commission as required by the Exclusive Listing Contract. The issue we determine is whether a real estate broker may collect a commission when he procures a buyer at a price acceptable to the seller, the seller refuses to do any repairs after the buyer's inspection, and the buyer terminates the agreement.

The facts of the case are as follows. On 15 May 1990, defendant engaged plaintiff as her exclusive agent to sell her home. Plaintiff and defendant signed an Exclusive Listing Contract which provided that the house was to be listed at a price of $194,900.00 and that defendant would pay plaintiff six percent of the gross sales price if plaintiff produced a purchaser within the exclusive listing period. The listing contract also contained a provision requiring defendant to cooperate with plaintiff to facilitate the sale of the house. About this time, plaintiff informed defendant that it was quite possible that she would have to make some repairs to the house in order to sell it. Defendant stated that the only defects of which she was aware were a faulty element in the stove, the garbage disposal, and the chimney flue. On 28 May 1990, plaintiff procured an offer to purchase in the amount of $170,000.00 by Mr. and Mrs. Thomas Koechlin. Plaintiff and defendant formulated a counter-proposal and presented the Koechlins with a written offer to sell and contract (the Contract) for a sale price of $182,500.00, with the closing to be held before 20 June 1990. The Koechlins accepted the offer and executed the Contract. Soon after the Contract was executed, defendant decided that she no longer wished to sell the house. She offered to pay plaintiff his commission and to pay the Koechlins $10,000.00 to be released from her obligation.

The Koechlins, however, wanted to go through with the sale. Defendant then consulted an attorney who advised her that the Contract was binding. Subsequently, defendant and the Koechlins entered into a written agreement modifying the Contract, but these modifications do not directly bear on the issues presented by this case.

Paragraph 8 of the Contract provided that the electrical, plumbing, heating, and cooling systems were to be in good working order at the time of closing and that the buyer had the right to have these systems inspected, at the buyer's expense, and that:

> If any repairs are necessary, Seller shall have the option of (a) completing them, (b) providing for their completion, or (c) refusing to complete them. If Seller elects not to complete or provide for the completion of the repairs, then Buyer shall have the option of (d) accepting the property in its present condition, or (e) terminating this contract.

Pursuant to this provision of the Contract, the Koechlins had professional inspections made of the plumbing, electrical, structural and heating systems of the house. These inspections indicated that some repairs needed to be made to the house. The combined total of the estimated costs for the repairs was approximately $4,900.00.

After receiving these inspection reports, defendant informed plaintiff that she would not make any repairs, insisting that she would "not pay one dime" toward repairs. Instead of accepting the property as it was or making a compromise offer to share the cost of repairs, the Koechlins exercised their right to terminate the Contract. The sale did not close and defendant released the Koechlins' earnest money.

Defendant first argues that the trial court erred in finding that the Koechlins were ready, willing and able purchasers. She contends that Paragraph 8 rendered the Contract conditional and neither the buyer nor the seller was willing to meet the condition.

The general rule is that when a broker produces a buyer who is ready, willing and able to buy the principal's land upon the terms offered by the principal, the broker is entitled to his commission. Carver v. Britt, 241 N.C. 538, 85 S.E.2d 888 (1955). Merely negotiating a conditional agreement, however, does not entitle a broker to a commission. 12 C.J.S. Brokers § 149 (1980); 12 Am.Jur.2d Brokers § 188 (1964). In Carver v. Britt, the defendant claimed that the plaintiff broker was not entitled to a commission because the acceptance message sent by the defendant had stated, "your telegram relative sale my property is accepted subject to details to be worked out…." 241 N.C. at 540, 85 S.E.2d at 889. In finding that the acceptance was not conditional, the Court distinguished between conditions going to the making of the contract and those which merely affect the execution of the contract. "Where an offer is squarely accepted in positive terms, the addition of a statement relating to the ultimate performance of the contract does not make the acceptance conditional and prevent the formation of the contract." Id. at 540, 85 S.E.2d at 890. On the other hand, a qualification "imposed as a part of the acceptance itself" would invalidate the contract. Id. at 541, 85 S.E.2d at 890.

In the instant case, the continuing validity of the Contract was conditioned on defendant's making any necessary repairs or the Koechlins' acceptance of the property as it was. We believe that a provision such as that contained in Paragraph 8 of the Contract, allowing a seller to refuse to make repairs to the property and the purchaser then to terminate the contract, was not a mere detail of execution, but went to the making of the contract. When a buyer and seller cannot work out these conditions of the contract, as the Koechlins and defendant were unable to do in this case, they invalidate the contract. Hence, we find that this contract was conditional and that, until the issue of repairs was resolved, it was not binding on the parties.

Defendant also disputes the trial court's other ground for awarding fees to the plaintiff. In its second conclusion of law, the court found that in refusing to even consider bargaining or negotiating with the Koechlins over the issue of repairs to the property and in adamantly refusing to spend "even one dime" on any repairs to the property after earlier acknowledging that at least some repairs would be required, the Defendant did not comply with her duty of good faith and fair dealing in attempting to resolve the issue of repairs. The sale of Defendant's house to the Koechlins was not closed as a consequence of the Defendant's failure to act in good faith or to make reasonable efforts to resolve the issue of repairs. The Defendant's failure to act in good faith also constituted a violation of her duties to the Plaintiff under the Exclusive Listing Contract. In support of the trial court's conclusion, plaintiff contends that the condition in Paragraph 8, like a condition of obtaining financing, carries with it an implied duty of good faith, citing Mezzanotte v. Freeland, 20 N.C.App. 11, 200 S.E.2d 410 (1973). In Mezzanotte, the sales agreement contained a provision stating that the agreement was contingent upon the buyer's obtaining satisfactory financing. The court found that even though the buyer had discretionary power affecting the seller's rights, the buyer's promise to purchase was not illusory because he had impliedly promised to make reasonable efforts to obtain financing. Mezzanotte, however, is distinguishable.

In this case, defendant made no promise, implicit or explicit, to make repairs, and the Contract imposed no such duty. Further, she did not have discretionary power to affect unilaterally the Koechlins' rights. The Contract gave defendant the right to refuse to make repairs, but the Koechlins could still have enforced the contract against her had they been willing to accept the property as it was. Neither party could unilaterally terminate the Contract. There was no implied promise to make a good faith effort to negotiate as to repairs.

Plaintiff, mindful of defendant's earlier attempt to terminate the Contract, believes that defendant's refusal to negotiate on the issue of repairs was her way of getting out of the Contract. It matters not what defendant's intentions were. Thompson-McLean, Inc. v. Campbell, 61 N.C. 310, 134 S.E.2d 671 (1964). Defendant was not legally bound to pay for repairs or to negotiate that condition.

Plaintiff finally argues that, by refusing to make repairs or negotiate the repairs, defendant breached her duty to cooperate, as contained in the Exclusive Listing Contract and that this fact alone is sufficient to support the judgment. However, once defendant signed the Contract, her duties under the Contract delimited her duty to cooperate under the Exclusive Listing Contract, i.e., her duty to cooperate was no more expansive than her general duty to abide by the terms of the Contract. The trial court, misunderstanding the nature of the Contract, erroneously found that there was a general duty of good faith with respect to repairs. As stated above, there was no such duty. Without that erroneously imposed duty, we find the evidence that defendant breached her duty to cooperate insufficient. In fact, the evidence tends to show the opposite: that defendant reduced the asking price of the house by more than $10,000.00, opened her house to the Koechlins and, later, to their inspectors, signed the contract, and, when she realized she was bound by it, placed her belongings in storage and took an apartment. The only evidence of any failure to cooperate was her refusal to make repairs or negotiate as to repairs. Since she had no duty in this regard, there was no evidence to support a finding that appellant breached her duty to cooperate under the Exclusive Listing Contract.

Based upon the foregoing, it is clear that defendant was well within her contractual rights to refuse to pay for the repairs demanded by the prospective buyers and that the Koechlins were not ready or willing to purchase the property until that condition was fulfilled. Having so determined, we reverse the trial court's judgment awarding commission fees to plaintiff.

Reverse.

Chapter Summary

The law of agency creates a unique relationship where one party is a principal and the other is an agent. An agent owes several duties to the principal, including the duty of obedience, care and loyalty. When an agency relationship is created in a real estate context, the real estate agent works for the seller who is regarded as the principal. The agent has training, education and experience that assist the principal in achieving a specific goal. Agents owe not only legal duties to their principal, but also ethical duties. Agents have fewer duties to third parties, but must avoid fraudulent and/or negligent misrepresentations of fact. When a real estate agent performs her duties by advertising and marketing the property and producing a buyer who is ready, willing and able to purchase the property, the agent is entitled to a commission, paid out of the sale price.

There are numerous professionals involved at every stage of a real estate transaction. Although this chapter focuses on real estate brokers and salespersons, other important professionals include attorneys, paralegals, appraisers, surveyors and inspectors. Real estate professionals are governed by the North Carolina Real Estate Commission, which not only licenses new agents, but also disciplines brokers and salespersons who violate the rules and regulations of the Commission.

Review Questions

1. Explain the law of agency.

2. What are three duties that an agent owes to a principal?

3. What are three duties that the principal owes to an agent?

4. Explain how the law of agency applies to a typical real estate transaction involving an agent and a homeowner.

5. What is the scope of a real-estate agent's authority in representing a homeowner?

6. What are some of the ways that investors make money off real estate?

7. What is the difference between a real estate broker and a real estate salesperson?

8. What qualifications are required for a person who wishes to become a real-estate broker in North Carolina?

9. Is an examination required to become a real-estate broker in North Carolina? If so, what type of examination is it?

10. What are some of the ethical duties owed by real estate brokers to their clients?

11. What is the Multiple Listing Service?

12. How has the Internet changed the way that houses are advertised and marketed?

13. Explain the role of a loan officer in a real estate transaction.

14. What are the duties of an appraiser?

15. How does a surveyor carry out his duties? What are those duties?

16. Explain the role of attorneys and paralegals in the real estate transaction.

17. How does one qualify as a contractor in North Carolina?

18. What are some of the duties of a property manager?

19. Explain the role of a house inspector in a typical real estate sales transaction.

20. What is a real estate investment trust?

21. What is the document that creates the agency relationship between a homeowner and a real estate broker?

22. What does an inspector do?

23. What are some of the methods used by appraisers to assess the value of real estate?

24. What systems in the home will a home inspector examine as part of a typical, residential inspection?

25. What is a comparative market analysis?

Assignment

1. Using the Internet resources, locate various Internet promotions for homes offered by various real-estate agencies. What type of information can you locate on these sites? How thorough are the sites? What types of visual aids do real estate companies use on the Internet to promote real estate?

2. Contact a local real-estate agent and ask him or her questions about the profession. For instance, what do they like best about what they do? What do they like least? Is this person a real estate broker or a salesperson? Is the profession something that they would recommend to others? If so, why? Are there any common misconceptions that people have about real-estate agents? What's the best way to locate a good real-estate broker?

Terms and Phrases

Agency

Ratification

Fraud

Negligent Misrepresentation

Material Fact

Puffing

Real Estate Investment Trust (REIT)

North Carolina Real Estate Commission

Real Estate Broker

Real Estate Salesperson

Multiple Listing Service

Appraiser

Surveyor

Contractor

Property Manager

Inspector

Chapter 3

Legal Estates in Property in North Carolina

Chapter Objectives

- Explain the legal elements of fee simple absolute estates
- Describe the creation and effect of fee simple determinable and fee simple on a condition subsequent estates
- Explain how and when a life estate is created
- Explain the differences between tenancies in common and joint tenancies
- Describe the features of tenancies in partnership and tenancies by entirety

I. What Is an Estate?

An estate is a right of immediate enjoyment in property.[1] When we speak of the various types of estates in real property, we are actually discussing the type and quality of the possessor's rights. Estates vary from fee simple absolute to life estates. Each has its own characteristics and its own unique method of creation.

Estates can be characterized as present estates or future estates. A present estate confers a benefit on the possessor immediately. A future estate, as the name suggests, will not confer a benefit until some point in the future. For example, John creates a will leaving all of his property to Maria. Maria has a future estate. She doesn't have the right to use the property now, but on John's death, she will. (Maria has a hope/expectation)

When there is a dispute about when an estate actually vests, North Carolina courts will construe an instrument as vesting an estate as early as possible.[2] This avoids any vacuum in ownership rights and confers the rights granted in an estate in such a way that they can be used.

Although we have characterized the term 'estate' as a right to use or enjoy property, this term has been interpreted in additional ways. For instance, some cases have defined an

---

1. *Ziegler v. Love*, 115 S.E. 887 (1923).
2. *Moore v. Hunter*, 265 S.E.2d 884 (1980).

estate as an interest in lands or property.[3] In other instances, an estate refers to the quality, extent of ownership, right to use and nature of ownership in property.[4]

For our purposes, we will define an estate in land as the quality of title, right to use and the extent of ownership in real property. This definition will help us to define one of the most important types of real property estates: Fee simple.

II. Fee Simple Estate

When we say that someone possesses fee simple ownership in property, this means that a person has the most complete set of rights that it is possible to have in real estate. "Ownership in fee simple is one in which the owner is entitled to the entire property, with unconditional power of disposition during one's life, and descending to one's heirs and legal representatives upon one's death intestate."[5] Among the rights that a fee simple owner possesses are:

Bundle of Rights

- The right to give the property away
- The right to sell the property
- The right to use and possess the property
- The right to raise and sell crops from the property
- The right to mortgage the property
- The right to rent the property to others.

Fee Simple Absolute: the name for the estate in which an owner has the highest quantity and quality of rights in real property

If we view fee simple ownership as a bundle of the various rights set out above, then we see that fee simple ownership possesses more rights in property than any other type of real estate rights. The fee simple owner not only possesses these rights, but also has the power to transfer some of them to others, while retaining the rest for himself. In chapter 4, when we explore landlord-tenant law, we will see that a leasehold estate is created when the property owner transfers the right to use and possess the property to someone else (the tenant), but retains the other rights. As long as the owners do not violate constitutional or statutory provisions, they are free to do with their property as they wish.

Sidebar: The concept of a 'fee' arose in the Middle Ages in England, where all land titles devolved from the King, who gave out large parcels to nobility, in exchange for the promise of military or monetary support to the monarchy.

In addition to these rights, North Carolina defines a fee simple estate as marketable and free of encumbrances.[6] There is no type of estate in land that has more extensive rights than that of fee simple absolute.

---

3. *Shoemaker v. Coats*, 10 S.E.2d 810 (1940).
4. *Shoemaker v. Coats*, 10 S.E.2d 810 (1940).
5. *Godette v. Godette*, 146 N.C.App. 737, 554 S.E.2d 8 (2001).
6. *Lea v. Bridgeman*, 228 N.C. 565, 46 S.E.2d 555 (1948).

When an instrument transfers title to land and there is any ambiguity or vagueness in the document vesting title, the law will presume that a fee simple estate was intended.[7] This is especially true when dealing with conditions placed on fee simple ownership.

A. Rights, Obligations and Limitations of Fee Simple Owners

Although an owner in fee simple has the most extensive rights in the property, these rights come at a price. A landowner in fee simple also assumes certain responsibilities along with these rights. Among those responsibilities is liability for injuries sustained by visitors to the property. We will discuss landowner liability in greater detail in a later chapter.

Although we have framed our discussion about fee simple estates as if there are no limitations on the quality of ownership, that is not entirely true. In later chapters, we will explore the types of public and private restrictions placed on fee simple ownership. However, before we proceed to that discussion, we must address the limitations that can be imposed on certain types of fee simple ownership.

B. Conditional Fee Simple Estates

Under North Carolina law, a grantor can place conditions on fee simple ownership, often referred to as fee simple defeasible estates. A fee simple defeasible falls into one of two categories:

1. Fee simple determinable
2. Fee simple subject to a condition subsequent[8]

In each of these categories, what would normally be a fee simple title is modified by some condition or limitation. Although fee simple absolute is the most common type of fee simple ownership, it is important to understand these other, lesser-known types of fee simple estates.

> Sidebar: The law does not favor construing the language of any title document that creates conditions or other impediments to taking possession of an estate.[9]

1. The Rules Used to Interpret Fee Simple Defeasible Estates

Before discussing the specifics of each of the various fee simple defeasible estates, there are some general guidelines that North Carolina courts use when considering these estates.

For instance, whenever a deed contains language purporting to create one of these estates, the language used must be specific. The wording must indicate the party's intent to

---

7. *Amerson v. Lancaster*, 106 N.C.App. 51, 415 S.E.2d 93 (1992).
8. *Elmore v. Austin*, 232 N.C. 13, 59 S.E.2d 205 (1950).
9. *Minor v. Minor*, 62 S.E.2d 60 (1950).

create a condition and the means to enforce it.[10] The law does not favor strict interpretations of restrictive language in deeds or wills. If the language is vague or uncertain, the courts will default to an interpretation that a fee simple estate was intended, and ignore any intention to create a fee simple determinable or other limited fee simple estate.[11]

2. Fee Simple Determinable

A fee simple determinable estate occurs when a person transfers property to another with a stipulation that the property should be used in a certain way. Suppose, for instance, that Al Able wishes to give his property to his church. He inserts a condition in the deed that reads, "Rights in fee simple are subject to the condition that the property should always be used for religious purposes." This transfer, although purportedly in fee simple, creates a clause that may revoke fee simple ownership. Modern real estate professionals do not use such language, preferring to use other methods to control the use of land, such as zoning and restrictive covenants, but there was a time when such limitations were popular.

The problem with a fee simple determinable is that on the happening of a specific event, the title to the property reverts to some other person. In our example above, if Al Able's property is ever used for non-religious purposes, whatever that might mean, then the fee simple ownership automatically vests in someone else, such as Al's heirs. This situation is fraught with difficulties in the modern world of real estate conveyances and is therefore strictly avoided. *ex future estate*

> Sidebar: "A fee simple determinable is converted into a fee simple absolute when the stated event on which it is limited becomes impossible of occurrence."[12]

Because the law does not favor a construction that creates fee simple determinable estates, the person inserting the condition in the deed must be very specific and also provide a mechanism for the transfer of title when the condition occurs.[13] For instance, in our previous example involving Al Able, you will notice that not only does the clause specify the type of use for the land, but also that the title will automatically revert to specific persons when the condition is violated. This type of express and unambiguous language is absolutely essential in creating a fee simple determinable estate.[14]

> Sidebar: Fee simple determinable estates are also referred to as 'base' or 'qualified fee' estates.[15]

Why would anyone wish to create a fee simple determinable title? The original owner might want the property to be used for a certain purpose. For example, the grantor might give valuable property to a local church and in exchange for this gift insist that the property be used for religious purposes. Such a condition substitutes for the money that the grantor might have made if he had simply sold the property.

When courts are called on to interpret language in a deed that supposedly creates a fee simple determinable, they strictly construe the wording. If the deed simply contains language that the property should be used for a certain purpose, this does not

---

10. *Braddy v. Elliott*, 146 N.C. 578, 60 S.E. 507.
11. *Hinton v. Vinson*, 104 S.E. 897 (1920).
12. *Lide v. Mears*, 2321 N.C. 111, 56 S.E.2d 404 (1949).
13. *Ange v. Ange*, 235 N.C. 506, 71 S.E.2d 19, 20 (1952).
14. *Station Associates, Inc. v. Dare County*, 350 N.C. 367, 513 S.E.2d 789 (1999).
15. *Charlotte Park and Recreation Commission v. Barringer*, 242 N.C. 311, 88 S.E.2d 114 (1955).

create a fee simple determinable or a fee simple on a condition subsequent.[16] The wording must also provide for some action when the condition is not met.

a. Court Tests for Fee Simple Determinable

One test used by the courts to determine if a deed contains a fee simple determinable estate, rather than a fee simple estate, is whether the language in the conveying instrument provides a mechanism for the owner (or his heirs) to re-enter the property, or to retake possession when the condition happens. Without this provision, the courts are likely to rule that no fee simple determinable was created.

Hypothetical #1.

Marvin is selling his property to Dana. He inserts the following language into the deed:

The property should be used for church reasons only.

Is this a fee simple determinable clause?

— No. A provision that simply states how the property should be used does not, by itself, create a fee simple determinable. In order to create that estate, the grantor must also include some language explaining what will happen when the property is no longer used according to the wording. For instance, the deed should contain a provision authorizing forfeiture of the title and repossession by others.[17] Because Marvin's deed clause did not contain this language, he has conveyed a fee simple absolute estate to Dana.

Relevant Case: Determining a Fee Simple Determinable Estate

Station Associates, Inc. v. Dare County, 350 N.C. 367, 513 S.E.2d 789 (1999)

PARKER, Justice.

This title dispute to approximately ten acres of land at the northern tip of Hatteras Island, Dare County, originates in an 1897 deed. In that year Jessie B. Etheridge conveyed the land in issue (hereinafter "the property") to the United States in the following deed:

Treasury Department

Life-Saving Service — Form No. 12. Whereas, The SECRETARY OF THE TREASURY has been authorized by law to establish the LIFE-SAVING STATION herein described;

And whereas, Congress, by Act of March 3, 1875, provided as follows, viz.: "And the Secretary of the Treasury is hereby authorized, whenever he shall deem it advisable, to acquire, by donation or purchase, [o]n behalf of the United States, the right to use and occupy sites for life-saving or life-boat stations, houses of refuge, and sites for pier-head Beacons, the establishment of which has been, or shall hereafter be, authorized by Congress;" And whereas, the said Secretary of the Treasury deems it advisable to acquire, on

---

16. *Ange v. Ange*, 235 N.C. 755, 71 S.E.2d 19 (1952).
17. *Station Associates, Inc. v. Dare County*, 350 N.C. 367, 513 S.E.2d 789 (1999).

behalf of the United States, the right to use and occupy the hereinafter-described lot of land as a site for a Life-Saving Station, as indicated by his signature hereto:

Now, this Indenture between Jessie B. Etheridge, party of the first part, and the United States, represented by the Secretary of the Treasury, party of the second part, WITNES-SETH that the said party of the first part, in consideration of the sum of two hundred dollars by these presents grant[s], demise[s], release[s], and convey[s] unto the said United States all that certain lot of land situate in Nags Head township, County of Dare and State of North Carolina, and thus described and bounded: Beginning at a cedar post bearing from the South West corner of the Oregon Life Saving Station South 40° West and distant 28.24 chains from said post South 68° West 10 chains to post, thence South 22° E. 10 chains to post, thence North 68° E. 10 chains to post, thence North 22° W. 10 chains to first Station containing 10 acres, be the contents what they may, with full right of egress and ingress thereto in any direction over other lands of the grantor by those in the employ of the United States, on foot or with vehicles of any kind, with boats or any articles used for the purpose of carrying out the intentions of Congress in providing for the establishment of Life-Saving Stations, and the right to pass over any lands of the grantor in any manner in the prosecution of said purpose; *369 and also the right to erect such structures upon the said land as the United States may see fit, and to remove any and all such structures and appliances at any time; the said premises to be used and occupied for the purposes named in said Act of March 3, 1875: To have and to hold the said lot of land and privileges unto the United States from this date.

And the said party of the first part for himself, executors, and administrators do[es] covenant with the United States to warrant and defend the peaceable possession of the above-described premises to the United States, for the purposes above named for the term of this covenant, against the lawful claims of all persons claiming by, through, or under Jessie B. Etheridge.

And it is further stipulated, that the United States shall be allowed to remove all buildings and appurtenances from the said land whenever it shall think proper, and shall have the right of using other lands of the grantor for passage over the same in effecting such removal.

> In witness whereof, the parties hereto have set their hands and seals this 8th day of March, A.D. eighteen hundred and ninety-seven.
>
> Signed, sealed, and delivered in presence of—
>
> s/ J.B. Etheridge
>
> s/ L.J. Gage
>
> Secretary of the Treasury

The United States took possession and duly established a life-saving station on the property operated by the Life-Saving Service, a part of the United States Treasury Department. The United States Coast Guard was thereafter created; and sometime prior to 1915 the Coast Guard took over operation of the station, which was then named the Oregon Inlet Coast Guard Station. In December of 1989, the U.S. Coast Guard abandoned the station. On 17 July 1992, the United States quitclaimed its interest in the property to Dare County.

Plaintiffs, who are the heirs of the original grantor, Jessie B. Etheridge, along with a corporation that purchased from the heirs an ownership interest in the land, claimed title to the property and instituted this action against Dare County.

The trial court granted judgment on the pleadings to defendant Dare County, concluding as a matter of law that Dare County had title to the property in fee simple absolute.

The Court of Appeals reversed and remanded holding that the United States was granted only a fee simple determinable by the 1897 deed and that a genuine issue of fact existed as to whether a condemnation proceeding by the United States in 1959 extinguished plaintiffs reversionary interest. We now reverse the Court of Appeals and reinstate the judgment of the trial court.

Before this Court defendant argues that the 1897 deed conveyed to the United States a fee simple absolute, but even if the estate conveyed was a fee simple determinable with a possibility of reverter, in 1959 when the United States created the Cape Hatteras National Seashore Recreation Area by condemning properties along the outer banks, plaintiffs' possibility of reverter in the property was extinguished by the condemnation. We do not need to address the second part of defendant's argument as we conclude that the 1897 deed conveyed to the United States not a fee simple determinable, but a fee simple absolute.

An estate in fee simple determinable is created by a limitation in a fee simple conveyance which provides that the estate shall automatically expire upon the occurrence of a certain subsequent event. Elmore v. Austin, 232 N.C. 13, 20–21, 59 S.E.2d 205, 211 (1950). "The law does not favor a construction of the language in a deed which will constitute a condition subsequent unless the intention of the parties to create such a restriction upon the title is clearly manifested." Washington City Bd. of Educ. v. Edgerton, 244 N.C. 576, 578, 94 S.E.2d 661, 664 (1956). "Ordinarily a clause in a deed will not be construed as a condition subsequent, unless it contains language sufficient to qualify the estate conveyed and provides that in case of a breach the estate will be defeated, and this must appear in appropriate language sufficiently clear to indicate that this was the intent of the parties." Ange v. Ange, 235 N.C. 506, 508, 235 N.C. 755, 71 S.E.2d 19, 20 (1952).

This Court has declined to recognize reversionary interests in deeds that do not contain express and unambiguous language of reversion or termination upon condition broken.

We have stated repeatedly that a mere expression of the purpose for which the property is to be used without provision for forfeiture or reentry is insufficient to create an estate on condition and that, in such a case, an unqualified fee will pass.

However, in those cases in which the deed contained express and unambiguous language of reversion or termination, we have construed a deed to convey a determinable fee or fee on condition subsequent.

Applying this law to the deed in the present case, we note that the 1897 document is completely devoid of any language of reversion or termination. Nowhere does the deed indicate that the United States' interest in the property would automatically expire or revert to the grantor upon the discontinued use of the property as a life-saving station. Plaintiffs contend, however, that the deed contains certain phrases expressive of the parties' intent that the estate was to be of limited duration: first, that the granting clause gives the United States the right only to "use and occupy" the property for the stated purposes; and second, that the word "term" within the warranty clause, in which the grantor warrants peaceable possession of the property "for the purposes above named for the term of this covenant," is sufficient to indicate that the parties intended that the United States' occupancy of the property would be for a limited duration. We disagree with plaintiffs' arguments. The use of the words "use and occupy" and "term" in this deed is not the equivalent of a clear expression that the property shall revert to the grantor or that the estate will automatically terminate upon the happening of a certain event.

Plaintiffs also state that for over one hundred years, the proper construction of deeds has focused on the intent of the parties and that a narrow focus on "technical" or "magic" words is inappropriate. They argue that the language of purpose contained within the deed, coupled with the language permitting the United States to "erect such structures on the said land as the United States may see fit, and to remove any and all such structures at any time," is inconsistent with the grant of a fee simple absolute. Such language of purpose and license, the argument runs, would be surplusage if a fee simple absolute were intended; thus, it follows that the deed conveys only a determinable fee since, "[if] possible, effect must be given to every part of a deed" and "no clause, if reasonable intendment can be found, shall be construed as meaningless." Mattox, 280 N.C. at 476, 186 S.E.2d at 382. In making this argument, plaintiffs rely on the reasoning employed by the District Court for the Eastern District of North Carolina in Etheridge v. United States, 218 F.Supp. 809 (E.D.N.C.1963). In Etheridge, the court attempted to apply North Carolina law in construing a deed nearly identical to the deed in this case; using a methodology of focusing on the parties' intent and giving effect to all parts of the deed, the court held that the deed conveyed a fee simple determinable. Id. at 811–13. This Court is not bound by decisions of a United States District Court interpreting or applying North Carolina law.

While discerning the intent of the parties is the ultimate goal in construing a deed, we disagree with plaintiffs' characterization of the test, requiring express and unambiguous language of reversion or termination, as a test that relies on "rigid technicality" and ignores the intent of the parties. Under our case law the use of some express language of reversion or termination is the usual manner in which parties intending to create a fee simple determinable manifest that intent. The language of termination necessary to create a fee simple determinable need not conform to any "set formula." Lackey, 258 N.C. at 464, 128 S.E.2d at 809. Rather, "any words expressive of the grantor's intent that the estate *374 shall terminate on the occurrence of the event" or that "on the cessation of [a specified] use, the estate shall end," will be sufficient to create a fee simple determinable. Barringer, 242 N.C. at 317, 88 S.E.2d at 120. In this case, however, no such language or expression can be found from which the Court can conclude, without speculation and conjecture, that "it is plainly intended by the conveyance or some part thereof, that the grantor meant to convey an estate of less dignity." N.C.G.S. § 39-1 (1984).

Accordingly, we reverse the decision of the Court of Appeals and remand to that court for further remand to the Superior Court, Dare County, for reinstatement of the judgment of the Superior Court.

REVERSED.

3. Fee Simple on a Condition Subsequent

A fee simple on a condition subsequent closely resembles, and is often confused with, fee simple determinable. The distinguishing feature between them is that where the fee simple determinable automatically transfers title on the happening of a specific event, a fee simple on a condition subsequent gives the grantor (or grantor's heirs) the right to challenge title.

The problem with both of these estates is that they create a host of problems in both interpreting the language creating them and clouding the title for future purchasers. The intent of both of these estates is to institute some type of control over the way that the property is used. However, there are other, more effective methods of achieving the same result. Fee simple determinable and fee simple on a condition subsequent estates have gradually disappeared from modern real estate practice, but are mentioned here because a real estate professional occasionally comes across them.

III. Life Estates

Unlike fee simple determinable estates, life estates are very common in real estate practice and a real estate professional should have a firm grasp of the concepts involved in creating, implementing and terminating life estates. A life estate is an estate that grants a person the use and enjoyment of property, but only during his life. On the person's death, title to the property passes to a pre-arranged person. A person who holds a life estate, usually referred to as a life tenant, cannot pass the property through probate to another. Instead, when the life tenant dies, the property vests in a person who has been designated to receive it.

> **Life Estate:** when a person possesses the right to use, possess, enjoy and take profits from a parcel of real estate, but only for the balance of his life.

When a person has a life estate, it means that he or she can use and enjoy the property, harvest crops from the property and, in many ways, do all of the activities normally associated with fee simple ownership. A life tenant is allowed to sell the property, but the buyer will only receive the rights possessed by the life tenant. In such a situation, the new buyer's rights in the land will extinguish on the death of the original life tenant. Given such a limitation, it is unlikely that anyone would be willing to buy the real property in question.

Life estates were an early creation of common law. Before the law was modified, a spouse had an automatic life estate when the other spouse died. This was a "common-law attempt to provide 'social security' for surviving spouses in the lands of deceased spouses."[18] These rights were termed Dower and Curtesy. Dower was the right of a surviving spouse to a life estate. Curtesy gave a life estate to a husband in the property owned by his wife. Dower and Curtesy were abolished in North Carolina in 1959, with the passage of a new statute defining intestate succession.[19] This statute established the rights of spouses and others to property owned by a person who died without a will.

A. Creating a Life Estate

The most common way of creating a life estate is by inserting language in a person's will such as:

> I leave my house and surrounding property to Martha for her life and then to my surviving heirs.

---

18. *Webster's Real Estate Law in North Carolina*, James Webster, Lexis Law Publishing, 1999, § 5-2, p. 85.
19. Intestate Succession Act. N.C.G.S. 29-1.

Once granted, the life tenant has the right to possess, use and enjoy almost all of the rights that we normally associate with fee simple ownership. However, there are some important limitations. Because the life tenant's right to the property terminates on her death, her right to sell, transfer or mortgage the property are extremely limited. Although there is some authority for a life tenant to transfer her estate to another, there is very little point in doing so. A person can only pass the quality of title that she possesses. If a person were to acquire a life tenant's interest in real estate, this interest would cease on the life tenant's death.

1. Elective Share for Spouses

Life estates usually arise in the context of a surviving spouse. If the deceased spouse has made no provision for the spouse in a will, or has died without a will, the surviving spouse has the right to seek an elective share of the marital estate.

Figure 3-1. Elective Share for Spouses

NCGS § 30-3.1. Right of elective share

(a) Elective Share.—The surviving spouse of a decedent who dies domiciled in this State has a right to claim an elective share, which means an amount equal to (i) the applicable share of the Total Net Assets, as defined in G.S. 30-3.2(4), less (ii) the value of Property Passing to Surviving Spouse, as defined in G. S. 30-3.3(a). The applicable share of the Total Net Assets is as follows:

(1) If the decedent is not survived by any lineal descendants, one-half of the Total Net Assets.

(2) If the decedent is survived by one child, or lineal descendants of one deceased child, one-half of the Total Net Assets.

(3) If the decedent is survived by two or more children, or by one or more children and the lineal descendants of one or more deceased children, or by the lineal descendants of two or more deceased children, one-third of the Total Net Assets.

Figure 3-2. Property Passing to Surviving Spouse

NCGS § 30-3.3. Property Passing to Surviving Spouse

(a) Property Passing to Surviving Spouse.—For purposes of this Article, "Property Passing to Surviving Spouse" means the sum of the following:

(1) One-half of the value of any interest in property held by the decedent and the surviving spouse as tenants by the entirety or as joint tenants with rights of survivorship;

(2) The value of any interest in property (outright or in trust, including any interest subject to a general power of appointment held by the surviving spouse, as defined in section 2041 of the Code) devised by the decedent to the surviving spouse, or which passes to the surviving spouse by intestacy, or by beneficiary designation, or by exercise of or in default of the exercise of the decedent's testamentary general or limited power of appointment, or by operation of law or otherwise by reason of the decedent's death, excluding any benefits under the federal social security system;

(3) Any year's allowance awarded to the surviving spouse;

---

a. Waiver of Elective Share

A spouse has the right to waive any claim on the marital estate, either before marriage (in the form of an ante-nuptial or pre-nuptial agreement) or after the marriage by a written waiver.

Figure 3-3. NCGS § 30-3.6. Waiver of Rights

(a) The right of a surviving spouse to claim an elective share may be waived, wholly or partially, before or after marriage, with or without consideration, by a written waiver signed by the surviving spouse.

(b) A waiver is not enforceable if the surviving spouse proves that:

(1) The waiver was not executed voluntarily; or

(2) The surviving spouse was not provided a fair and reasonable disclosure of the property and financial obligations of the decedent, unless the surviving spouse waived, in writing, the right to that disclosure.

B. Remaindermen

The person who is designated to receive title to the property on the death of the life tenant is referred to as the remainderman. A remainderman has a future interest in the property, not a present one. This means that the remainderman has no right to challenge the life tenant's use of the premises, except in very narrow circumstances. The remainderman's interest does not trigger until the life tenant's death. Therefore, all of the remainderman's rights in the property are future interests.

Remainderman: A person with a future, unvested interest in property.

C. Waste

One exception to the general rule that remainderman cannot challenge the life tenant's use of the property applies to the concept of waste. In this state, 'waste' has been defined as any practice that spoils or destroys the land or its innate value. Examples of waste include destroying timber, failure to maintain the premises and any other action that affects the value of the property that the remainderman will eventually receive.[20]

Besides waste, a remainderman may also bring suit to avoid the seizure of the land to satisfy a judgment.[21]

Waste: Any practice that spoils or destroys the land or its value.

The obligation to avoid waste includes the responsibility of the life tenant to pay taxes on the property.[22] A life tenant cannot, for instance, conveniently forget to list or pay the property taxes and then use this as a means of acquiring fee simple title to the property at a tax auction, circumventing the entire structure of the life estate and cutting off the interests of the remaindermen.[23]

---

20. *Fleming v. Sexton*, 172 N.C. 250, 90 S.E. 257 (1916).

21. *Narron v. Musgrave*, 236 N.C. 388, 73 S.E.2d 6 (1952).

22. *Thompson v. Watkins*, 285 N.C. 616, 620, 207 S.E.2d 740, 743 (1974)

23. *Smith v. Smith*, 261 N.C. 278, 134 S.E.2d 331 (1964); *Meadows v. Meadows*, 216 N.C. 413, 5 S.E.2d 128 (1939)

Figure 3-4. § 105-302. In Whose Name Real Property Is to Be Listed

(a) Taxable real property shall be listed in the name of the owner, and it shall be the owner's duty to list it unless the board of county commissioners shall have adopted a permanent listing system as provided in G.S. 105-303(b). For purposes of this section, the board of county commissioners may require that real property be listed in the name of the owner of record as of the day as of which property is to be listed under G.S. 105-285 ...

(c) For purposes of this Subchapter:

(8) A life tenant or tenant for the life of another shall be considered the owner of real property, and it shall be his duty to list the property for taxation, indicating on the abstract that he is a life tenant or tenant for the life of another named individual.*

* NCGS§ 105-302.

D. Merger

There are some important concepts that change the nature of a life estate. One such limitation is the doctrine of merger. Under merger, when a single person is both the life tenant and the remainderman, the estates merge and this person becomes the owner in fee simple. This situation might arise as follows:

> A dies, leaving B with a life estate. The provisions of A's will clearly state that on B's death, the property should go to A's heirs. B is A's only heir, therefore the doctrine of merger mandates that the life estate and the remainder interest merge together, giving B an immediate fee simple interest in the property. Closely related to the doctrine is a rule that once caused no end of consternation for North Carolina Real Estate practitioners: the Rule in Shelley's Case.

E. Rule in Shelley's Case

The Rule in Shelley's case was an old common law rule that required merger of life estates and future interests where D leaves his estate to A and to D's heirs, and there is no other language clarifying exactly who D's heirs are. If A was also one of D's heirs, then A would not take a life estate. Instead, A would take fee simple absolute, even though this would preclude D's other heirs. The Rule in Shelley's case was abolished in 1987 for all transactions coming after that date. The rule still applies to transactions prior to that date, but as time passes, the rule fades into much-deserved obscurity.

F. Renouncing a Life Estate

A person who has been granted a life estate is always entitled to renounce it. North Carolina General Statute § 46-1 provides the mechanism for renouncing a life tenancy. See Figure 3-5.

Figure 3-5. Renouncing a Life Estate

NCGS § 46-1. Life estate renunciation

While a holder of a life estate in property may renounce his or her life estate where there is a contingent interest in the remainder to the holder's unborn children and brothers and sisters, the holder of the life estate may not renounce the interests of his or her unborn children for the benefit of the holder's brothers and sisters

---

G. Life Estate Pur Autre Vie

North Carolina also recognizes a different type of life estate. In a life estate pur autre vie, an owner in fee simple conveys a life estate to one person that terminates on the death of another person. The language used to create it is: "to A for the life of B."[24]

Pur Autre Vie: (French) "For another's life."

IV. Concurrent Ownership in Real Estate

So far, our discussion has proceeded on the assumption that there is only one owner for a particular parcel. What happens when, as is common, there is more than one owner? How are the rights of ownership divided among them? In the next section, we will examine the various types of concurrent ownership estates in real property.

A. Tenants in Common

Under North Carolina law, a tenancy in common is created when real property is conveyed to two or more persons and there is no clear indication about the type of co-tenancy involved. In many ways, tenancy in common is the 'default' co-tenancy. As we will see later, if the parties intend to create a joint tenancy, they must specifically declare their intention to do so.[25]

> Sidebar: "A tenancy in common is a tenancy by two or more persons, in equal or unequal undivided shares, each person having an equal right to possess the whole property but no right of survivorship."[26]

A tenancy in common can be created in any number of ways, either through sale, gift or probate. The tenants are not required to possess equal shares in the land. One could possess 75% of the property, while the other possesses 25%. The parties may transfer their interest in the property as they see fit and upon the death of a co-tenant, his or her

---

24. Watson v. Smoker, 138 N.C.App. 158, 530 S.E.2d 344 (2000).
25. Powell v. Malone, 22 F. Supp. 300 (M.D.N.C. 1938).
26. Godette v. Godette, 146 N.C.App. 737, 554 S.E.2d 8 (2001).

share is transferred to the heirs. We will also see that tenants in common do not enjoy the right of survivorship. Once created, the co-tenant's ownership interest can be subject to actions by creditors, including liens.[27]

Figure 3-6. Summarizing Tenancy in Common

- Tenants in common have a separate, undivided interest in the property. Each tenant has the right to possess and use the property.
- No right of survivorship
- Each tenant may transfer ownership interest to another
- May own unequal shares in the property

B. Joint Tenancy

Joint tenancy is the second type of concurrent estate. Under a joint tenancy, two or more people own an undivided, equal share in property. Joint tenancy has the right of survivorship.

1. The Right of Survivorship

The right of survivorship is a simple device with profound implications. When two people own property as joint tenants and one dies, the other owner receives the decedent's share. Unlike tenancy in common, where the co-tenant's interest in the property is transferred to the heirs, a co-tenant's interest in a joint tenancy automatically reverts to the surviving co-tenant, thus cutting out the decedent's heirs. Because this raises a host of issues, joint tenancy is never presumed under North Carolina law. If the co-tenants wish to create a joint tenancy, and enjoy the benefit of survivorship, they must clearly state their intention to do so.

The automatic right of survivorship, a feature of old common law transactions, was abolished by statute. If the parties wish to create joint tenancy in real property ownership, they must specifically state their intention in writing.[28] See Figure 3-7.

Figure 3-7. NCGS § 41-2. Survivorship in Joint Tenancy Defined;
Proviso as to Partnership

Except as otherwise provided herein, in all estates, real or personal, held in joint tenancy, the part or share of any tenant dying shall not descend or go to the surviving tenant, but shall descend or be vested in the heirs, executors, or administrators, respectively, of the tenant so dying, in the same manner as estates held by tenancy in common ... Nothing in this section prevents the creation of a joint tenancy with right of survivorship in real or personal property if the instrument creating the joint tenancy expressly provides for a right of survivorship, and no other document shall be necessary to establish said right of survivorship.

Figure 3-8. Example of Language Used to Create a Joint Tenancy

Example: To A and B as joint tenants, not as tenants in common, with the right of survivorship.

---

27. *Martin v. Roberts*, 177 N.C.App. 415, 628 S.E.2d 812 (2006)
28. *Matter of Estate of Heffner*, 99 N.C.App. 327, 392 S.E.2d 770 (1990); N.C.G.S. § 41-2.

Sidebar: Under joint tenancy, an owner can re-convey the property to himself and others, creating a joint tenancy.

Figure 3-9. Comparing and Contrasting Various Concurrent Ownership Estates

Tenancy in Common	Joint Tenancy
Unequal interests are permissible	Each co-tenant owns an equal, undivided interest
No right of survivorship	Has the right of survivorship
When in doubt, this estate is assumed under the law	Must be created by special action of the parties
Co-tenant's interest conveyed to heirs on death	Co-tenant's interest conveyed to surviving co-tenant on death

---

Sidebar: The Right of Survivorship provides that on the death of the last co-tenant, the remaining owner acquires the property in fee simple absolute.

C. Tenancy by Entirety

Tenancy by entirety is a joint tenancy that is only available to legally married persons. It has all of the features of any joint tenancy, but it also has overtones of domestic law. In many ways, tenancy by the entirety is the successor to the old concepts of dower and curtesy. When spouses own property in this co-tenancy, the death of either places fee simple ownership in the survivor.

D. Tenancy in Partnership

Tenancy in partnership is the last type of co-tenancy we will discuss. Under this scenario, a legally established partnership creates a co-tenancy among the partners that is similar to joint tenancy. In order to qualify for this tenancy, the partners must have a partnership agreement and actually be in business together. When this minimal standard is met, the consequences of a tenancy in partnership are:

1. No single partner can sell, transfer or mortgage the property without the consent of the other partners

2. No single partner's creditors can attach the partner's share of the partnership property.

3. The partner's interest cannot be inherited; instead, the interest is split among the surviving partners.

North Carolina has adopted the Uniform Partnership Act. Under this Act, "The property rights of a partner are (1) his rights in specific partnership property, (2) his interest in the partnership, and (3) his right to participate in the management."[29]

---

29. N.C.G.S. § 59-54.

Figure 3-10. North Carolina Uniform Partnership Act

NCGS § 59-55. Nature of a partner's right in specific partnership property

(a) A partner is co-owner with his partners of specific partnership property holding as a tenant in partnership.

(b) The incidents of this tenancy are such that:

(1) A partner, subject to the provisions of this Act and to any agreement between the partners, has an equal right with his partners to possess specific partnership property for partnership purposes; but he has no right to possess such property for any other purpose without the consent of his partners.

(2) A partner's right in specific partnership property is not assignable except in connection with the assignment of rights of all the partners in the same property.

(3) A partner's right in specific partnership property is not subject to attachment or execution, except on a claim against the partnership. When partnership property is attached for a partnership debt the partners, or any of them, or the representatives of a deceased partner, cannot claim any right under the homestead or exemption laws.

(4) On the death of a partner his right in specific partnership property vests in the surviving partner or partners, except where the deceased was the last surviving partner, when his right in such property vests in his legal representative. Such surviving partner, or partners, or the legal representative of the last surviving partner, has no right to possess the partnership property for any but a partnership purpose.

E. Partition

A partition is the break up of a parcel by the percentage of ownership for the tenants. Partition can take two different forms. The first type is the physical breakup of a parcel of land owned by two or more persons. In this situation, the land is sub-divided and each co-tenant is given a wholly owned parcel that is no longer a co-tenancy with any other owners. The second type of partition is the sale of the entire parcel to some third party and a split of the profits in line with the percentage of ownership. Such actions are commonly referred to as "partition proceedings." Partition is a right recognized in concurrent owners, such as tenants in common.[30]

> Sidebar: Partitions are commonly seen in the dissolution of joint tenancies and tenancies in common.

Figure 3-11. Sale in Lieu of Partition

NCGS § 46-22. Sale in lieu of partition

(a) The court shall order a sale of the property described in the petition, or of any part, only if it finds, by a preponderance of the evidence, that an actual partition of the lands cannot be made without substantial injury to any of the interested parties.

(b) "Substantial injury" means the fair market value of each share in an in-kind partition would be materially less than the share of each cotenant in the money equivalent that would be obtained from the sale of the whole, and if an in-kind division would result in material impairment of the cotenant's rights.

(c) The court shall specifically find the facts supporting an order of sale of the property.

(d) The party seeking a sale of the property shall have the burden of proving substantial injury under the provisions of this section.

---

30. *Robertson v. Robertson*, 126 N.C.App. 298, 484 S.E.2d 831 (1997).

Chapter Summary

When an owner possesses fee simple absolute title in real estate, it means that he or she possesses the highest and best type of ownership that a person can possess in real estate. Fee simple absolute owners possess many rights, including the right to sell, give away, mortgage and rent out the real estate. When more than one owner possesses title to property, this is referred to as concurrent ownership. In North Carolina, there are various types of concurrent ownership. Under tenancy in common, two or more owners possess unequal, divided interest in a property. Tenants in common may transfer their ownership to others and there is no right of survivorship. Under joint tenancy, two or more owners possess an undivided interest in property that does possess the right of survivorship. The right of survivorship is a legal term that authorizes the transfer of all interest in property to a surviving owner when the other dies. The result of the right of survivorship is that the surviving tenant takes complete title to the property, effectively excluding the heirs of the deceased tenant. Another form of concurrent ownership is tenancy by entirety. This tenancy is only available to married couples and possesses many of the features of joint tenancy. The fourth type of concurrent ownership mentioned in this chapter is tenancy by partnership. This is a form of concurrent ownership that recognizes the rights and duties of partners to one another. Like joint tenancy, tenancy by partnership authorizes the transfer of title to a surviving partner instead of a deceased partner's heirs.

Review Questions

1. Define 'estate' as that term applies to North Carolina real estate.
2. What is the difference between a present and a future estate?
3. Describe the features of fee simple absolute title.
4. List and explain the rights conveyed to a person who possesses fee simple title in land.
5. What are conditional fee estates?
6. Explain the features of fee simple determinable estates.
7. Compare and contrast fee simple determinable estates with fee simple on a condition subsequent estates.
8. What rules do the courts in this state follow when interpreting language purporting to create condition fee estates?
9. Provide examples of the type of language required to create a fee simple determinable estate.
10. Explain the result and reasoning in *Station Associates, Inc. v. Dare County* (this chapter's case).
11. What is a life estate?
12. How is a life estate normally created?
13. What types of rights does a life tenant have?
14. What is 'elective share' for spouses and how does it relate to life estates?
15. What is a remainderman?
16. What is the legal action referred to as 'waste?'
17. What is the merger doctrine as it applies to life estates?
18. What is the Rule in Shelley's case?
19. What is a life estate pur autre vie?
20. Compare and contrast a tenancy in common with a joint tenancy.
21. What is the right of survivorship?
22. Has North Carolina abolished joint tenancy in all situations? Explain your answer.
23. What is a tenancy by entirety and when does it apply?
24. What rights do general partners have in a tenancy by partnership?
25. Explain partition.

Assignments

1. Barbara and Jerry are considering marriage, however they have decided to live together for a while before taking the next step. They wish to buy a home together. Should they acquire the home as tenants in common or as joint tenants? Explain your answer.

2. Draft clauses that could be inserted in a deed or a will that create the following estates:

- Life estate

- Joint tenancy

- Tenancy in common

3. Answer the following questions about this chapter's highlighted case, *Station Associates, Inc. v. Dare County.*

- Under what theory did the plaintiffs claim the right to the property in dispute?

- What was their theory of why they were entitled to title in the land?
- Why did the court determine that the original transaction was not a fee simple determinable but a fee simple absolute transaction?

- Is there any language that could have been included in the original transaction that would have changed the outcome in this case?

- Draft a deed provision that would satisfy the court's requirements for a fee simple determinable estate.

Terms and Phrases

Fee Simple Absolute	Life Estate Pur Autre Vie
Fee Simple Determinable	Tenants in Common
Fee Simple With a Condition Subsequent	Joint Tenancy
Life Estate	The Right of Survivorship
Waste	Tenancy By Entirety
Remainderman	Tenancy in Partnership
Merger	Partition

Chapter 4

Landlord-Tenant Law

Chapter Objectives

At the conclusion of this chapter, you should be able to:

- Explain the basic legal relationship between a landlord and a tenant
- Define the elements of an estate for years and an estate from year-to-year
- Describe the features of a tenancy at will and a tenancy at sufferance
- Explain how these various tenancies are terminated
- Describe the important considerations that go into drafting a residential lease

I. Introduction

In this chapter, we will examine landlord-tenant law. In the previous chapter, we explored the rights associated with various types of real estate ownership. For fee simple owners, these rights include the power to occupy, use and possess property, among many others. An owner also has the right to transfer a limited portion of these rights to another person. In a landlord-tenant situation, a fee simple owner, the landlord, transfers the rights to occupy, use and possess the property to another individual, the tenant. The original owner, the landlord, retains all of the other rights. The transfer of the rights to use and enjoy the property is usually for a specified lease period. In this chapter, we will examine the various ways that the landlord-tenant relationship is established as well as the different types of tenancies that are created. We will begin our discussion with an examination of Freehold estates and non-Freehold estates.

II. Freehold versus Non-Freehold Estates

We have already seen that an owner who possesses fee simple absolute title may transfer that title to another person. The owner's ability to freely transfer title to the property is the main characteristic of a freehold estate. An owner in freehold possesses complete title to the property and there are no liens or other encumbrances on it. When a person possesses only a few of the rights normally associated with fee simple title, this is referred to as a non-freehold estate. Holders of non-freehold estates, the most common example being a tenant, cannot freely transfer those rights to others. Because they hold these rights for limited periods of time, their rights will expire and revert to the original owner. However, during the lease period, they have the right to occupy, use and enjoy the property in many of the ways that a fee simple owner would. We will examine the limits of these rights throughout this chapter.

III. Residential Rental Agreements Act

Perhaps the most important legislation in the area of landlord-tenant law in North Carolina is the Residential Rental Agreements Act. This Act governs nearly every aspect of the landlord-tenant relationship, and also specifically states the duties of the landlord to the tenant and the types of civil actions that each party may bring against the other.

A. Landlords and Tenants Have Mutual Obligations

To many people, the landlord-tenant relationship appears to be one-sided. The tenant pays rent, while the landlord enjoys all the fruits of ownership. The landlord retains the right to sell, mortgage and inspect the property, while the tenant merely has a temporary right to possess the property. It is interesting to note, however, that North Carolina law specifically states that the parties have mutual obligations to one another. Landlords have a host of duties and obligations to the tenant, including the duty to repair damage and to take necessary steps to keep the premises clean, safe and habitable, while tenants also have obligations to the landlord that extend beyond the payment of monthly rent. Under North Carolina law, this arrangement is referred to as "mutuality of obligations,"[1] with each party bound to the other.

Figure 4-1. § 42-41. Mutuality of Obligations

The tenant's obligation to pay rent under the rental agreement or assignment and to comply with G.S. 42-43 and the landlord's obligation to comply with G.S. 42-42(a) shall be mutually dependent.

B. Landlord Duties under the Residential Rental Agreements Act

Under the North Carolina Residential Rental Agreements Act, landlords have specific duties imposed on them. These duties include:

---

1. NCGS § 42-41.

- Making all repairs and doing whatever is necessary to keep the premises in a fit and habitable condition
- Keeping all common areas in a safe condition
- Maintaining electrical, plumbing, heating and ventilating systems
- Providing smoke detectors

Before the passage of the Residential Rental Agreements Act, North Carolina common law imposed duties on landlords. Interestingly enough, the Act is considered to be an additional burden on landlords and was not intended to replace the previous, common law obligations that required the landlord to refrain from acts of negligence in maintaining the property.[2] Among the old common law obligations was the duty to use due care in making repairs to the leased property.[3] Courts in this state have also construed the landlord's common law duty to include not only the obligation to warn visitors about unsafe conditions, but to actually repair those conditions.[4] The question of negligence raises a whole host of issues, not only about the landlord's duty to the tenant but also the specter of contributory negligence.[5]

Although an extensive discussion of negligence law here would take too much time and push the subject far away from landlord-tenant issues, real estate professionals should be aware of the fact that negligence law is binding on both landlords and tenants. The rules of contributory negligence, which bars recovery to an injured plaintiff who has in any way contributed to his own injuries, will continue to be an important issue in North Carolina real estate law.

The Act also provides that the landlord is not released of any obligation in the landlord-tenant relationship by the tenant's explicit or implicit acceptance of the landlord's failure to comply with the Act. The landlord cannot attempt to waive the residential rental agreements in a lease provision. Any language in the lease that attempts to do so is void. A tenant is allowed to bring an action under the Residential Rental Agreements Act (RRAA) when a landlord fails to maintain the premises in a habitable manner. The tenant may sue to recover special damages.

Sidebar: The statutory provisions of the Residential Rental Agreements Act (RRAA) do not apply to transient hotels, motels or similar lodgings.[6]

Hypothetical #1.

Tracy lives in an upstairs apartment. One of the steps on the stairway is loose. One evening, Tracy slips on the stairway to her apartment and then brings suit under the Residential Rental Agreements Act. Tracy never attempted to repair the step herself and never notified the landlord about the loose step. Can she succeed with her suit?

Answer: No. Because she did not notify the landlord, she failed to prove that the landlord had any knowledge about the loose step and therefore that the landlord failed to live up to the standard set out in the Residential Rental Agreements Act.[7]

---

2. *Collingwood v. General Elec. Real Estate Equities, Inc.*, 324 N.C. 63, 376 S.E.2d 425 (1989).
3. *Bolkhir v. North Carolina State University*, 321 N.C. 706, 365 S.E.2d 898 (1988).
4. *Allen v. Equity & Investors Management Corp.*, 56 N.C.App. 706, 289 S.E.2d 623 (1982).
5. *Baker v. Duhan*, 75 N.C.App. 191, 330 S.E.2d 53 (1985).
6. NCGS § 42-39.
7. *DiOrio v. Penny*, 331 N.C. 726, 417 S.E.2d 457 (1992).

Figure 4-2. §42-42. Landlord to Provide Fit Premises

(a) The landlord shall:

(1) Comply with the current applicable building and housing codes, whether enacted before or after October 1, 1977, to the extent required by the operation of such codes; no new requirement is imposed by this subdivision (a)(1) if a structure is exempt from a current building code.

(2) Make all repairs and do whatever is necessary to put and keep the premises in a fit and habitable condition.

(3) Keep all common areas of the premises in safe condition.

(4) Maintain in good and safe working order and promptly repair all electrical, plumbing, sanitary, heating, ventilating, air conditioning, and other facilities and appliances supplied or required to be supplied by the landlord provided that notification of needed repairs is made to the landlord in writing by the tenant, except in emergency situations.

(5) Provide operable smoke detectors, either battery-operated or electrical, having an Underwriters' Laboratories, Inc., listing or other equivalent national testing laboratory approval, and install the smoke detectors in accordance with either the standards of the National Fire Protection Association or the minimum protection designated in the manufacturer's instructions, which the landlord shall retain or provide as proof of compliance. The landlord shall replace or repair the smoke detectors within 15 days of receipt of notification if the landlord is notified of needed replacement or repairs in writing by the tenant. The landlord shall ensure that a smoke detector is operable and in good repair at the beginning of each tenancy. Unless the landlord and the tenant have a written agreement to the contrary, the landlord shall place new batteries in a battery-operated smoke detector at the beginning of a tenancy and the tenant shall replace the batteries as needed during the tenancy. Failure of the tenant to replace the batteries as needed shall not be considered as negligence on the part of the tenant or the landlord.

(b) The landlord is not released of his obligations under any part of this section by the tenant's explicit or implicit acceptance of the landlord's failure to provide premises complying with this section, whether done before the lease was made, when it was made, or after it was made, unless a governmental subdivision imposes an impediment to repair for a specific period of time not to exceed six months. Notwithstanding the provisions of this subsection, the landlord and tenant are not prohibited from making a subsequent written contract wherein the tenant agrees to perform specified work on the premises, provided that said contract is supported by adequate consideration other than the letting of the premises and is not made with the purpose or effect of evading the landlord's obligations under this Article.

---

1. Tenant Suits under Residential Rental Agreements Act

When a landlord violates the RRAA, the tenant is entitled to damages. If tenants can prove their case, then they are entitled to damages that are calculated by the difference between the fair rental value of the leased premises as they should have been, versus the fair rental value of the leased premises in their unfit condition. The tenant is also entitled to recover special and consequential damages. These are damages that refer to the tenant's out-of-pocket expenses directly related to the landlord's duty to provide a safe and habitable residence.[8]

---

8. *Miller v. C.W. Myers Trading Post, Inc.*, 85 N.C.App. 362, 355 S.E.2d 189 (1987).

2. *Unfair or Deceptive Trade Practices*

The Unfair or Deceptive Trade Practices Act has also been applied to residential landlords. This act prohibits fraud and other deceptions in dealing with tenants.[9]

Figure 4-3. § 75-1.1. Methods of Competition, Acts and Practices Regulated;
          Legislative Policy

(a) Unfair methods of competition in or affecting commerce, and unfair or deceptive acts or practices in or affecting commerce, are declared unlawful.

Figure 4-4. The Landlord's Duties to the Tenant Include

• Making sure that the premises comply with applicable building and housing codes
• To make any repairs as necessary to keep the premises safe and in working condition
• To keep all common areas free of garbage and trash in any other impediments.

C. The Tenant's Duties to the Landlord

Because the landlord-tenant relationship is mutual, the tenant also owes some duties to the landlord. These duties include the obligation to keep the leased premises clean, to dispose of garbage, to refrain from damaging the property beyond normal wear and tear and, obviously, to pay rent.

Among the tenant's obligations are to keep the premises clean and safe and not allow any unsafe or unsanitary conditions to develop on the leased premises. As part of an obligation, the tenant must dispose of all garbage and other rubbish in a clean and safe manner, keep all plumbing fixtures clean and not deliberately destroy or deface any part of the premises. In the event that the tenant violates these obligations, the tenant is responsible for all damage done to the property. The tenant's obligation does not apply to normal wear and tear. It also does not apply to damage done by natural forces or accidents.[10]

Figure 4-5. What Duties Does a Tenant Owe to the Landlord?

• The obligation to keep the leased premises clean and safe
• The obligation to dispose of garbage
• To keep plumbing fixtures clean
• The obligation not to destroy, alter, damage or deface the leased premises
• The obligation to pay for any damages above normal wear and tear
• The obligation to pay rent on an agreed-upon basis.

---

9. *Friday v. United Dominion Realty Trust, Inc.*, 155 N.C.App. 671, 575 S.E.2d 532 (2003).
10. NCGS § 42-42.

Figure 4-6. Tenant's Statutory Obligations

§ 42-43. Tenant to maintain dwelling unit

(a) The tenant shall:

(1) Keep that part of the premises that the tenant occupies and uses as clean and safe as the conditions of the premises permit and cause no unsafe or unsanitary conditions in the common areas and remainder of the premises that the tenant uses.

(2) Dispose of all ashes, rubbish, garbage, and other waste in a clean and safe manner.

(3) Keep all plumbing fixtures in the dwelling unit or used by the tenant as clean as their condition permits.

(4) Not deliberately or negligently destroy, deface, damage, or remove any part of the premises, nor render inoperable the smoke detector provided by the landlord, or knowingly permit any person to do so.

(5) Comply with any and all obligations imposed upon the tenant by current applicable building and housing codes.

(6) Be responsible for all damage, defacement, or removal of any property inside a dwelling unit in the tenant's exclusive control unless the damage, defacement or removal was due to ordinary wear and tear, acts of the landlord or the landlord's agent, defective products supplied or repairs authorized by the landlord, acts of third parties not invitees of the tenant, or natural forces.

(7) Notify the landlord, in writing, of the need for replacement of or repairs to a smoke detector. The landlord shall ensure that a smoke detector is operable and in good repair at the beginning of each tenancy. Unless the landlord and the tenant have a written agreement to the contrary, the landlord shall place new batteries in a battery-operated smoke detector at the beginning of a tenancy and the tenant shall replace the batteries as needed during the tenancy. Failure of the tenant to replace the batteries as needed shall not be considered as negligence on the part of the tenant or the landlord.

(b) The landlord shall notify the tenant in writing of any breaches of the tenant's obligations under this section except in emergency situations.

---

1. Ordinary Wear and Tear

Although the tenant is responsible for damages done to the leased premises, this liability does not extend to "ordinary wear and tear." This is a phrase that refers to the minor damage done to any premises over a period of time. Examples of ordinary wear and tear would include:

- Scratches and dents in doors
- Signs of wear in carpeting or flooring
- General dirt and grime that accumulates during normal living
- Nail holes in walls

IV. The Tenant Security Deposit Act

The Tenant Security Deposit Act regulates the manner in which landlords can collect and subsequently use tenant deposits. The act requires that security deposits must be placed in a trust account. The landlord can use a security deposit to pay outstanding rent or for damages done that exceed normal wear and tear on the premises. The landlord can also apply the security deposit toward a lease term where the tenant leaves early or for unpaid bills. The maximum amount set by the statute for a month-to-month estate is two month's rent.[11]

If the landlord uses the deposit proceeds, he or she must make an accounting to the tenant itemizing the damages and mail this accounting to the tenant within 30 days of the estate termination.[12] The Act also permits tenants to bring suit against landlords who fail to refund the deposit.[13]

Figure 4-7. § 42-50. Deposits from the Tenant

Security deposits from the tenant in residential dwelling units shall be deposited in a trust account with a licensed and insured bank or savings institution located in the State of North Carolina or the landlord may, at his option, furnish a bond from an insurance company licensed to do business in North Carolina. The security deposits from the tenant may be held in a trust account outside of the State of North Carolina only if the landlord provides the tenant with an adequate bond in the amount of said deposits. The landlord or his agent shall notify the tenant within 30 days after the beginning of the lease term of the name and address of the bank or institution where his deposit is currently located or the name of the insurance company providing the bond.

A. Pet Deposits

Under the Act, landlords are permitted to charge a "reasonable, nonrefundable" fee as a pet deposit.[14] This deposit is the landlord's way not only to seek compensation for the unique types of damages caused by pets, but also a way to control the nature, quantity and size of the pets that the tenant brings onto the property.

B. Late Fees

When rent is due in monthly installments, the maximum late fee that can be charged is $15 or 5% of the monthly rent, whichever is greater. If the rent is due in weekly installments, the late fee is either four dollars or 5% in weekly rent, whichever is greater.

V. Discriminatory Practices

Under North Carolina General Statute 41A (The State Fair Housing Act) it is unlawful to discriminate against tenants on the basis of race, color, religion, etc.

---

11. NCGS § 42-51.
12. NCGS § 42-52.
13. NCGS § 42-55.
14. NCGS § 42-53.

Figure 4-8. § 41A-4. Unlawful Discriminatory Housing Practices

(a) It is an unlawful discriminatory housing practice for any person in a real estate transaction, because of race, color, religion, sex, national origin, handicapping condition, or familial status to:

    (1) Refuse to engage in a real estate transaction;

    (2) Discriminate against a person in the terms, conditions, or privileges of a real estate transaction or in the furnishing of facilities or services in connection therewith;

        (2a) Refuse to permit, at the expense of a handicapped person, reasonable modifications of existing premises occupied or to be occupied by the person if the modifications are necessary to the handicapped person's full enjoyment of the premises; except that, in the case of a rental unit, the landlord may, where it is reasonable to do so, condition permission for modifications on agreement by the renter to restore the interior of the premises to the condition that existed before the modifications, reasonable wear and tear excepted;

        (2b) Refuse to make reasonable accommodations in rules, policies, practices, or services, when these accommodations may be necessary to a handicapped person's equal use and enjoyment of a dwelling

---

VI. Lead-Based Disclosure

Under the Federal Residential Lead-Based Hazard Reduction Act of 1992,[15] landlords who own and lease houses built prior to 1978 must make specific disclosures to potential tenants. These disclosures include: a lead hazard information pamphlet, disclosure of any known lead-based paint, and the requirement to give the tenant 10 days to conduct his own risk assessment or to inspect the premises for lead-based paint.

VII. Specific Types of Tenancies

There are four types of non-freehold, landlord-tenant relationships. They are:

- A tenancy for years (estate for a stated term)
- A tenancy from year-to-year (estate from period to period)
- A tenancy at will
- A tenancy at sufferance

A. Tenancy for Years (Estate for a Stated Period)

An estate or tenancy for years is classified as any tenancy that will expire at a specific time. Many legal commentators have suggested that a more appropriate name for this tenancy would be an Estate for a Stated Period, for the simple reason that an estate for years could actually be for a period considerably less than one year, such as a month, a week or even a day.

---

15. 42 U.S.C. § 4851.

An estate for a stated period is created by the express terms of the lease. Viewed in this way, the lease is actually a contract between the landlord and the tenant setting out the specific rights of each and also the date upon which the leasehold terminates.

1. Termination of an Estate for a Stated Period of Time

Because an estate for a stated period is created by the specificity of the termination date, this tenancy expires by its own terms. No notice of cancellation is required by either party to terminate the lease. Although notice of cancellation is not required, such leases often contain provisions setting a deadline for a notice of renewal or extension of the lease.

2. Notice of Termination

The notice required to cancel the different types of tenancies depends on their legal status. For instance, in a tenancy from year-to-year, notice to cancel must be received at least one month prior to the stated term of the lease. On the other hand, tenancies from month-to-month or period-to-period require seven day's notice. In tenancies from week to week, two day's notice is required.

Figure 4-9. § 42-14. Notice to Quit in Certain Tenancies

A tenancy from year to year may be terminated by a notice to quit given one month or more before the end of the current year of the tenancy; a tenancy from month to month by a like notice of seven days; a tenancy from week to week, of two days. Provided, however, where the tenancy involves only the rental of a space for a manufactured home as defined in G.S. 143-143.9(6), a notice to quit must be given at least 30 days before the end of the current rental period, regardless of the term of the tenancy.

B. Estate from Year to Year (Estate from Period to Period)

Tenancies from period to period are created by the agreement among the parties or, in some cases, court action. Courts may interpret a lease as a tenancy from year-to-year when a lease does not provide a specific termination date. These tenancies are also created when a tenant holds over from an original estate for years and there is no new agreement between the landlord and tenant.

1. Termination of an Estate from Year to Year

These tenancies do not terminate automatically. Instead, the parties must give notice to cancel a tenancy from period to period. Generally, either party must give notice at least one month prior to the end of a year-to-year lease. When the lease is month-to-month, the required cancellation notice is seven days. Unless there is a cancellation, the tenancy will continue for an indefinite period of time.

C. Tenancy at Will

A tenancy at will is created when the landlord and tenant enter into a lease agreement where the term is not definite.[16] This tenancy is also created when the parties agree that the estate will last "as long as the parties desire." Either party can terminate such a tenancy at any time.[17] The only requirement is that the parties receive "reasonable notice." When the landlord gives reasonable notice of cancellation or makes a demand for possession of the property and the tenant remains, the estate classification changes from a tenancy at will to a tenancy at sufferance.[18]

1. Termination of a Tenancy at Will

Any party can terminate a tenancy at will at any time. There is no minimum statutory period of time required, except that the tenant should be given reasonable time to remove her personal objects from the premises.

D. Tenancy at Sufferance

Unlike the other tenancies we have discussed, a tenancy at sufferance is not created by agreement of the parties. Instead, a tenancy of sufferance comes into existence when a tenant holds over on a lease without the landlord's consent. In such a situation, the landlord is free to begin eviction procedures. However, if the landlord accepts rental payments from the tenant, a tenancy at will is created.

1. Termination of a Tenancy at Sufferance

A tenancy at sufferance is not a true estate at all. The tenant is on the premises unlawfully and therefore there is no notice requirement at all to terminate the tenant's status. However, the landlord must follow eviction procedures as they are set out under North Carolina law and discussed later in this chapter.

VIII. Real Estate Leases

Because the lease is the embodiment of the contractual agreement between the landlord and tenant, the lease contains not only basic contractual elements, but also some specifics that are required by the unique nature of real property law. In this section, we will discuss not only the various types of leases, but also the minimum legal requirements of leases under North Carolina law. We will begin our discussion with the various types of leases commonly seen between landlords and tenants.

---

16. *Barbee v. Lamb*, 225 NC 211, 34 SE2d 65 (1945).
17. *Davis v. Lovick*, 226 NC 252, 37 SE2d 680 (1946).
18. *Sappenfield v. Goodman*, 215 NC 417, 2 SE2d 13 (1939).

A. Types of Leases

Leases come in a wide variety of arrangements, from fixed rent leases to agricultural leases. Each has its own specific features and entitlements.

1. Fixed Rent Leases

A fixed rent lease, which is one of the common forms of a lease, the landlord charges a flat fee that must be paid at a regular interval by the tenant. In residential fixed rent leases, for example, the regular interval is monthly.

2. Percent Leases

A percentage lease is a lease in which some or all of the rental payment is calculated based on the gross receipts of the tenant's business. Usually, it is a percentage of the tenant's sales and is used in commercial leases. In some situations, a landlord would charge a minimum flat rental plus a percentage of monthly or annual gross sales in addition to that flat fee.

3. Net Leases

In a net lease, the tenant is responsible not only for paying rent but also for all costs associated with the premises, such as utility bills and property taxes.

4. Ground Leases

A ground lease is an arrangement between a landlord and tenant where the tenant leases vacant land for a specific period of time. Ground leases can last for decades and usually have some provision that during the tenant's possession he will construct a building on the premises.

5. Mineral Leases

A mineral lease allows the tenant to evaluate the parcel for possible extraction of minerals, ores and other materials. According to North Carolina's Statute of Frauds, mineral leases for any period of time must be in writing.

6. Oil and Gas Leases

Oil and gas leases allow the tenant to explore the property for oil, natural gas and related products and to use those resources in production.

B. Creating the Landlord-Tenant Relationship

The landlord-tenant relationship often can be a verbal agreement between the parties, but it usually takes the form of a written contract, otherwise known as a lease. The lease has outlines duties and obligations of each of the parties, details the mechanism that each party has to bring action against the other for default under the agreement and also sets the length of the agreement between the landlord and tenant. In the next few sections, we will examine specific parts of the residential lease agreement, beginning with the minimum requirements of the lease set out by North Carolina law and other typical lease provisions commonly provided in residential leases.

1. Required Provisions under North Carolina Law

The minimum requirements of a lease in North Carolina are:

- Identifiable landlord
- Identifiable tenant
- Clearly identified leased premises
- Specific term of the lease

Recitation of the consideration involved in the lease[19]

2. Common Lease Clauses and Provisions

In the following sections, we will examine common lease clauses and provisions that are found in most residential rental agreements. This list is, by no means, exhaustive.

a. Renewal

Many leases contain clauses that allow for the parties to renew the lease when it expires. The parties may simply give notice that they intend to create a new lease term that is identical to the previous one. In some situations, the lease agreement may contain an automatic renewal provision. For instance, a year-to-year lease might contain a provision that creates a month-to-month lease once the original term has expired and the tenant remains on the premises.[20]

b. Deposits

Earlier in this chapter we saw that not only can landlords require a deposit, but also that North Carolina law has strict requirements governing how these deposits may be used. Landlords frequently require deposits as a means of ensuring tenants' behavior as well as a way to compensate themselves for damages caused by the tenant during the lease term.

c. Persons Permitted to Be on the Premises

Another common provision found in leases concerns the people who are permitted to be on the premises. Obviously, landlords have a vested interest in reducing the overall number of people who are permitted to live on the site. More people means more wear and tear on the premises. When there are more than the allotted number of residents, there may also be implications for safety reasons, such as fire code regulations. As a result, landlords frequently insert provisions in residential leases that enumerate exactly who, and who is not, allowed to be on the premises.

---

19. *Carolina Helicopter Corp. v Cutter Realty Co.*, 263 NC 139, 139 SE2d 362 (1964).
20. *Stanley v. Harvey*, 90 N.C.App. 535, 369 S.E.2d 382 (1988).

d. Fixtures

The parties will also wish to define the nature of fixtures. A fixture is an item of personal property that has become permanently attached to real property. When this occurs, the personal property is reclassified as real property and is referred to as a fixture. Residential tenants are not allowed to remove fixtures and take them with them.

You will find examples of all of these lease provisions in the apartment lease agreement provided in Figure 4-10.

Figure 4-10. Apartment Lease Agreement

This is a residential rental agreement between Larry Landlord, Inc (hereafter referred to as "Landlord" and _____, (hereafter referred to as "Tenant." The terms "Landlord" and "tenant" shall apply with equal force to males or females. Throughout this document, both tenant and landlord are referred to with male pronouns; however, these terms encompass male, female usage, singular and plural.

The consideration for this lease is the rent that you, as the tenant, will pay to the landlord. The amount of the rent is _____ for the premises, more particularly described as _____ (hereafter referred to as "premises."

TENANT hereby agrees to lease the above premises and to the following, numbered provisions.

1. Lease Period.

The period of this lease runs for ___ months. The lease period begins on the ___ day of _____, 20__ and ends on the ___ day of _____, 20__. This period shall be referred to as the initial term of the lease.

a. The lease will terminate without the requirement of any cancellation notice by either side on the final date of the initial term of the lease.

b. The lease may be renewed, subject to the renewal provisions set out later in this document.

c. If the tenant remains on the premises after the expiration of the lease term, the tenancy shall automatically be deemed a month-to-month tenancy as that tenancy is described under North Carolina law.

2. Rental Payments and Late Fees.

The Tenant hereby agrees to make rental payments, and to make such payments with notice or demand by Landlord. The rental amount is $_____.

The first rental payment is due on the date that this lease agreement is signed and shall be due in monthly installments on the first day of each month. The rental payment is due in advance for the month of occupancy in the leased premises.

Late Fees

If the Tenant fails to pay the full amount due under this lease agreement by the fifth day of the month, Landlord will assess a late fee equal to $15, which fee shall be added to the total amount of the rent due for that month. If the Tenant fails to make payment on the rent by the 10th day of the month, Landlord shall begin eviction procedures as set out in North Carolina General Statute § 42-25, et seq.

3. Security Deposit(s).

The Tenant shall deposit with the Landlord a security deposit in the amount of $_____. This deposit is required to secure the Tenant's payment on the rent and to reimburse the Landlord for any damages caused by the Tenant.

The security deposit shall be deposited in a trust account with a licensed and insured bank or savings institution located in the State of North Carolina. The deposit will be held in Everyman Bank and Trust, located on 1200 Main Street, Anytown, North Carolina. The security deposit, less any assessed damages, shall be returned to Tenant no less than 30 days following the expiration of the lease term.

Pet Deposit

In addition to the security deposit required above, Tenant shall also furnish a pet deposit in the amount of $_____. Tenant may keep only one pet on the leased premises. Said pet may not exceed 30 lbs in weight.

4. Acceptance of Leased Premises by Tenant.

Tenant acknowledges that he has inspected the leased premises and agrees that the premises are in safe, fit and habitable condition. Tenant also acknowledges that all electrical, plumbing, sanitation, HVAC and other systems/appliances are in good, working order.

5. Permitted Occupants of Leased Premises.

Tenant shall not allow the leased premises to be occupied or used as residence by anyone other than himself and the following listed persons:

_____

_____

6. Tenant's Duties During the Period of the Lease Agreement.

Tenant hereby agrees that, during the full term of the lease agreement, he will

❑ Keep the leased premises clean and safe
❑ Dispose of garbage, rubbish, ashes and other wastes
❑ Keep all fixtures and appliances clean
❑ Not to destroy, alter, damage or deface the leased premises
❑ Pay for any damages above normal wear and tear
❑ Pay rent on an agreed-upon basis
❑ Allow the Landlord reasonable access to the premises for the purposes of inspecting the leased premises and making repairs

7. Tenant's Insurance.

Landlord is not an insurer of the Tenant's personal property or possessions located in, near or on the leased premises. Tenant is responsible for insuring his own possessions. Landlord makes no representations concerning indemnification of Tenant's losses due to fire, accident, injury or destruction that are not caused by negligence imputed to the Landlord. Tenant is responsible for obtaining renters' insurance and paying all costs associated with such insurance, including premiums.

8. Modifying or Altering the Physical Structure.

Tenant agrees that he will not modify, alter or in any way change the physical structure of the leased premises, except for ordinary wear and tear. This provision does not apply to normal activities such as hanging framed photographs or draperies. Any work carried out by Tenant will be done in a workman-life manner and may only be commenced after written consent by the Landlord.

9. Assignments and Sub-Leasing.

The Tenant hereby agrees that he will not assignment, transfer or sub-let the leased premises without the prior, written consent of the Landlord.

10. Notice Provisions.

In the event that any notice shall be required to be mailed, or hand-delivered by Landlord to Tenant, or Tenant to Landlord, both parties agree that such notices will be mailed, hand-delivered or sent by courier to the following addresses:

Tenant: _____

Tenant hereby agrees to provide a new address to Landlord within ten days of the termination of the lease agreement.

Landlord: _____

Landlord's address is also the address where rental payments should be made.

11. Default and Eviction.

In the event of Tenant's default, Landlord will commence eviction procedures as set out in North Carolina General Statutes.

IN WITNESS WHEREOF, this Apartment Lease Agreement is signed this the ___ day of _____, 20___

_____

Tenant

_____

Tenant

_____

Tenant

_____

Landlord

3. Commercial Leases

Obviously the parties concerned in commercial leases are different than those found in residential leases. Commercial leases often involve warehouses or retail spaces and, as a result, many of the issues normally seen in residential leases do not surface here. Instead, commercial leases have their own, unique concerns. For instance, in commercial leases, the focus of the lease has more to do with how the property will be used and what will occur in the event that the tenant's business declares bankruptcy or ends in some other unforeseen way. Another issue that is commonly seen in commercial leases is the issue of trade fixtures.

a. Trade Fixtures

Earlier in this chapter, we defined a "fixture" as an item of personal property that becomes permanently attached to real property. When this occurs, the personal property becomes real property, with all that entails. Like any other form of real property, the tenant is not allowed to remove the fixture. However, the rules about fixtures change when the lease involves commercial property.

A "trade fixture" is an item of personal property that becomes more or less permanently affixed to the real estate, but is used to further the tenant's business. "Trade fixtures are distinct from the land and are treated as belonging to the tenant."[21] Under this ruling, a tenant is allowed to remove trade fixtures during the lease term and for a reasonable time after the lease expires.

C. Lease Assignments and Sub-Letting

A tenant may assign or sublet an estate for a stated term, unless the lease provides specific language limiting these rights. An example of limiting language would include a landlord's provision in the lease stating that the tenancy cannot be assigned without the

---

21. *Harris v. Lamar Co.*, 150 N.C.App. 437, 563 S.E.2d 642 (2002).

written permission of the landlord. Most landlords include provisions limiting a tenant's ability to assign or sublet the lease. You see an example of such limiting language in Figure 4-10.

D. Statute of Frauds Concerns in Leases

North Carolina's Statute of Frauds requires certain types of contracts to be in writing before they can be enforceable. Categories of transactions that fall under the Statute of Frauds include pre-detrimental agreements, transfer of ownership and real estate interests, and any contract that, by its provisions, cannot be performed in less than a year. When a lease encompasses a period of time that is greater than one year, the Statute of Frauds requires it to be in writing. If the landlord and the tenant negotiate a lease agreement in excess of one year and fail to put the agreement in writing, neither party may bring suit to enforce the lease provisions. However, putting a lease agreement into writing is always a good idea, even when the lease period is for less than a year.

Figure 4-11. § 22-2. Contract for Sale of Land; Leases

All contracts to sell or convey any lands, tenements or hereditaments, or any interest in or concerning them, and all leases and contracts for leasing land for the purpose of digging for gold or other minerals, or for mining generally, of whatever duration; and all other leases and contracts for leasing lands exceeding in duration three years from the making thereof, shall be void unless said contract, or some memorandum or note thereof, be put in writing and signed by the party to be charged therewith, or by some other person by him thereto lawfully authorized.

IX. Eviction

When the tenant fails to live up to the obligations set out in the lease, such as failing to make monthly rental payments, the landlord may take action against the tenant to enforce the lease terms. The landlord may assess late fees against the tenant for failure to pay the rent by a specified time, but if the tenant has completely stopped making regular monthly rental payments, the only real option left to the landlord is to evict the tenant. Under North Carolina law, the landlord is not free to simply go to the leased premises, haul the tenant onto the street, throw the tenant's personal belongings after him, and then rent the premises to someone else. North Carolina has a very strict procedural method used to evict tenants and must be followed in every case.

Figure 4-12. § 42-25.6. Manner of Ejectment of Residential Tenants

It is the public policy of the State of North Carolina, in order to maintain the public peace, that a residential tenant shall be evicted, dispossessed or otherwise constructively or actually removed from his dwelling unit only in accordance with the procedure prescribed in Article 3 or Article 7 of this Chapter.

A. Eviction Procedures

Eviction is a court procedure, normally carried out under the auspices of the Small Claims Court. As such, that court's rules should be followed in regards to preparation of a complaint and service of summons on the tenant.

Figure 4-13. § 42-26. Tenant Holding over May Be Dispossessed in Certain Cases

(a) Any tenant or lessee of any house or land, and the assigns under the tenant or legal representatives of such tenant or lessee, who holds over and continues in the possession of the demised premises, or any part thereof, without the permission of the landlord, and after demand made for its surrender, may be removed from such premises in the manner hereinafter prescribed in any of the following cases:

(1) When a tenant in possession of real estate holds over after his term has expired.

(2) When the tenant or lessee, or other person under him, has done or omitted any act by which, according to the stipulations of the lease, his estate has ceased.

(3) When any tenant or lessee of lands or tenements, who is in arrear for rent or has agreed to cultivate the demised premises and to pay a part of the crop to be made thereon as rent, or who has given to the lessor a lien on such crop as a security for the rent, deserts the demised premises, and leaves them unoccupied and uncultivated.

B. Wrongful Eviction

When a landlord fails to abide by North Carolina's statute governing eviction, the landlord may be liable for sanctions, such as allowing the tenant to recover possession of the leased premises and for damages to the tenant. Under North Carolina law, a landlord's damages do not include punitive damages.[22]

When a tenant has been wrongfully evicted, she has several possible remedies including:

- Recover possession of the leased premises
- Terminate the lease
- Recover damages against the landlord for costs associated with the tenant's removal[23]

C. Act Prohibiting Retaliatory Eviction

The process of eviction cannot be used as a means to retaliate against the tenant. Put another way, landlords are not free to evict tenants who complain about the state of the premises. The practical result of the act is to give tenants the right to raise the affirmative defense of retaliatory eviction. If the tenant prevails on a claim of retaliatory eviction, the court may reinstate the tenant in the leased premises and assess other damages against the landlord.

---

22. NCGS § 42-25.9.
23. NCGS § 42-25.9.

Figure 4-14. §42-37.1. Defense of Retaliatory Eviction

(a) It is the public policy of the State of North Carolina to protect tenants and other persons whose residence in the household is explicitly or implicitly known to the landlord, who seek to exercise their rights to decent, safe, and sanitary housing. Therefore, the following activities of such persons are protected by law:

(1) A good faith complaint or request for repairs to the landlord, his employee, or his agent about conditions or defects in the premises that the landlord is obligated to repair under G.S. 42-42;

(2) A good faith complaint to a government agency about a landlord's alleged violation of any health or safety law, or any regulation, code, ordinance, or State or federal law that regulates premises used for dwelling purposes;

(3) A government authority's issuance of a formal complaint to a landlord concerning premises rented by a tenant;

(4) A good faith attempt to exercise, secure or enforce any rights existing under a valid lease or rental agreement or under State or federal law; or

(5) A good faith attempt to organize, join, or become otherwise involved with, any organization promoting or enforcing tenants' rights.

(b) In an action for summary ejectment pursuant to G.S. 42-26, a tenant may raise the affirmative defense of retaliatory eviction and may present evidence that the landlord's action is substantially in response to the occurrence within 12 months of the filing of such action of one or more of the protected acts described in subsection (a) of this section.

(c) Notwithstanding subsections (a) and (b) of this section, a landlord may prevail in an action for summary ejectment if:

(1) The tenant breached the covenant to pay rent or any other substantial covenant of the lease for which the tenant may be evicted, and such breach is the reason for the eviction; or

(2) In a case of a tenancy for a definite period of time where the tenant has no option to renew the lease, the tenant holds over after expiration of the term; or

(3) The violation of G.S. 42-42 complained of was caused primarily by the willful or negligent conduct of the tenant, member of the tenant's household, or their guests or invitees; or

(4) Compliance with the applicable building or housing code requires demolition or major alteration or remodeling that cannot be accomplished without completely displacing the tenant's household; or

(5) The landlord seeks to recover possession on the basis of a good faith notice to quit the premises, which notice was delivered prior to the occurrence of any of the activities protected by subsections (a) and (b) of this section; or

(6) The landlord seeks in good faith to recover possession at the end of the tenant's term for use as the landlord's own abode, to demolish or make major alterations or remodeling of the dwelling unit in a manner that requires the complete displacement of the tenant's household, or to terminate for at least six months the use of the property as a rental dwelling unit.

D. Expedited Evictions

North Carolina law does provide for expedited eviction in certain cases. For instance, if a tenant is a convicted felon, the landlord may seek expedited eviction of the tenant under the provisions of North Carolina General Statute §42-59. In order to take advantage of this new and improved eviction process, the landlord must show that the tenant is involved in illegal activity, such as drug dealing or has been convicted of a felony, as those terms are defined in the statute.[24]

---

24. NCGS §42-62.

Figure 4-15. §42-59.1. Statement of Public Policy

The General Assembly recognizes that the residents of this State have the right to the peaceful, safe, and quiet enjoyment of their homes. The General Assembly further recognizes that these rights, as well as the health, safety, and welfare of residents, are often jeopardized by the criminal activity of other residents of rented residential property, but that landlords are often unable to remove those residents engaged in criminal activity. In order to ensure that residents of this State can have the peaceful, safe, and quiet enjoyment of their homes, the provisions of this Article are deemed to apply to all residential rental agreements in this State.

Sidebar: Under Expedited Eviction Act, landlords are permitted to bring civil actions to evict tenants who have been convicted of felonies.

Relevant Case

Conley v. Emerald Isle Realty, Inc., 350 N.C. 293, 513 S.E.2d 556 (1999)

LAKE, Justice.

The question presented for review is whether the Court of Appeals erred in reversing the trial court's order entering summary judgment for all defendants. In support of its decision, the Court of Appeals ruled that plaintiffs' forecast of the evidence could support a finding that defendants breached their implied warranty affirming that the premises was suitable for tenant occupancy. Since we decline to impose an implied warranty of suitability on landlords who lease a furnished residence for a short period, we reverse the decision of the Court of Appeals.

Plaintiffs made the following basic allegations in the complaint filed in this action. Plaintiffs are Charles and Anna Conley; their three sons, Charles, Robert and William; their sons' spouses, Regina, Patricia and Janet; and three of Charles and Anna's grandchildren. Defendants are the Ingram family (hereinafter "defendants Ingram") and also Emerald Isle Realty, Inc., a real-estate company located in Emerald Isle, which is in the business of renting beach condominiums and cottages. The subject property is the "Janus Cottage," an oceanfront house located in Emerald Isle and owned by defendants Ingram. Defendants Ingram listed their cottage for weekly rental through defendant Emerald Isle Realty. Defendant Emerald Isle Realty provided defendants Ingram with an itemized list of all maintenance work and repairs and consulted with defendants Ingram before the beginning of each tourist season with regard to recommended repair work for the cottage.

Plaintiffs William and Janet Conley rented the Janus Cottage through defendant Emerald Isle Realty for a two-week period during the summer of 1994. The rental was for the purpose of a family vacation. Even though only William and Janet Conley signed the rental agreement, all of the plaintiffs Conley were vacationing at the cottage. After dinner on the night of 30 July 1994, the plaintiffs went onto the second-story deck on the sound side of the cottage to have their picture taken. Anna Conley had the camera and stood closest to the house. As the remaining members of the Conley family gathered for the photograph, the deck separated from the house. The deck then collapsed, causing the plaintiffs to fall from the second floor to a first floor deck, which also collapsed.

On 22 February 1996, plaintiffs instituted this action against defendant Emerald Isle Realty and defendants Ingram to recover damages for plaintiffs' injuries which resulted from the collapsed deck. On 6 August 1997, defendant Emerald Isle Realty and defendants Ingram filed separate motions for summary judgment. The motions were heard at the 18 August 1997 Civil Session of Superior Court, Carteret County. On 19 August 1997, the trial court entered an order granting both motions for summary judgment. Plaintiffs then appealed to the Court of Appeals.

The Court of Appeals reversed the trial court's order granting summary judgment. Conley v. Emerald Isle Realty, Inc., 130 N.C.App. 309, 502 S.E.2d 688 (1998). Defendant Emerald Isle Realty and defendants Ingram each petitioned this Court for discretionary review. On 5 November 1998, this Court entered orders allowing discretionary review for all defendants.

Defendant Emerald Isle Realty and defendants Ingram contend that the Court of Appeals erred in reversing the trial court's order of summary judgment for defendants on the grounds that North Carolina has never imposed an implied warranty of suitability upon the lessor of a short-term leasehold. For the reasons stated herein, we agree.

In the decision below, the Court of Appeals correctly noted that the North Carolina Residential Rental Agreements Act (the Act), codified at chapter 42, article 5 of the North Carolina General Statutes, does not apply to the facts of this case. Conley, 130 N.C.App. at 312, 502 S.E.2d at 690. The Act obligates landlords to "[m]ake all repairs and do whatever is necessary to put and keep the premises in a fit and habitable condition." N.C.G.S. §42-42(a)(2) (Supp.1998). However, the scope of the Act extends only to premises which are "normally held out for the use of residential tenants who are using the dwelling unit as their primary residence." N.C.G.S. §42-40(2) (1994). The parties to the case at bar do not dispute that the rented beach cottage was not plaintiffs' primary residence.

Since the Act specifically does not apply to short-term vacation rentals such as the one involved here, North Carolina's common law rules concerning the landlord-tenant relationship control. This Court has long applied the enactment of our legislature in this regard:

> All such parts of the common law as were heretofore in force and use within this State, or so much of the common law as is not destructive of, or repugnant to, or inconsistent with, the freedom and independence of this State and the form of government therein established, and which has not been otherwise provided for in whole or in part, not abrogated, repealed, or become obsolete, are hereby declared to be in full force within this State.

The "common law" which we have held is to be applied in North Carolina "is the common law of England to the extent it was in force and use within this State at the time of the Declaration of Independence; is not otherwise contrary to the independence of this State or the form of government established therefor; and is not abrogated, repealed, or obsolete." Gwathmey, 342 N.C. at 296, 464 S.E.2d at 679. Historically, North Carolina has applied the rule of caveat emptor to landlord-tenant relations. Robinson v. Thomas, 244 N.C. 732, 736, 94 S.E.2d 911, 914 (1956). Therefore, under the common law, the "landlord is under no duty to make repairs." Id. In addition, "[t]he owner is not liable for personal injury caused by failure to repair."

In the decision below, the Court of Appeals modified the common law by adopting an implied warranty of suitability as an exception to the common law rule. After noting that a landlord-tenant relationship exists when there is a short-term lease of furnished premises, the Court of Appeals stated:

In recognizing this landlord-tenant relationship, however, [other] courts have rejected the common law rule absolving the landlord from all liability for unknown dangerous defects in the premises. Instead, these courts hold that the landlord who leases a furnished residence for a short period "impliedly warrants that the furnished premises will be initially suitable for tenant occupancy." We agree with this exception to the common law rule.

The Court of Appeals then reasoned that since a jury could conclude that the Ingrams breached this implied warranty of suitability, summary judgment for the Ingrams was improper. Id. Further, with regard to defendant Emerald Isle Realty, the Court of Appeals concluded that there was a genuine issue of fact as to whether Emerald Isle Realty, acting as the Ingrams' agent, agreed to assume part or all of the Ingrams' duty to repair or maintain the premises. We disagree as to both conclusions.

This Court has never adopted an implied warranty of suitability doctrine as an exception to our traditional landlord-tenant law, and we decline to do so now. Therefore, because the Act does not control in this case and because defendants Ingram owe no duty to plaintiffs under North Carolina's common law, summary judgment for the defendants Ingram was appropriate. Also, since North Carolina does not recognize the implied warranty of suitability and since the defendants Ingram did not owe a duty to the plaintiffs, we conclude that defendant Emerald Isle Realty is also free from liability.

Finally, we address the defendants' argument suggesting that there is some distinction between defendants' duty to plaintiffs William and Janet Conley as opposed to the rest of the Conley family. As stated by the Court of Appeals:

The basis for the defendants' argument is that the vacation home was leased only to William and Janet Conley and thus there was no landlord-tenant relationship with the remainder of the Conley family. It follows, the defendants contend, that the members of the Conley family were licensees and that "absent some active negligence" on the part of the defendants, their recourse is against William and Janet Conley.

Conley, 130 N.C.App. at 314, 502 S.E.2d at 692. The Court of Appeals disagreed with this argument and held that any guests of the tenants should also enjoy the protection provided under the implied warranty of suitability.

It is important to note that the facts of this case present a unique situation which does not appear to have been contemplated by our legislature. Since we have held that North Carolina does not recognize the implied warranty of suitability, defendants Ingram and defendant Emerald Isle Realty owe the guests of William and Janet Conley the same duty that exists under the common law. Therefore, because the controlling law imposes no duty upon the landlord to repair or maintain the leased premises for the short-term tenants' benefit, we cannot conclude that the landlord failed to reasonably maintain the premises for the protection of the tenants' visitors.

Unless the General Assembly amends the Residential Rental Agreements Act to cover short-term leases which do not serve as the tenants' "primary residence," landlords and rental agencies providing leases in this context must continue to be subject to our common law and are thus absolved from liability for personal injury caused by a failure to repair.

For the foregoing reasons, we conclude that the trial court correctly ordered summary judgment in favor of all defendants on the ground that North Carolina will not impose an implied warranty of suitability on landlords and their agents who lease a furnished residence for a short term. Therefore, the decision of the Court of Appeals is reversed, and this case is remanded to that court for further remand to the Superior Court, Carteret County, for reinstatement of the order granting summary judgment in favor of all defendants.

REVERSED AND REMANDED.

Chapter Summary

In this chapter, we have seen that a landlord-tenant relationship is created when an owner transfers certain rights out of a freehold estate and assigns them to a tenant. Among these rights is the right to use and possess the property. The landlord retains the other rights. During the time that a tenant is in possession of the property, referred to as a tenancy, the tenant has both rights and obligations that derive from that possession. The tenant and the landlord are bound to one another in a legally-recognized relationship. This relationship requires that the landlord maintain the premises in a safe and habitable way, while the tenant is required to pay the landlord for the right to use and possess the property. There are various tenancy relationships that can exist. An estate for years has a specific termination date. When a specific date or period of time lapses, the tenant ceases to hold any rights in the property. Those rights then revert to the landlord who is free to transfer them to a different tenant. An estate from year-to-year is the term used to describe a tenancy that runs for a specific period of time. This term could be as short as one week or as long as a year. A tenancy at will is created when the parties do not create specific terms for the lease, especially the lease period. Either party may terminate a tenancy at will at any time. A tenancy at sufferance, on the other hand, is not the product of a voluntary agreement between the landlord and tenant. In fact, it arises when the tenant wrongfully remains on the premises after the lease has expired.

The legal agreement that sets out the mutual obligations between the landlord and tenant is the lease. Under North Carolina law, a residential lease must meet certain minimum requirements. These requirements include: clearly identifiable landlord and tenant, a description of the lease terms, a description of the property that is to be leased and a recitation of the consideration for the lease contract.

Review Questions

1. If a landlord owns property in fee simple, what rights does he transfer to a tenant in order to create a landlord-tenant relationship?

2. Larry Landlord decides that rather than follow statutory eviction process, he will simply place a padlock on the front door of his tenant's apartment while his tenant is at work. Is this permissible?

3. Larry Landlord is in desperate need of money and uses the tenant security deposit to pay some of his personal expenses. He fully intends to repay the money before the lease term is out. Has Larry landlord violated any North Carolina legal provisions?

4. One of Larry Landlord's tenants has filed suit against Larry for discriminatory practices. Before the case comes to trial, Larry evicts the tenant. Is this action in violation of North Carolina law, and, if so, why?

5. What are the characteristics of an estate for years?

6. What are the legal elements of an estate from year-to-year?

7. When is an estate at will created?

8. When is an estate at sufferance created?

9. Are there specific types of leases that must be in writing according to the statute of frauds? If so, what are they?

10. Explain assignment of leases.

11. What type and length of notice must be given to terminate an estate for years and how does this compare with cancellation provisions for an estate from year-to-year?

12. Explain the difference between a fixed rent lease and a percentage lease.

13. What are some examples of "ordinary wear and tear?"

14. Are there any limits on the maximum amount that a landlord can require as a security deposit? Explain.

15. What is "self-help eviction?"

16. What is a ground lease?

17. What is a tenancy at will?

18. Name at least three different statutes that are important in residential leasing and explain why they are important.

19. What is a mineral lease?

20. Compare and contrast an estate for years with an estate from year-to-year.

Assignment

Using the form provided in this chapter, create a residential lease for Terry Tenant and his dog, Buster, who will live in the premises from January 1 of next year through December 31 of next year. The rent is $500 per month. The landlord will assess the maximum possible late fees, which you should calculate based on the statutes and information presented in this chapter. The landlord will also require a 10% pet fee. The landlord's name is Larry Landlord.

Terms and Phrases

Freehold
Residential Rental Agreements Act
Landlord
Tenant
Wear and Tear
Tenant Security Deposit Act
Discriminatory Practices
Lead-Based Disclosure
Estate for a Stated Term
Estate from Period to Period
Tenancy at Will
Tenancy at Sufferance
Fixed Rent Leases
Percent Leases

Net Leases
Ground Leases
Mineral Leases
Oil and Gas Leases
Deposits
Fixtures
Commercial Leases
Trade Fixtures
Assignments
Sub-letting
Eviction
Retaliatory Eviction
Expedited Evictions

Chapter 5

Buying, Selling and Transferring Interest in Real Estate

Chapter Objectives

At the conclusion of this chapter, you should be able to:

- Explain the basic procedures involved in voluntary real estate transfers
- Describe the various ways that title to real estate is transferred
- Explain how title to property can be lost involuntarily
- Explain adverse possession
- Describe the process of foreclosure

I. Introduction

In this chapter, we will explore not only the ways that owners voluntarily transfer title to property, but also the ways that property can be taken from them. Voluntary transfers include gifts, probate and wills. In each case, the owner willingly surrenders title to the real estate to another. However, there are several situations where an owner's legal rights to real estate are transferred involuntarily, such as in foreclosures, condemnation actions, accretion and adverse possession. We will explore all of these topics in this chapter, beginning with voluntary transfers.

A. Voluntary Transfers

A voluntary transaction occurs when a person who has fee simple ownership in property decides to transfer title to another person. The most common form of voluntary transfer is sale.

1. By Sale

A real estate sale embodies several different aspects of law. On the one hand, a sale is a contract between two parties. A buyer makes an offer to a seller to purchase the property. At its core, this sale arrangement is the same as any buyer-seller transaction. A buyer promises to produce a specific amount of money in exchange for the seller's promise to produce clear title to the property. On a specific day, the buyer will hand over his money to the seller and the seller will hand over title. This is the common way that almost all items are sold, from cars to houses. Although there are important differences in the sale of real estate, those differences surface later.

A real property sale, then, must satisfy the elements of a contract, including offer, acceptance, consideration, capacity and legality. On the other hand, a sale of real property is also something more. It is the transfer of a bundle of rights, from the right to mortgage to the right to leave the property to one's heirs. In these ways, a real estate sale merges different areas of law into one transaction, including contract law, the Statute of Frauds, title concerns, title insurance and federal regulations. In future chapters, we will examine these other aspects of real property transfers. Here, we will limit discussion to the nature of a real property sale, including contract law considerations.

a. A Real Estate Sale Is a Contract

Sales of real estate occur just like sales of any other item. There is a buyer and a seller. The buyer and seller negotiate with one another for the purchase of the item. The actual transaction, where the deed is delivered to the buyer in exchange for money, is referred to as the closing. We devote the entirety of chapter 12 to a discussion of real estate closings.

If a real estate sale is, at least on some level, a contract, then it must satisfy the same legal requirements as any other contract. Those elements consist of the following:

- Offer

- Acceptance

- Consideration for the promises exchanged

- Legal capacity for both parties to the transaction

- Legality of the subject contemplated in the contract

i. Offer

An offer to purchase real estate usually arises in the following way: An owner decides to sell her property and either places a "For Sale" sign in her yard, or contacts a real estate agent to arrange to have the house listed for sale. In either event, the house is advertised. This advertisement is not an offer. The "For Sale" sign is merely an invitation to submit an offer. Consider the following scenario:

Jean has decided to sell her home. She purchases a "For Sale By Owner" sign and puts it in her front yard. Tom sees the sign and contacts Jean. He asks how much the house is being sold for and Jean responds, "What are you offering?" Tom thinks it over and then makes an offer on the house of $95,000. Which person made an offer, Jean or Tom?

Answer: Tom. Jean's sign was simply an invitation to make an offer.

If the scenario set out above seems confusing, we can clear it up with a short inquiry. A legally valid offer is specific as to terms and manner of acceptance. Put another way, the legal test for what constitutes an offer is very simple: can another person accept the statement and create a binding contract? If the answer to this question is yes, then the original statement must have been an offer. If the answer to this question is no, the statement could not be an offer. Let's examine the situation involving Jean to see if we can decide whether or not her for-sale sign constituted an offer. Could anyone appear at Jean's house and say "I accept" and create a binding contract? The answer is obviously no. There are no specifics about price, the manner of acceptance or who may accept. Without the specifics, there can be no offer. If you look at Tom's statement to Jean, we see that there is an offer. Tom's statement contains all of the necessary elements for a successful offer. It is specific as to amount and who may accept. His offer of $95,000 is made to Jean. If Jean accepts the offer, a binding contract has been created.

ii. Acceptance

A legally binding acceptance creates a contract. In the scenario above, Jean's acceptance of Tom's offer creates a legally enforceable contract. In a later chapter, when we discuss the details of a real estate contract, we will see that there are some additional requirements in this transaction. However, at this point, Jean's acceptance of Tom's offer creates a legally binding contract.

iii. Consideration

The requirement of consideration is an ancient contract law prerequisite to the creation of a valid contract. Consideration refers to the requirement that both parties to a contract give up something of value in order to receive something of value. This is often referred to as "bargained for exchange" between the parties. In our example, Jean will surrender title to her property in exchange for money and Tom will exchange money for title to the property. If both parties receive something of value in the transaction the legal requirement of consideration is met. Consideration ensures that both parties have a vested interest in seeing the contract through to fruition.

iv. Capacity

Another important contractual requirement in any real estate transaction is the legal capacity of both parties. Capacity refers to the parties' ability to know and understand the consequences of their transaction. A party must be aware of his or her actions, understand those actions and be able to intelligently interact with others. A party who lacks legal capacity is incapable of entering into a contract. Examples of individuals who lack capacity include children and people who have been declared insane.

v. Legality of Subject

Finally, all contracts must have a legal subject in order to be enforced. Although this usually is not a difficult requirement to meet, legality of subject can be invoked to cancel a contract. Examples of contracts that do not have a legal subject include contracts that violate public policy or statutes. A contract that violates a statute will not be enforced. Examples of such contracts would include mortgages where the interest rates are higher than is allowed by state or federal law.

b. Other Legal Aspects of a Real Estate Sale

A real estate sale is more than a mere contract. A real estate transaction also involves the transfer of rights from one person to another. In a typical real estate transaction, these rights consist of all of the rights we associate with fee simple absolute title including the right to use, possess, enjoy, mortgage, takes crops or profits from and leave to one's heirs. Later, we will see that these additional requirements, such as satisfying the Statute of Frauds, must also be satisfied before a legally binding transaction is created.

2. By Will

Another very common method of transferring title to real property is by leaving it to another person in a will. A will is a written document in which an owner indicates his or her desire to transfer title to a specific individual on the owner's death. When a person (testator) dies with a will, he or she is said to have died testate. A will is commonly referred to as a testamentary document.

> **Will:** A written document expressing the testator's desires about the division of his or her property after death.

> **Testator:** The term for the person who writes a will that directs disposition of his or her property.

After the testator dies, the provisions of the will are put into effect. Unless the will contains an unlawful clause, the testator's wishes will be honored. Generally, the person designated in the will to receive the testator's property will receive it.

In order to be valid, a will must meet certain minimum requirements. These requirements are:

- The will must be in writing
- The will must be signed
- The will must be witnessed
- The testator must have mental capacity to decide on the dispositions of property

Probate is the process of distributing a decedent's assets after death. When a person dies with a will, his or her executor is permitted to submit the will for probate. Property may not be distributed under a will's provisions until a court has passed on its provisions. In order to be effective against bona fide purchasers, the will must be offered for probate within two years of the decedent's death.[1]

Under North Carolina law, the Clerk of the Superior Court in the county where the will is probated must notify the legatees and devisees under the will.[2] Copies of probated wills, as well as lists of beneficiaries or devisees under probated wills are kept in the Clerk's office.

Wills remain on file in the clerk's office, where they become part of the public record and play an important role in title examinations.[3] We will explore the topic of probate, wills and the indexes where this information can be located when we discuss title examinations in Chapter 11.

a. By Intestate Succession

If a landowner dies without leaving a will, he is said to have died intestate. When this occurs in North Carolina, courts must refer to the Intestate Succession Act to determine

---

1. NCGS § 31-12.
2. NCGS § 31-14.
3. NCGS § 31-20.

Figure 5-1. § 31-16. Applications for Probate must Contain

(1) That such applicant is the executor, devisee or legatee named in the will, or is some other person interested in the estate, and how so interested.

(2) The value and nature of the testator's property, as near as can be ascertained.

(3) The names and residences of all parties entitled to the testator's property, if known, or that the same on diligent inquiry cannot be discovered; which of the parties in interest are minors, and whether with or without guardians, and the names and residences of such guardians, if known.

---

which people qualify as the landowner's heirs and thus who should receive his property. In such a case, an administrator will be appointed by the court to handle the decedent's affairs and to dispose of his or her property as dictated by the statute.

Figure 5-2. Intestate Succession

N.C.G.S. § 29-14. Share of surviving spouse

(a) Real Property.—The share of the surviving spouse in the real property is:

    (1) If the intestate is survived by only one child or by any lineal descendant of only one deceased child, a one-half undivided interest in the real property;

    (2) If the intestate is survived by two or more children, or by one child and any lineal descendant of one or more deceased children or by lineal descendants of two or more deceased children, a one-third undivided interest in the real property;

    (3) If the intestate is not survived by a child, children or any lineal descendant of a deceased child or children, but is survived by one or more parents, a one-half undivided interest in the real property;

    (4) If the intestate is not survived by a child, children or any lineal descendant of a deceased child or children, or by a parent, all the real property.

(b) Personal Property.—The share of the surviving spouse in the personal property is:

    (1) If the intestate is survived by only one child or by any lineal descendant of only one deceased child, and the net personal property does not exceed thirty thousand dollars ($30,000) in value, all of the personal property; if the net personal property exceeds thirty thousand dollars ($30,000) in value, the sum of thirty thousand dollars ($30,000) plus one half of the balance of the personal property ...

---

3. By Gift

A landowner has the right to give away her land if she wishes. There is no requirement that the landowner always transfer title for value. An owner in fee simple is fully authorized to give property to another. However, there are some limitations on the power to give land as a gift. For instance, the landowner cannot give away land as a way of avoiding creditors or as a way to dodge a civil judgment. When the landowner gives property to the government, it is referred to as a dedication.

> **Dedication:** The process for giving or donating property to federal, state or local government.

Just as we saw in discussing real estate sales, the owner must have capacity to transfer title, even in a gift situation. A purported gift made by someone who is legally incompetent can be voided by the courts.

B. Involuntary or Unwilling Title Transfers

In this section, we will explore the various methods of transferring title when the owner is not a willing participant in the process. Like the previous section, these transfers are listed in the order of the most common to the least common.

1. By Foreclosure

When land is used as the collateral for a loan, the landowner gives the right of foreclosure to the lending institution. This right can be triggered when the borrower fails to make payments on the mortgage. In North Carolina, the most common method of financing real estate is through the use of a Deed of Trust, which we discuss in much greater detail in chapter 9.

When a lending institution forecloses on real estate, it is authorized to conduct an auction of the property for the outstanding balance of the loan. When a person bids on the property at the auction, he or she acquires fee simple title to the property in exchange for the bid.

a. Deeds of Trust

Deeds of Trust are the most common type of lender financing arrangements in North Carolina. Although we explore real estate financing in greater detail in a later chapter, it is important to understand the provisions of deeds of trust as they apply to foreclosures in North Carolina. A Deed of Trust is an instrument that pledges the real estate as security for the loan. In the typical Deed of Trust scenario, the purchaser signs an agreement to a trustee who will act on the lending institution's behalf in the event that the borrower defaults on the loan payment. Unlike mortgages, where there are usually only two parties, the lending institution and the borrower, in a Deed of Trust there are three parties. These parties are the lending institution, the trustee and the borrower. The trustee has the power to foreclose on the loan for the lending institution and is authorized to both advertise the property for sale and to place the property for auction, but only in the event that the borrower defaults on the loan. The most common way for a borrower to default is by failing to make regular, monthly mortgage payments to the lending institution. Although Deeds of Trust were once very common in the United States, only a handful of states continue to use them. In most states, mortgages are the preferred method of financing.

b. Foreclosing a Deed of Trust

One of the advantages of a Deed of Trust is that it takes foreclosure away from a court proceeding to a private, contractual remedy. Decisions in North Carolina clearly establish that by agreeing to the terms of the Deed of Trust, the borrower is agreeing to sidestep the technicalities of judicial foreclosure in favor of private foreclosure.[4] In states that use mortgages, foreclosure is a court remedy, involving the filing of an action and the application of Civil Rules of Procedure.

> Sidebar: Foreclosure by power of sale is a special proceeding commenced without formal summons and complaint and with no right to jury trial.[5]

---

4. *In re Foreclosure of Michael Weinman Associates*, 333 N.C. 221, 227, 424 S.E.2d 385, 388 (1993).
5. *United Carolina Bank v. Tucker*, 99 N.C.App. 95, 392 S.E.2d 410 (1990).

Figure 5-3. § 45-21.16. Notice and Hearing

(a) The mortgagee or trustee granted a power of sale under a mortgage or deed of trust who seeks to exercise such power of sale shall file with the clerk of court a notice of hearing in accordance with the terms of this section. After the notice of hearing is filed, the notice of hearing shall be served upon each party entitled to notice under this section. The notice shall specify a time and place for the hearing before the clerk of court and shall be served not less than 10 days prior to the date of such hearing. The notice shall be served and proof of service shall be made in any manner provided by the Rules of Civil Procedure for service of summons, including service by registered mail or certified mail, return receipt requested. However, in those instances that publication would be authorized, service may be made by posting a notice in a conspicuous place and manner upon the property not less than 20 days prior to the date of the hearing, and if service upon a party cannot be effected after a reasonable and diligent effort in a manner authorized above, notice to such party may be given by posting the notice in a conspicuous place and manner upon the property not less than 20 days prior to the date of hearing. Service by posting may run concurrently with any other effort to effect service. The notice shall be posted by the sheriff ...

(c) Notice shall be in writing and shall state in a manner reasonably calculated to make the party entitled to notice aware of the following:

(1) The particular real estate security interest being foreclosed, with such a description as is necessary to identify the real property, including the date, original amount, original holder, and book and page of the security instrument.

(2) The name and address of the holder of the security instrument at the time that the notice of hearing is filed.

(3) The nature of the default claimed.

(4) The fact, if such be the case, that the secured creditor has accelerated the maturity of the debt.

(5) Any right of the debtor to pay the indebtedness or cure the default if such is permitted.

(5a) The holder has confirmed in writing to the person giving the notice, or if the holder is giving the notice, the holder shall confirm in the notice, that, within 30 days of the date of the notice, the debtor was sent by first-class mail at the debtor's last known address a written statement of the amount of principal and interest that the holder claims in good faith is owed as of the date of the written statement, a daily interest charge based on the contract rate as of the date of the statement, and the amount of other expenses the holder contends it is owed as of the date of the statement.

---

i. Requirements of Foreclosure Sales

When it becomes necessary to foreclose on a Deed of Trust, there are specific statutory requirements that the trustee must follow. The statutes set out the following requirements:

- Foreclosure Notice
- Notice of Sale
- Advertising the Foreclosure
- The Legal Procedures at the Sale

Foreclosure Notice

North Carolina statutes provide that before a foreclosure can be brought, a foreclosure hearing must be scheduled. Notice for such a hearing must be served on all parties concerned at least 10 days prior to the hearing date. The notice must contain information identifying which real estate parcel is being foreclosed upon as well as the date, original amount of the loan and the deed book and page where the Deed of Trust can be located. Once a hearing has been held, the next step in a foreclosure is a notice of sale.

Notice of Sale

The sale or auction to foreclose property must take place in the county where the property is actually located. A foreclosure notice of sale designates the date, hour and place where the sale will occur under the provisions of the Deed of Trust. The notice usually contains a provision that the property is sold subject to any outstanding taxes and special assessments that remain unpaid. One of the requirements of the notice is that the foreclosure sale must be advertised in the local newspaper.

Figure 5-4. § 45-21.4. Place of Sale of Real Property

(a) Every sale of real property shall be held in the county where the property is situated unless the property consists of a single tract situated in two or more counties.

Figure 5-5. § 45-21.16A. Contents of Notice of Sale

The notice of sale shall—

(1) Describe the instrument pursuant to which the sale is held, by identifying the original mortgagors and recording data. If the record owner is different from the original mortgagors, the notice shall also list the record owner of the property, as reflected on the records of the register of deeds not more than 10 days prior to posting the notice. The notice may also reflect the owner not reflected on the records if known;

(2) Designate the date, hour and place of sale consistent with the provisions of the instrument and this Article;

(3) Describe the real property to be sold in such a manner as is reasonably calculated to inform the public as to what is being sold, which description may be in general terms and may incorporate the description as used in the instrument containing the power of sale by reference thereto. Any property described in the instrument containing the power of sale which is not being offered for sale should also be described in such a manner as to enable prospective purchasers to determine what is and what is not being offered for sale;

(5) State the terms of the sale provided for by the instrument pursuant to which the sale is held, including the amount of the cash deposit, if any, to be made by the highest bidder at the sale;

(6) Include any other provisions required by the instrument to be included therein;

(7) State that the property will be sold subject to taxes and special assessments if it is to be so sold; and

(8) State whether the property is being sold subject to or together with any subordinate rights or interests provided those rights and interests are sufficiently identified.

Advertising the Foreclosure

You can find foreclosure notices in the legal classifieds section of your local newspaper. The legal classifieds come out once a week, usually on Fridays. If you peruse these legal classifieds, you will see an abundance of foreclosure notices. Publishing the notice is required by North Carolina statutes. The foreclosure notice must be published in a local newspaper for at least two successive weeks prior to the date of the foreclosure auction. Advertising provisions also include the requirement that a notice of foreclosure must be posted at the local courthouse. When you visit the local courthouse, you often find a bulletin board or other public area covered with all types of legal notices. Among these legal postings you will usually find many legal notices captioned "Notice of Sale" or "Notice under Power of Sale."

Figure 5-6. § 45-21.17. Posting and Publishing Notice of Sale of Real Property

In addition to complying with such provisions with respect to posting or publishing notice of sale as are contained in the security instrument,

(1) Notice of sale of real property shall

    a. Be posted, in the area designated by the clerk of superior court for posting public notices in the county in which the property is situated, at least 20 days immediately preceding the sale.

    b. And in addition thereto,

        1. The notice shall be published once a week for at least two successive weeks in a newspaper published and qualified for legal advertising in the county in which the property is situated.

        2. If no such newspaper is published in the county, then notice shall be published once a week for at least two successive weeks in a newspaper having a general circulation in the county.

        3. In addition to the required newspaper advertisement, the clerk may in his discretion, on application of any interested party, authorize such additional advertisement as in the opinion of the clerk will serve the interest of the parties, and permit the charges for such further advertisement to be taxed as a part of the costs of the foreclosure.

The Legal Procedures at the Sale

On the day of the actual sale, members of the public may gather and bid on the property. The original borrower is entitled to bid on his own property at the foreclosure sale, but if the original owner could not afford to make monthly mortgage payments, it is very unlikely that he or she will be able to come up with the entire loan balance at the sale. The trustee is not authorized to bid on the property, only to conduct the sale. The successful bidder at the sale must post a cash deposit of 5% of the sales price. Following the sale, statutes provide a 10 day window for others to place an upset bid on the property.

Figure 5-7. § 45-21.10. Requirement of Cash Deposit at Sale

(a) If a mortgage or deed of trust contains provisions with respect to a cash deposit at the sale, the terms of the instrument shall be complied with.

(b) If the instrument contains no provision with respect to a cash deposit at the sale, the mortgagee or trustee may require the highest bidder immediately to make a cash deposit not to exceed the greater of five percent (5%) of the amount of the bid or seven hundred fifty dollars ($750.00).

(c) If the highest bidder fails to make the required deposit, the person holding the sale may at the same time and place immediately reoffer the property for sale.

Figure 5-8. § 45-21.27. Upset Bid on Real Property; Compliance Bonds

(a) An upset bid is an advanced, increased, or raised bid whereby any person offers to purchase real property theretofore sold, for an amount exceeding the reported sale price or last upset bid by a minimum of five percent (5%) thereof, but in any event with a minimum increase of seven hundred fifty dollars ($750.00). Subject to the provisions of subsection (b) of this section, an upset bid shall be made by delivering to the clerk of superior court, with whom the report of sale or last notice of upset bid was filed, a deposit in cash or by certified check or cashier's check satisfactory to the clerk in an amount greater than or equal to five percent (5%) of the amount of the upset bid but in no event less than seven hundred fifty dollars ($750.00) ...

2. By Condemnation (Eminent Domain)

The federal and state constitutions give governments the power of eminent domain. This power allows the government to seize private land for public use. When the government seizes land for a project, such as building a highway, this is called condemnation. The government has the right to seize anyone's property for such a purpose, but when the seizure occurs, the owner must be compensated for the loss. The payment to the owner must recognize the fair market value of the property. Calculating the fair market value is often the most hotly contested issue in a condemnation action, with the owner claiming a higher fair market value than the amount calculated by the government.

a. Inverse Condemnation

An interesting offshoot to the issue of condemnation is inverse condemnation. An inverse condemnation claim is one in which the landowner claims that the government has taken the property (or rendered it useless) through some action. The landowner's action claims that the government has seized this property without using proper channels.

Sidebar: Inverse condemnation is "a cause of action against a governmental defendant to recover the value of property which has been taken in fact by the governmental defendant, even though no formal exercise of the power of eminent domain has been attempted by the taking agency."[6]

First of all, we should clarify some of the terms used in eminent domain. "Eminent domain" is the power to "divest right, title or interest from the owner of property and vest it in the possessor of the power against the will of the owner upon the payment of just compensation for the right, title or interest divested."[7] "Condemnation," for instance, refers to the procedure through which eminent domain is exercised.[8]

Although we often think of the power of condemnation as a power reserved exclusively to the government, it can also be exercised by certain private corporations. Many utility companies have limited powers of condemnation in order to build railroads, power stations and to lay power and telephone lines[9] and gas lines.[10] General Statutes also place strict limitations on private companies and the purpose for which they condemn property.[11]

The North Carolina legislature sets out the procedures used by local and state government agencies in taking land. The owners must be reimbursed for the taking. The reimbursement comes in the form of the fair market value of the land taken.[12] A proposed taking can be invalidated by the court if it is found to be arbitrary and capricious.[13]

Once the property has been taken, not only is the owner entitled to payment for the seizure, but also to a pro rata reimbursement for any taxes already paid on the parcel.[14]

---

6. *Charlotte v. Spratt*, 263 N.C. 656, 140 S.E.2d 341 (1965).
7. NCGS § 40A-2 (3).
8. NCGS § 40A-2 (1).
9. NCGS § 40A-3.
10. NCGS § 62-190.
11. NCGS § 40A-3.
12. *North Carolina State Ports Authority v. Southern Felt Corp.*, 1 N.C. App. 231, 161 S.E.2d 47 (1968).
13. *Onuska v. Barnwell*, 140 N.C. App. 590, 537 S.E.2d 840 (2000).
14. NCGS § 40A-6.

3. Partition

We have already discussed partition in the context of the break-up of a co-tenancy. In a partition, the cotenants request a court to physically divide ownership of the property between them, creating two separate, individually-owned parcels. Although this does sometimes happen, it is more common for the property to be sold and the proceeds divided between the cotenants according to their percentage of ownership.

4. Accretion

Accretion is the process of acquiring additional property through natural forces, such as the gradual deposit of soil along one side of a riverbed. This soil is coming from somewhere else and the landowner who is losing her soil is gradually losing part of her parcel to the benefit of the other landowner downstream. When this process occurs naturally, the boundaries of the properties are adjusted to reflect the consequent loss for one and gain for the other. The North Carolina Supreme Court uses a colorful phrase to describe this process. When the lot grows increasingly smaller, the title is divested by "the sledge-hammering seas the inscrutable tides of God."[15]

5. Escheat

When a landowner dies without heirs, who gets the property? Without some way to identify an heir through intestate succession laws or by other means, there is the potential for title to simply languish. No one would be able to use the property. To avoid this dilemma, North Carolina, like most states, has created a statutory scheme called escheat. Under escheat procedures, title to the property is eventually vested in the local government, but only after specific procedures have been strictly followed.

Figure 5-9. § 29-12. Escheats

If there is no person entitled to take under G.S. 29-14 or G.S. 29-15, or if in case of an illegitimate intestate, there is no one entitled to take under G.S. 29-21 or G.S. 29-22 the net estate shall escheat as provided in G.S. 116B-2.

Figure 5-10. § 116B-1. Escheats to Escheat Fund

All real estate which has accrued to the State since June 30, 1971, or shall hereafter accrue from escheats, shall be vested in the Escheat Fund. Title to any such real property which has escheated to the Escheat Fund shall be conveyed by deed in the manner now provided by G.S. 146-74 through G.S. 146-78, except as is otherwise provided herein: Provided, that in any action in the superior court of North Carolina wherein the State Treasurer is a party, and wherein said court enters a judgment of escheat for any real property, then, upon petition of the State Treasurer in said action, said court shall have the authority to appoint the State Treasurer or his designated agent as a commissioner for the purpose of selling said real property at a public sale, for cash, at the courthouse door in the county in which the property is located, after properly advertising the sale according to law. The said commissioner, when appointed by the court, shall have the right to convey a valid title to the purchaser of the property at public sale. The funds derived from the sale of any such escheated real property by the commissioner so appointed shall thereafter be paid by him into the Escheat Fund.

---

15. *Shell Island Homeowners Ass'n, Inc. v. Tomlinson*, 134 N.C.App. 217, 517 S.E.2d 406 (1999).

Figure 5-11. Adverse Possession in North Carolina

The elements of adverse possession are that the new possession be:
- Hostile (without permission)
- Actual
- Open
- Exclusive
- Notorious and
- Continuous during the statutory period*

* *Curd v. Winecoff*, 88 N.C.App. 720, 364 S.E.2d 730 (1988); *Chicago Title Ins., Co. v. Wetherington*, 127 N.C.App. 457, 490 S.E.2d 593 (1997).

---

6. Adverse Possession

There are times when a person can acquire title to property through the process of adverse possession. This process is triggered when a person who is not the landowner moves onto the land and takes possession of it. Once possession is acquired, the new possessor must hold the land in open, actual and continuous ownership from that point onward. Courts in this state have also stated that this possession must be 'notorious.' This requirement means that a person's possession must not be secret, but must instead be obvious. The new owner proclaims his right to the property by setting up fences or other structures and holding it against the claims of others. If the new possessor maintains this possession for twenty years he can file an action in court asking to be awarded fee simple ownership.

The period varies depending on the circumstances that placed the claimant on the land in the first place. If the claimant takes possession without color of title, then he must possess the land for a minimum of twenty years. If he enters under color of title, then he must possess the land for a minimum of seven years.

> Sidebar: Local and state governments can acquire title under adverse possession in the same way that private individuals can.[16]

What Is Color of Title?

Color of title refers to a document that purports to convey interest in land but, in reality, does not. A document that grants color of title could be a voided deed, a commissioner's tax deed or any document that describes the property but does not effectively create legal title in the land.

"Color of title is that which gives the semblance or appearance of title, but is not title in fact that which on its face, professes to pass title, but fails to do so because of a want of title in the person from whom it comes or the employment of an ineffective means of conveyance."[17]

Proving Adverse Possession

When a person wishes to acquire title through adverse possession, he or she must first bring a court action. This court proceeding is referred to as an action to quiet title or, under the old Latin phrase, an action 'quia timet.'[18]

---

16. *Williams v. North Carolina State Bd. of Ed.*, 266 N.C. 761, 147 S.E.2d 381, (1966).
17. *Hensley v. Ramsey*, 283 N.C. 714, 199 S.E.2d 1 (1973); *Adams v. Severt*, 40 N.C.App. 247, 252 S.E.2d 276 (1979).
18. *Williams v. Weyerhaeuser Co.*, 378 F.2d 7 (C.A.N.C. 1967).

Figure 5-12. NCGS § 1-38. Seven Years' Possession under Color of Title

(a) When a person or those under whom he claims is and has been in possession of any real property, under known and visible lines and boundaries and under color of title, for seven years, no entry shall be made or action sustained against such possessor by a person having any right or title to the same, except during the seven years next after his right or title has descended or accrued, who in default of suing within that time shall be excluded from any claim thereafter made; and such possession, so held, is a perpetual bar against all persons not under disability: Provided, that commissioner's deeds in judicial sales and trustee's deeds under foreclosure shall also constitute color of title.

(b) If

(1) The marking of boundaries on the property by distinctive markings on trees or by the implacement of visible metal or concrete boundary markers in the boundary lines surrounding the property, such markings to be visible to a height of 18 inches above the ground, and

(2) The recording of a map prepared from an actual survey by a surveyor registered under the laws of North Carolina, in the book of maps in the office of the register of deeds in the county where the real property is located, with a certificate attached to said map by which the surveyor certifies that the boundaries as shown by the map are those described in the deed or other title instrument or proceeding from which the survey was made, the surveyor's certificate reciting the book and page or file number of the deed, other title instrument or proceeding from which the survey was made, then the listing and paying of taxes on the real property marked and for which a survey and map have been certified and recorded as provided in subdivisions (1) and (2) above shall constitute prima facie evidence of possession of real property under known and visible lines and boundaries. Maps recorded prior to October 1, 1973 may be qualified under this statute by the recording of certificates prepared in accordance with subdivision (b)(2) above. Such certificates must contain the book and page number where the map is filed, in addition to the information required by subdivision (b)(2) above, and shall be recorded and indexed in the deed books. When a certificate is filed to qualify such a recorded map, the register of deeds shall make a marginal notation on the map in the following form: "Certificate filed pursuant to G.S. 1-38(b), book .... (enter book where filed), page ..."

(c) Maps recorded prior to October 1, 1973 shall qualify as if they had been certified as herein provided if said maps can be proven to conform to the boundary lines on the ground and to conform to instruments of record conveying the land which is the subject matter of the map, to the person whose name is indicated on said recorded map as the owner thereof. Maps recorded after October 1, 1973 shall comply with the provisions for a certificate as hereinbefore set forth.

§ 1-40. Twenty years adverse possession

No action for the recovery or possession of real property, or the issues and profits thereof, shall be maintained when the person in possession thereof, or defendant in the action, or those under whom he claims, has possessed the property under known and visible lines and boundaries adversely to all other persons for 20 years; and such possession so held gives a title in fee to the possessor, in such property, against all persons not under disability.

When the possessor brings a quiet title action, he or she has the burden of proving all of the elements of adverse possession. The claimant must prove the first and most obvious element—actual possession. North Carolina courts have held on numerous occasions that intermittent possession, occasional trespasses or prospecting for gold do not satisfy this first element of adverse possession.[19]

---

19. *Davis v. Federal Land Bank of Columbia*, 219 N.C. 248, 13 S.E.2d 417 (1941).

How does a possessor prove that he has been in continuous possession of the property for the required time period? He can certainly call witnesses to testify to this fact, but he can also rely on the public records. The fact that the claimant has paid property taxes on a steady basis is certainly one factor that will weigh heavily in his favor. However, this by itself does not establish possession. The claimant must present additional proof showing that he was in possession of the property during the period required by the statute. This evidence will vary considerably from case to case.[20] The claimant must prove possession within clearly set out, known and visible boundary lines.[21]

Possession Must Be Deliberate

A person claiming title under adverse possession must also show that his possession was a deliberate action, not simply an error. The possessor must show a conscious decision to take the property and hold it against the claims made by others, including the original owner. In situations where a person takes possession mistakenly, the term of his adverse possession only begins when he discovers his mistake and then continues to hold the property. The time calculated under adverse possession will begin running at this point, not when he originally, and mistakenly, took possession.[22]

Tacking

Can a person claiming title by adverse possession rely on the possession of others? Put another way, if A takes possession of the property under color of title and holds it for three years adversely to the original owner, can B then hold the property for an additional four years and then claim title through adverse possession? The term for this is tacking and is allowed, under certain circumstances. Tacking is permissible where the successive owners can establish privity with one another.[23]

What Is Privity?

Before a party can use tacking as a method to establish the minimum time period under adverse possession, he must show privity with the previous owner. Privity is a legal relationship between the parties, such as grantor-grantee or decedent-heir. This shows that there was a recognizable legal relationship between these parties that will justify a ruling that the possession of the prior accrues the benefit of the latter. Without this showing, the succeeding owner might simply be viewed as an adverse possession against the original owner and the previous possessor.[24]

How Much Property Is Acquired under Adverse Possession?

When a person claims title under adverse possession, how much of the property will he actually receive? Does he receive title to the entire parcel, however large it may be, simply by possessing a tiny portion of it? In most cases, the adverse possessor can only claim title to the land that he actually possessed.[25] However, the rule changes when a person takes possession under a colorable claim of title that actually describes the entire tract, specifying boundary lines. Under this scenario, the adverse possessor can take title to the entire parcel.[26]

---

20. *Chisholm v. Hall*, 255 N.C. 374,121 S.E.2d 726, (1961).
21. *Mizzell v. Ewell*, 27 N.C.App. 507, 219 S.E.2d 513 (1975).
22. *Enzor v. Minton*, 123 N.C.App. 268, 472 S.E.2d 376 (1996).
23. *Lancaster v. Maple Street Homeowners Ass'n*, Inc., 156 N.C.App. 429, 577 S.E.2d 365 (2003).
24. *Atwell v. Shook*, 133 N. C. 387, 45 S. E. 777 (1903).
25. *Sessoms v. McDonald*, 237 N.C. 720, 75 S.E.2d 904 (1953).
26. *Morehead v. Harris*, 262 N.C. 330, 137 S.E.2d 174 (1964).

Exceptions to the 7-Year/20-Year Rule

There are some exceptions to these statutory periods. One such exception concerns owners who are either incompetent or minors. In either case, the incapacitated owner has three years from the removal of the disability to bring an action challenging possession.[27]

7. Tax Auctions

In our final examples of involuntary transfer of title, we come to tax auctions. Real estate taxes are assessed on virtually every type of property. Owners are legally obligated to pay their taxes and the local government is authorized to file a lien on the property to enforce payment. When an owner still fails to pay outstanding taxes, the local government is authorized to auction the property at a tax sale. The highest bidder can receive fee simple absolute title at such an auction, but courts in this state have been scrupulous is requiring strict compliance with all statutory provisions and have frequently disallowed tax deeds for features that might pass muster in other types of deeds.

Figure 5-13. Foreclosing a Tax Lien

§ 43-48. Foreclosure of tax lien
The lien for ad valorem taxes may be foreclosed and the property sold pursuant to G.S. 105-375. A note of the sale under this section shall be duly registered, and a certificate shall be entered and an owner's certificate issued in favor of the purchaser in whom title shall be thereby vested as registered owner, in accordance with the provisions of this Chapter. Nothing in this section shall be so construed as to affect or divert the title of a tenant in reversion or remainder to any real estate which has been returned delinquent and sold on account of the default of the tenant for life in paying the taxes or assessments thereon.

§ 105-375. In rem method of foreclosure
(a) Intent of Section.—It is hereby declared to be the intention of this section that proceedings brought under it shall be strictly in rem. It is further declared to be the intention of this section to provide, as an alternative to G.S. 105-374, a simple and inexpensive method of enforcing payment of taxes necessarily levied, to the knowledge of all persons, for the requirements of local governments in this State; and to recognize, in authorizing this proceeding, that all persons owning interests in real property know or should know that the tax lien on their real property may be foreclosed and the property sold for failure to pay taxes …

Relevant Case: Adverse Possession

Willis v. Johns, 55 N.C.App. 621, 286 S.E.2d 646 (1982)

WHICHARD, Judge.

Plaintiffs instituted this action in June 1977 to recover possession of real property, alleging fee simple title in themselves and wrongful and unlawful possession by defendants. Defendants answered, alleging they purchased the property in 1964 from Wake County at a public sale for delinquent taxes and claiming that the judgment of Superior Court and the Commissioner's Deed pursuant thereto constituted color of title. The Commissioner's

---

27. NCGS § 1-17.

Deed indicated that Wake County had obtained the property upon failure of the owners, heirs at law of one Henry Sanders, to pay taxes; and that defendant Jackie Johns had been the last and highest bidder at the sale. As a further defense, defendants asserted that since acquiring the property they had erected a dwelling house thereon, and that plaintiffs' recovery thereof thus would constitute unjust enrichment. Defendants sought a judgment declaring the property described in their deed free and clear of plaintiffs' claims.

The court appointed a referee-surveyor to survey and map the property. At trial, without a jury, the surveyor testified for plaintiffs that the residence occupied by defendants was situated on the Isom Cook tract which had been conveyed to plaintiffs. He further stated that the boundary description found in defendants' deed did not coincide precisely with the property in question and that the name of Henry Sanders, predecessor in title to the delinquent taxpayers through whom defendants claimed, did not appear in the files on the Isom Cook tract.

Plaintiff Allen Willis, Sr. testified that before he purchased the tract he had walked over it, had had the title searched, and had been satisfied with the title. Until the year of trial, he had paid taxes on the property. When he discovered that defendants were building a home on his property, he tried several times to contact defendant Jackie Johns and did, in fact, discuss the problem with him. Plaintiff Lucy G. Willis offered corroborative testimony.

Defendants' evidence tended to show that, in 1964, defendant Jackie Johns had purchased his tract of land, which included the property claimed by plaintiffs; that he had had it surveyed and marked; and that he had paid property taxes on it ever since. In October 1968, he had the basement of his house excavated on the disputed portion of his property, and he had a driveway constructed from the location of the house to the street. Johns could not recall talking to Allen Willis about the disputed portion until after his home had been completed and he had lived in it for approximately ten years.

The court found as facts that, in 1963, Wake County commenced a foreclosure action against the heirs at law of Henry Sanders for delinquent taxes on lands described in plaintiffs' complaint; that, in 1964, defendant Jackie Johns received a deed to lands completely encompassing plaintiffs' tract; that, in 1968, defendants commenced construction of their home by excavating for a basement; and that, while excavating, defendants received but ignored plaintiffs' warnings that defendants were on plaintiffs' property. It concluded that defendants acquired good and sufficient title only to that portion of the tract described in the tax deed which did not encompass plaintiffs' land; that, although the tax deed as to the portion embracing plaintiffs' land was defective and conveyed nothing to defendants, it did constitute color of title to plaintiffs' land; that defendants' possession of plaintiffs' land was for a period greater than seven years next preceding institution of this action; and that, by virtue of defendants' adverse possession under color of title, fee simple title had vested in defendant Jackie Johns prior to filing of the lawsuit. The court decreed defendant Jackie Johns the fee simple owner and dismissed plaintiffs' complaint.

Plaintiffs contend the Commissioner's Deed, and the judgment of Superior Court from which it originated, did not contain a description of the land either certain in itself or capable of being made certain so that the deed would constitute color of title. While a commissioner's deed in a judicial sale constitutes color of title, G.S. 1-38(a) (Cum.Supp.1981), a party who uses a deed to establish color of title must prove that the boundaries in the deed cover the land in dispute, Skipper v. Yow, 238 N.C. 659, 78 S.E.2d 600 (1953). When the description leaves uncertain what property is embraced, parol evidence is admissible to fit the description to the land.

The description in defendants' deed referred to land "situated in Raleigh Township, Wake County," and read:

> Bounded on the east by Montague Street
>
> Bounded on the north by its land described in Book 289, Page 359; Book 1264, Page 342; Book 1112, Page 284 and Book 1112, Page 285.
>
> Bounded on the west by the land of Graham Morgan.
>
> Bounded on the south by land described in Book 1196, Page 96; Book 912, Page 301; Book 1238, Page 513.
>
> Defendants concede that the deed "is not artfully drawn." In light of other evidence at trial, however, it was sufficient to permit an accurate determination of the tract conveyed.

The description begins by setting forth the eastern boundary as Montague Street, which the evidence showed to be in St. Mary's Township in Garner. Some of the deeds mentioned in the description refer to St. Mary's Township in Garner, and since the description otherwise places the property in that township, error in describing the township was not fatal. The description continues by setting forth the northern boundary as identifiable lands deeded to Mary Stewart (Book 289, Page 359) and C. G. Irving, Jr. (Book 1264, Page 342). The northern boundary is also described by reference to two other parcels which lie too far west to form a boundary with the disputed property but which do aid in defining its northwest corner. On the west, the property is bounded by property of Graham Morgan, which was established not only by testimony of the surveyor but also by testimony of a woman who lived in the vicinity, knew Morgan, and knew the location of the branch forming Morgan's eastern boundary, which was defendants' western boundary. By reference to one deed (Book 1196, Page 96), the commissioner's conveyance established the southwestern corner. Finally, the southern boundary is defined by two deeds, the first to property of the Sallie Whitaker subdivision (Book 912, Page 301) and the second to a lot in the Sallie Whitaker Land Subdivision deeded to Bernice Walton (Book 1238, Page 513).

Additionally, the surveyor testified that, as to defendants' tax deed, he was "satisfied that part of the land is described in the deed which is outlined in blue." A blue line demarcated the land defendants claimed on the survey by which the surveyor illustrated his testimony. Although White expressed reservations about the deeds establishing the northwest and southwest corners because they defined no boundary, the map he prepared otherwise clearly showed the boundaries of defendants' property.

The court was able from the foregoing to establish with sufficient certainty the boundaries of the property defendants claimed. The evidence supports its findings establishing the boundaries. This assignment of error is, therefore, overruled.

Plaintiffs also contend the court erred in determining that defendants, whose home occupied only a portion of the disputed property, adversely possessed the entire tract. Where, as here, one enters upon land and asserts ownership of the whole under an instrument constituting color of title, the law will extend his occupation of a portion thereof to the outer bounds of his deed, provided no part of the premises is held adversely by another. See Price v. Tomrich Corp., 275 N.C. 385, 167 S.E.2d 766 (1969); Price v. Whisnant, 232 N.C. 653, 62 S.E.2d 56 (1950); J. Webster, Real Estate Law in North Carolina § 264 (1971 & Supp.1977). Exclusive possession of a portion, if continued without interruption for seven years, will ripen title to all the land embraced in the deed. Id. It is undisputed here that defendants' exclusive adverse possession of a part of the disputed property continued well beyond seven years. Their title by adverse possession under color of title, therefore, extended to all the property described in the Commissioner's Deed, which embraced all of plaintiffs' tract.

Plaintiffs' final assignment of error attacking the judgment as a whole depends upon their first two assignments, and is therefore without merit.

Affirmed.

Chapter Summary

There are numerous ways for title to real estate to be transferred. Title may be transferred through voluntary means by sale, probate or gift. In a sale transaction, real estate law encompasses contractual and other legal elements. In order to create a valid real estate conveyance, many of the contractual elements, such as offer, acceptance, capacity and legality must be met. Title to real estate can also be involuntarily or unwillingly taken from an owner. Involuntary transfer of real estate involves actions such as foreclosure, eminent domain, partition, accretion, adverse possession and tax sales. Foreclosure is the process of removing an owner's title through the clause in the Deed of Trust that allows a trustee to auction property off for past due mortgage payments. North Carolina statutes provide extensive requirements for how and when a foreclosure sale can proceed. Among the statutory requirements are the notice of foreclosure, the foreclosure hearing, provisions requiring advertising of the notice of foreclosure and procedures to be followed at the foreclosure sale. Eminent domain refers to the power of the government to seize individual property for governmental use. When an owner loses property through eminent domain, he or she must be compensated for the loss. Accretion is the process of losing a portion of one's property to natural forces, such as the action of tides that gradually wear away a parcel's boundaries. Title to property can also be lost through adverse possession. Adverse possession is a legal doctrine that allows a person who enters upon someone else's land and holds that land openly, notoriously and against other claims to bring action within a specific period of time to have the parcel declared to be the possessor's in fee simple absolute. The period of time that the possessor must hold the property varies according to the circumstances surrounding the initial acquisition. In some instances, for example, the period of time is 7 years, while in others it is 20 years. Title to property can also be lost through foreclosure of a tax lien. Governments have the power to assess real property taxes and to enforce those taxes through use of liens or tax auctions. Acquiring possession of property by means of a tax auction is one method to acquire adverse possession.

Review Questions

1. What are three methods of voluntary transfer of title?
2. What are three methods of involuntary transfer of title?
3. What is accretion?
4. When is foreclosure authorized?
5. What is a deed of trust and how does it compare to a mortgage?
6. Explain eminent domain.
7. List and describe the three parties involved in a deed of trust arrangement.
8. What are the advertising requirements in a foreclosure notice?
9. What is the minimum amount that a person must deposit after being the successful bidder at a foreclosure auction?
10. Are certain private companies allowed to exercise eminent domain in North Carolina? Explain.
11. What is inverse condemnation?
12. When a person loses a portion of his real property through accretion can he or she petition neighbors to ask them to give up some of their property to make up for the property that he has lost? Explain your answer.
13. What is escheat and when is it required under the law?
14. What is intestate succession?
15. What are the elements of adverse possession in North Carolina?
16. Explain "color of title" as that term is used in adverse possession.
17. What is "tacking" as that term applies to adverse possession?
18. Explain the court's decision in this chapters relevant case.
19. When is a tax auction of property authorized?
20. Why is it important to establish a grantor's legal capacity prior to transfer of title?

Assignment

1. Go to the local courthouse and locate a foreclosure notice. What are the details of this notice?

2. Locate a foreclosure notice in the legal classifieds of the local newspaper. List the relevant details of this foreclosure notice, including: the time and place the foreclosure sale will be held, the amount outstanding and any other important provisions in the notice.

Terms and Phrases

Will

Testator

Dedication

Foreclosure

Deeds of Trust

Condemnation

Eminent Domain

Partition

Accretion

Escheat

Adverse Possession

Color of Title

Tacking

Privity

Tax Lien

Chapter 6

Deeds

Chapter Objectives

- Explain the function of deeds
- Explain the important differences between various types of deeds
- List and explain the minimum requirements that any deed must have under North Carolina law
- Describe various deed clauses
- Describe the rules that courts follow in construing the language in deeds

I. Introduction to Deeds

In this chapter, we will examine the many aspects of deeds under North Carolina law. A deed is the written expression of the legal transfer of rights from one party to another. Before we can explain the modern deed provisions, it is useful to briefly explore the history of real estate transactions, especially those surrounding the transfer of ownership rights.

In ancient times, a real estate transaction was a symbolic ceremony in which a grantor transferred property and title to a grantee. We have already seen that there are important differences between real property and personal property and this distinction becomes readily apparent when we examine the laws surrounding transfer of title between these two different types of property. In personal property, a physical transfer of the object almost always accompanies title transfer. If you think about the process involved in buying a laptop computer, you acquire title to the laptop after you pay the sale price and take physical possession of it. Although your receipt and accompanying paperwork will help prove your claim, the best way to establish your ownership of the item is by physical possession of it. This old common-law rule is the source of the maxim, "possession is 9/10 of a Law." However, we run into some immediate difficulties when we apply this type of reasoning to real property. Because real property is fixed and immovable, and because it isn't always possible for an owner to be in physical possession of his real property, the courts had to recognize a different type of title transfer process.

In past centuries, transferring title to real estate was accomplished by removing some physical object from the land, such as a clod of earth, and actually surrendering physical possession of that clod to the buyer. The clod of earth acted as a physical symbol of the land and the buyer's acceptance of the symbol served to signify his acceptance of title. The courthouse records simply confirmed this physical act.

In modern times, we have abandoned the idea of removing some physical object from the land to show transfer of ownership, but the idea has not gone away. Instead, deeds have taken over much of the symbolism that once accompanied a real estate transaction.

A. Defining a Deed under North Carolina Law

In this chapter, we will examine various types of deeds that have very different legal significance. However, all deeds have features in common. North Carolina law defines a deed as: "an instrument that is designed to convey interests in real estate. Deeds are written, signed, delivered by the grantor and accepted by the grantee."[1] But deeds are more than simple documents that record transactions. Deeds are also contracts between grantors and grantees. They set out the terms of the contractual agreement between the parties. This means that a deed serves two functions: it records the details of a transaction while also serving as the written contract for that transaction. As a result of this dual nature, deeds must satisfy two divergent requirements: the legal requisites of deeds (including execution and acknowledgment) and contract law (including offer, acceptance, consideration and capacity).

Deed: an instrument designed to convey interests in real estate.

Throughout this chapter, we will use the terms "grantor" and "grantee." A grantor is the person who transfers the property and the grantee is the person who receives the property interest. Grantors and "sellers" are often, but not always, synonymous.

1. Deeds Have a Dual Nature

A deed is both a document that details a transaction between a grantor and a grantee and it is also a substitute for the old symbolic ceremony of the transfer of physical possession of the land. This dual nature in deeds accounts for some of the peculiarities we will see later when we examine some of their technical requirements. If deeds were simply another form of contract, there would be no need for some of these particular provisions. For instance, when we discuss delivery and acceptance of a deed, if you keep in mind that this provision is a substitute for the more ancient right of physical transfer of ownership, many of the requirements will make more sense.

a. Contractual Elements of Deeds

When we say that deeds have a contractual component, this becomes very clear when discussing the aspects of competence and capacity. The grantor in a deed transaction must meet many of the same requirements as a contractual party, including the requirement of legal capacity. A person who is considered competent enough to enter into a contract is competent enough to transfer real estate interests, and vice versa. Under these guidelines, certain classifications of individuals are barred from entering into deeds. Examples of these individuals include:

- Anyone under the age of 18

---

1. *Williams v. North Carolina State Bd. of Ed.*, 284 N.C. 588, 201 S.E.2d 889 (1974).

- Anyone under the influence of drugs to the extent that it impairs his or her mental abilities

- Anyone declared to be mentally incompetent

In situations where a person lacks capacity and transfers property through a deed, the court may declare the deed void and cancel the transaction. Interestingly enough, these rules about capacity apply to the grantor, but not the grantee. There is no requirement that a grantee have contractual capacity in order to receive a legal interest in a real estate transaction. We will discuss the legal requirements imposed on grantees later in this chapter.

b. Statutory Requirements of Deeds

Deeds must be in writing under the Statute of Frauds. Deeds must also meet other technical requirements such as the type of rights conveyed and the manner in which they are executed.[2] We will explore these requirements after we discuss the various types of deeds.

B. Types of Deeds

In the following sections, we will explore various types of deeds commonly seen in real estate practice.

1. Gift Deeds

When a person gives real estate to another, this transfer is recorded in a gift deed. When the transaction is a gift, the parties have two years to record it. If the parties wait longer than two years to record the gift deed, the transaction is void and the title to the estate is transferred back to the original grantor.[3] Although North Carolina law is generally liberal on its construction of gift deeds, there are important Internal Revenue Service administrative rules that can affect a gift transaction. For instance, section 1031 of the Internal Revenue Code may impose a tax liability on the value of the property transferred by gift.

2. Quitclaim Deeds

A quitclaim deed makes no assurances or warrantees by the person who executes the deed. In essence, a quitclaim deed does exactly what its title suggests: it surrenders any rights or interests that the person executing the deed may have in the property. Quitclaim deeds are often sought in situations where a probate matter has created a potential cloud on the title. For instance, in an intestate proceeding, a distant relative might legitimately claim a tiny, fractional interest in property based on his or her legal status as an heir of the deceased grantor. However, in practical terms, this fractional interest is nearly worth-

---

2. *Ballard v. Ballard*, 230 N.C. 629, 55 S.E.2d 316 (1949).
3. *Ferguson v. Ferguson*, 225 N.C. 375, 35 S.E.2d 231 (1945).

less. In order to clear up this potential cloud on the title, the attorney conducting the title examination and closing will seek a quitclaim deed from this relative. Attorneys routinely seek quitclaim deeds from any person who might even arguably have a claim on the property, even when the person's claim is tenuous, at best. Most attorneys and title insurance companies opt for the cautious approach and obtain quitclaim deeds in order to quell any possibility of a claim on the property at a future date.

A quitclaim deed conveys only the interest held by the grantor. The grantor makes no claims about the nature or quality of the title and no representations to the grantee about the legal status of the property.[4]

3. General Warranty Deeds   *The Best*

General warranty deeds contain a series of warrantees or promises that the grantor makes to the grantee about various aspects of the property. These warrantees give the grantee a potential cause of action against the grantor if, at the time of delivery and acceptance of the deed, one or more of them is not true. Here is a summary of the typical warrantees made in a general warranty deed:

- That the grantor is seized of the premises
- That the grantee has the warranty of quiet enjoyment
- That there are no encumbrances on the property
- That the grantor will provide further assurance
- That the grantor will warrant forever the grantee's rights

a. Seizin

The covenant or warranty of seizin is the grantor's assurance that he or she is in legitimate possession of the property and is able to transfer that interest to another.

b. Quiet Enjoyment

The warranty of quiet enjoyment is the grantor's promise that there are no outstanding claims or unresolved interests in the property that would affect the grantee's ability to use and enjoy it. It is this warranty, coupled with several of the succeeding warrantees that create the necessity for a title examination to determine the current state of the property's title before any transfer of ownership occurs.

c. Against Encumbrances

The warranty against encumbrances is the grantor's assurance that there are no outstanding liens, judgments or other legal actions that will affect the grantee's ownership in the property.

---

4. *Heath v. Turner*, 309 N.C. 483, 308 S.E.2d 244 (1983).

d. Further Assurance

This warranty is the grantor's promise that should some claim arise against the property, the grantor will give further evidence, testimony or additional materials to prove that the transaction was legitimate and that the grantee has full title to the property.

e. Warranty Forever

In addition to all of the previous promises made by the grantor, this provision is the grantor's promise that he or she will take no action to undermine the grantee's title in the property after the conveyance is made.

4. Special Warranty Deeds *Not as good as the best*

A special warranty deed only contains one or two warrantees from the grantor to the grantee. These deeds are often executed in specific circumstances where there is a potential cloud on the title or some other factor that might affect the marketability of the title. This deed is the grantor's assurance that he or she has not done anything during the ownership period to affect the grantee's interest.

5. Deeds of Trust

A Deed of Trust is the deed used by a lender to protect its rights to the property in the event that the buyer/borrower defaults on a mortgage payment. We discuss Deeds of Trusts and mortgages in much greater detail in chapter 9.

6. Timber Deeds

A timber deed does exactly what its title suggests, it transfers interest in the trees found on the property. This deed gives the grantee the right to remove and harvest timber.

7. Deed of Correction

A deed of correction is usually created after a title search has revealed a defect in one of the deeds that forms the chain of title. It is fairly common for a deed of correction to be issued to correct an invalid property description.

8. Sheriff's Deed

A Sheriff's deed is usually issued after an auction to transfer some or all of the interest in a parcel to the successful bidder.

9. Tax Deeds

Tax deeds are issued when a property is auctioned off for past due taxes. A person who bids on the property at a tax sale receives a tax deed that arguably creates colorable claim of title on the property. However, there are some potential problems with tax deeds, especially when they are used as the basis for an adverse possession claim. For instance, courts insist that the tax auction must be strictly complied with before it will be deemed effective. Because many tax auctions do not meet the statutory requirements, the deeds received have questionable legal authority.

II. Minimum Legal Requirements of Deeds

All deeds must meet certain minimum, legal requirements. These include:

A. They must be in writing as required under the Statute of Frauds

B. They must meet basic contractual elements, such as capacity

C. They must have clearly identifiable grantors and grantees

D. They must contain an adequate description of the property conveyed

E. The grantor must sign them ⟋Q

F. They must contain language of conveyance

G. They must be properly executed

H. They must be delivered by the grantor and accepted by the grantee ⟋Q

A. Deeds Must Be in Writing

Under North Carolina's Statute of Frauds, NCGS § 22-2, deeds must in writing to be legally effective. We will discuss the Statute of Frauds in much greater detail in the next chapter.

B. Contractual Elements

As we discussed earlier, a deed must meet certain contractual elements. For instance, the grantor must have the legal capacity to transfer property. This means that the grantor must be of sound mind at the time that he or she transfers the property and understand the significance of the transaction.

C. Clearly Identifiable Parties ⟋Q

The rules about identifying the parties to a real estate transaction vary according to the party. The rules about the grantor are far stricter than those that apply to the grantee.

1. Grantor

The grantor must be identified by name and the grantor's signature must appear on the deed. The grantor's failure to sign the deed is a fatal error and will result in a void transaction.

2. Grantee

The strict rules about identifying the grantor do not apply to the grantee. Under North Carolina law, the grantee must be identified in such a way that the property vests in a specific person.[5] This does not mean that the grantee is required to be named, as long as the person can be identified. Because the grantee's signature is not required on a deed, there is no requirement that the grantee is legally sane or even that the grantee is an adult. However, a deed to a dead person is invalid and will not pass title.[6]

> Sidebar: Although it is not fatal to a deed if the grantor does not specifically name the grantee, this is obviously the better practice.

a. Misnomer

A common problem in deeds is the concept of "misnomer." This occurs when the grantor incorrectly identifies the grantee in the deed. If the courts can determine the party intended to receive the real estate, that person will receive title to the property, even if incorrectly named in the deed.[7] This is as true for individuals as it is for corporations.[8]

D. Description of the Property Conveyed

Although we explore the topic of legal and adequate property descriptions in the next chapter of this book, a word or two about them here is also appropriate. The property described in the deed must be sufficiently clear and specific to identify this parcel from any other. A mere street address is not legally sufficient. The traditional method used to meet this legal standard is a metes and bounds description. This description, which sets out the distance and direction of each of the boundary lines is one of the best ways to meet the North Carolina standard for adequate legal description in a deed.

> Sidebar: Incorrect property descriptions are one of the most common errors in deeds. All real estate professionals should pay particular attention to the metes and bounds description in a deed to make sure that it is accurate.

Although metes and bounds descriptions are one of the best ways to describe property, they are not the only method. Other methods include reference to plats and other public documents.

> Sidebar: To be legally valid, a property description must be valid as of the date that it was recorded.

1. Plat Reference

When a deed contains a reference to a plat or other map, the plat is incorporated into the deed and becomes an official part of it.[9] "A map or plat, referred to in a deed, becomes part of the deed, as if it were written therein."[10]

---

5. *Byrd v. Patterson*, 229 N.C. 156, 48 S.E.2d 45 (1948).
6. *Campbell v. Everhart*, 139 N.C. 503, 52 S.E. 201 (1905).
7. *Asheville Division No. 15 v. Aston*, 92 N.C. 578 (1885).
8. *Tomika Investments, Inc. v. Macedonia True Vine Pentecostal Holiness Church of God, Inc.*, 524 S.E.2d 591 (2000).
9. *Parrish v. Hayworth*, 138 N.C. App. 637, 532 S.E.2d 202 (2000).
10. *Stines v. Willyng, Inc.*, 81 N.C.App. 98, 101, 344 S.E.2d 546, 548 (1986).

2. *Reference to Other Public Records*

Although it is common to describe property by a metes and bounds description or by reference to a plat, there are other, legally valid ways of doing so. For instance, it is also possible to create a legally adequate property description by referring to other public records, such as other deeds.

When the courts are faced with an ambiguous property description, they rely on their rules of construction in interpreting boundaries. These rules are, in order of preference:

- Natural landmarks
- Survey monuments
- Boundaries of adjacent properties
- Courses and distances, such as is found in a metes and bounds description
- Total acreage

E. Signature

One of the most important legal requirements of a deed is the grantor's signature. It must be present on the deed to make it legally effective.[11] There is no requirement that the grantee sign the deed. The reason for this disparity is that it is the grantor who is conveying his or her interest in the property to another. In this situation, the focus is on the grantor, the grantor's mental ability, the grantor's rights and interests in the property and the grantor's intent in the transaction. The North Carolina Statute of Frauds also requires the grantor's signature. Agents may sign for the principal/grantor, but only when the agent has been given express authority to do so.

F. Words of Conveyance TQ

The deed must contain some words of conveyance, indicating the grantor's intent to transfer interest to the grantee. These words of intent can be as simple as "the grantor does hereby grant, bargain, sale or transfer" to the grantee.

G. Deed Must Be Properly Executed

In addition to the requirements set out above, the deed must also be correctly executed. In modern real estate practice, attorneys rely heavily on deed forms that have been approved by the North Carolina Bar Association. There is no requirement that these forms must be used. Obviously, the approved forms contain all of the statutory elements necessary and are used by real estate professionals on a daily basis throughout the state. However, parties can create perfectly legal and binding deeds without the use of these forms.

---

11. *Matter of Mills*, 68 N.C. App. 694, 315 S.E.2d 716 (1984).

H. Delivery and Acceptance

Returning to our earlier discussion about the history of real estate transactions, we see that modern deeds still have some elements of the old symbolic ceremony of transferring rights to real estate. This symbolism has now been incorporated into modern deeds in the delivery and acceptance requirement. When a grantor has executed all of the written requirements of a deed, the transaction is still not legally effective until the deed has actually been delivered to and accepted by the grantee. In this regard, the deed substitutes for the physical clod of earth that once traded hands to symbolize transfer ownership. Here, the deed serves that function. Case law in this state is quite clear on the point that a validly executed deed is not effective until it has been delivered to the grantee. Until that event has occurred, title to the property has not been transferred. The practical effect of this rule is that until the deed is delivered, the grantor's homeowner's insurance remains liable for any damages done to the home until the point in time when the deed is delivered and accepted by the grantee. Once delivery and acceptance has occurred, even if the grantee has not actually moved into the home, the grantee's homeowner's insurance becomes liable for any damages done to the structure.

Sidebar: Without delivery, there is no valid transaction.[12]

1. Proving Delivery

In order to show a valid delivery according to North Carolina law, three criteria must be met:

1. The grantor intended that the deed transfer real property to the grantee.
2. The grantor's action places the deed beyond his possession and control.
3. The grantee accepts the deed.[13]

Sidebar: An indication of delivery by the grantor is his recording the deed, even if the grantee has no knowledge that the deed has been recorded.[14]

When the grantee accepts the deed, he or she becomes bound by the terms contained in it. This is true even though the grantee never signed the deed. If the grantor places the deed with a third person and never gives directions to that third person to make delivery of the deed, then no delivery has occurred and title does not pass.[15] When a deed has been recorded, courts will presume a valid delivery and acceptance.[16]

2. Delivery in Escrow

In an escrow closing, the grantee delivers the deed to a third person who holds it in escrow. The person who holds the deed in escrow has specific instructions from the grantor to deliver the deed to the grantee at a specific time or after a specific event has occurred. A grantor who cannot be physically present at the closing might use escrow closings. In such a situation, the grantor would sign all necessary paperwork and deliver the deed to the escrow agent who would then transfer the deed to the grantee at a later time. The law

---

12. *Williams v. North Carolina State Bd. of Ed.*, 284 N.C. 588, 201 S.E.2d 889 (1974).
13. *Jones v. Saunders*, 254 N.C. 644, 119 S.E.2d 789 (1961).
14. *Corbett v. Corbett*, 249 N.C. 585, 107 S.E.2d 165 (1959).
15. *Fortune v. Hunt*, 149 N.C. 358, 63 S.E. 82 (1908).
16. *Williams v. North Carolina State Board of Education*, 284 N.C. 588, 201 S.E.2d 889 (1974).

creates a legal fiction that the closing that occurs in escrow happens contemporaneously, even though the grantor may have executed the paperwork days or even weeks prior to the actual date of closing. A legal 'fiction' is a court doctrine where a court will recognize something as having occurred at a specific time, even when it actually did not. In this case, an escrow closing creates the legal fiction that both parties were present and that delivery and acceptance occurred at the time stated in the agreement, when in fact it did not. We will discuss escrow closings in greater detail in Chapter 12.

I. Non-Essential Deed Terms

So far, we have limited our discussion to the minimum legal requirements for any deed. In the next few sections, we will focus on clauses and features that are commonly found in deeds, even though they may not be strictly required.

1. Consideration

Although we have said that a deed resembles a contract in many ways, there are important differences. While contracts require consideration, deeds do not. The issue of consideration sometimes becomes important when dealing with gift deeds, especially when the deed has not been recorded in the two-year period of time required, but in most other situations, consideration is not an issue.[17]

Although consideration is not a requirement for a valid deed, when the deed fails to list any consideration, there is a possibility that the deed is a gift. Such a deed must be recorded within two years, or it is ineffective.

2. Acknowledgment

An acknowledgment is the grantor's execution of the deed in the presence of a certified officer, such as a Notary Public, Clerk of Court or the Registrar of Deeds. Valid acknowledgment occurs when a person witnesses the grantor's signature.

Acknowledgments are not an official requirement of a deed under North Carolina law. However, an acknowledgment is required before a deed can be recorded. Given the dire consequences for a grantee who fails to record a deed, we could easily argue that acknowledgements are indirectly required in all deeds.[18]

Sidebar: The most common way to acknowledge a deed is for it to be notarized.

3. Seal *extends SoL to 10 years*

Until 1999, a seal was required on all deeds. The requirement of a seal was in addition to the requirement of the grantor's signature. The law surrounding seals has a rich history, primarily derived from the fact that throughout most of human history the vast majority of citizens could not write their names. Placing a document under seal had a significant legal impact. Even today, contracts under seal enjoy specific evidentiary and other advantages over contracts that do not have a seal. However, because this require-

---

17. *Mills v. Dunk*, 263 N.C. 742, 140 S.E.2d 358 (1965).
18. *Ballard v. Ballard*, 230 N.C. 629, 55 S.E.2d 316 (1949).

ment has been removed in North Carolina law, seals are no longer required on deeds. Even when they were a requirement, the word "seal" next to the grantor's signature was sufficient to meet this requirement.

Figure 6-1. § 39-6.5. Elimination of Seal

The seal of the signatory shall not be necessary to effect a valid conveyance of an interest in real property; provided, that this section shall not affect the requirement for affixing a seal of the officer taking an acknowledgment of the instrument.

> Sidebar: The North Carolina Bar Real Property Section was a major advocate behind the requirement that all deeds bear a seal.

4. Witnesses

There is no requirement that a deed must be witnessed in order to be legally effective. The grantor's signature is sufficient, especially if it has been acknowledged.

5. Revenue Stamps

Effective July 1, 2000, revenue stamps are no longer required. Instead of revenue stamps, registrars simply note the tax assessed as a percentage of the transaction price.

6. Date

Although there is no requirement that a deed be dated, the existence of a date on a deed creates a rebuttable presumption that the deed was delivered.

III. Specific Deed Clauses

Now that we have discussed both the essential and non-essential elements of deeds, we will focus on the clauses found in most deeds. Two of the most important clauses are the granting clause and the habendum clause.

A. Granting Clause

As we have already seen, a deed must contain language that indicates the grantor's intent to convey an interest to another. The granting clause is one way to establish this intent.

The granting clause is language that indicates the grantor's intention to transfer some or all of his interest in the property to the grantee. Typical language found in a granting clause includes "the grantor has and by these presents does grant, bargain, sell and convey onto the grantee in fee simple."

B. Habendum Clause 𝘛𝑄

While a granting clause indicates the grantor's intent and identifies the nature of the estate transferred, the habendum clause indicates the extent of the estate conferred on the grantee. Consider the language set out in Figure 6-2.

Figure 6-2. Habendum Clause

TO HAVE AND TO HOLD the aforesaid tract or parcel of land, and all of the privileges and appurtenances thereto belonging, to the said party of the second part, its successors and assigns, to its only use and behoof forever. And the said party of the first part, for its successors or assigns, COVENANTS with the said party of the second part, its successors and assigns, that it is seized of said premises in fee and has the right to convey in fee simple; that the same is free and clear from all encumbrances, and that it does hereby WARRANT and will forever DEFEND the said title to the same against the claims of all persons whomsoever.*

* *Ives v. Real-Venture, Inc.*, 97 N.C.App. 391, 388 S.E.2d 573 (1990).

C. Exceptions and Exclusions

The deed may also contain exceptions and exclusions. These are provisions that the grantor inserts to limit the extent of his promises or warranties. For instance, a grantor might include an exception stating that the property is free and clear of all encumbrances with the exception of an existing easement. These exceptions and exclusions serve two purposes: they put the grantee on notice of specific situations and insulate the grantor from claims that he failed to provide full disclosure about the nature of the title.

IV. Construing the Language in Deeds

Courts are frequently called upon to interpret ambiguous language in deeds. This situation can arise with both prepared forms and "do it yourself" deed forms, although it occurs more frequently with the latter than the former. North Carolina has had two divergent approaches to the issue of interpreting language in deeds. The old method, in existence prior to 1968, paid less attention to the intent of the parties and gave more credence to the formalities of the deed itself.

Under the old rule where the habendum and granting clauses referred to fee simple title, while other clauses made contrary references to a lesser estate, the courts ignored the "lesser" clauses and followed the wording in the main clauses. The problem with this rule is that it often ignored the plain intent of the parties.

This situation changed in 1968 when the North Carolina Legislature adopted NCGS § 39-1.1. This statute redefines deed construction by requiring the courts to put the parties' intention into effect when it can be determined.

Figure 6-3. NCGS § 39-1.1. In construing Conveyances Court Shall Give Effect to Intent of the Parties

(a) In construing a conveyance executed after January 1, 1968, in which there are inconsistent clauses, the courts shall determine the effect of the instrument on the basis of the intent of the parties as it appears from all of the provisions of the instrument.

(b) The provisions of subsection (a) of this section shall not prevent the application of the rule in Shelley's case.

The courts are also guided by other statutes in the methods they use to interpret deeds. Once such example is NCGS § 39-2.

Figure 6-4. § 39-2. Vagueness of Description Not to Invalidate

No deed or other writing purporting to convey land or an interest in land shall be declared void for vagueness in the description of the thing intended to be granted by reason of the use of the word "adjoining" instead of the words "bounded by," or for the reason that the boundaries given do not go entirely around the land described: Provided, it can be made to appear to the satisfaction of the jury that the grantor owned at the time of the execution of such deed or paperwriting no other land which at all corresponded to the description contained in such deed or paper-writing.

Under modern laws of deed construction, courts must give precedence to the stated intention of the parties as expressed by them in the actual documents, not by a strict and perhaps misguided devotion to legal phrases that might contradict parties' intentions.

"In the interpretation of a deed, the intention of the grantor or grantors must be gathered from the whole instrument and every part thereof given effect, unless it contains conflicting provisions which are irreconcilable or a provision which is contrary to public policy or runs counter to some rule of law."[19]

This principle underlies the approach now used by courts in this state. "The rigid technicalities of the common law have gradually yielded to the demand for a more rational mode of expounding deeds. Hence to discover the intention of the parties is now regarded as the chief essential in the construction of conveyances."[20]

> Sidebar: The language used in deeds, even in standardized forms, should be closely scrutinized to make sure that the parties are not conveying a partial interest or making some other claim inconsistent with the overall focus of the document.

---

19. *Lackey v. Hamlet City Bd. of Ed.*, 258 N.C. 460, 128 S.E.2d 806 (1963).
20. *Springs v. Hopkins*, 171 N.C. 486, 88 S.E. 774 (1916).

Figure 6-5. Deed Checklist

1. Have you identified the kind of deed you are dealing with?
2. Have you identified the parties to the transaction?
3. Must have the complete legal name of the grantor
4. Must have an identifiable buyer (name is obviously preferred)
5. Is there a habendum clause?
6. Did the grantor sign the deed? If not, is there a power of attorney permitting someone else to sign for him?
7. Are the appropriate covenants listed?
   a. Covenant of seizin?
   b. Covenant of further assurance?
   c. Covenant of quiet enjoyment?
   d. Covenant of warranty forever?
   e. Covenant against encumbrances?
8. Has it been notarized?
9. Is there an acknowledgment?
10. Are there words of conveyance?
11. Is this a standard deed form or one that has been created by the parties?

V. Recording Statutes

North Carolina's recording statute is found in NCGS § 47-18. Originally enacted in 1885, it is sometimes referred to as the Connor Act. Our state follows the "race" recordation statute scheme, which means that if the grantor deeds the property to two different individuals, the first one to record the deed at the courthouse is the grantee of record and has full rights to the property. The other party does not have valid title, but may very well have an action for fraud against the grantor.

Under North Carolina law there is no requirement that the deed be recorded to be legally effective; however, the grantee's failure to file the deed can have disastrous consequences. For example, if the grantee fails to record the deed, third parties, creditors and purchasers may behave as though the deed does not exist. The effective result of NCGS § 47-18 is to make third parties only responsible for what has actually been filed in the public records. NCGS § 47-18 also makes the deed's date important. This statute provides that the date that the deed was recorded is of vital concern. It determines who has priority; the first to file is given priority over later filers. In this way, North Carolina's deed recordation statute is actually "race-notice." Third parties may rely on the public record only in order to establish claims, but claims are given priority based on the dates that they are recorded. Essentially, the first person to the courthouse to file any lien or other encumbrance on property has top priority over anyone who files later.

Relevant Cases

Mason-Reel v. Simpson 100 N.C.App. 651, 397 S.E.2d 755 (1990)

LEWIS, Judge.

The issue in this case is whether the trial judge, upon a motion made after the denial of a summary judgment, correctly used N.C.G.S. § 39-1.1 when he interpreted, as a matter of law, the intent of the parties in a deed which contained inconsistent clauses.

The plaintiffs filed a complaint alleging in their first claim for relief that the defendants had fraudulently schemed to acquire title to the plaintiffs' property. The plaintiffs also alleged that due to the defendants' fraud, there exists a cloud on plaintiffs' title to their property. In the plaintiffs' second claim for relief, the plaintiffs asked the court to "declare the effect of the [deed] … to be a timber deed …" pursuant to N.C.G.S. § 39-1.1.

The deed in controversy was typed, i.e., not on a form, and was executed on 24 March 1986. It was prepared by the defendants' attorney and was signed by the plaintiff-grantors. The granting clause states in part:

> [t]hat said parties of the first part, for and in consideration of the sum of TEN DOLLARS, and other good and valuable considerations to them in hand paid, the receipt of which is hereby acknowledged, have bargained and sold and by these presents do bargain, sell, and convey unto the said party of the second part and his heirs and assigns all merchantable timber and a certain tract or parcel of land as hereinafter defined, lying or standing upon a certain tract of land in Pamlico County, North Carolina, and more fully described as follows:

The deed then describes the tract of land in detail. The habendum clause provides the following:

> [t]o have and to hold, said timber, together with the rights and privileges hereinabove set out, to him, the said party of the second part and his heirs and assigns in fee simple forever.

The warranty clause states as follows:

> [a]nd said parties of the first part do covenant that they are seized of said timber and the lands upon which it is situated in fee simple, and have the right to convey the same, that the same are free and clear of all encumbrances and that they will warrant and defend the title herein conveyed against the lawful claims of all persons whomsoever.

The defendants made a motion for summary judgment, arguing that there was no genuine issue of material fact as to the plaintiffs' claims of fraud. Judge Reid denied the summary judgment motion. At a separate hearing later, before Judge Barefoot, the plaintiffs moved that the judge interpret the meaning of the words of the deed and find, as a matter of law, pursuant to N.C.G.S. § 39-1.1, that the parties intended to convey only timber rights and not the fee simple. The defendants asked for a jury trial.

After reading the pleadings which included a copy of the deed in controversy the trial judge, without a jury and without hearing any evidence, ruled that there was an error in the granting clause and that the parties intended the word "and" to be "on" so that the clause would read: "merchantable timber on a certain tract or parcel of land…." Thus, the trial judge ruled that it was the intent of the parties to convey only timber.

"The intention of the parties as apparent in a deed should generally control in determining the property conveyed thereby; but, if the intent is not apparent from the deed,
resort may be had to the general rules of construction." When the legislature passed
N.C.G.S. § 39-1.1, it was their primary intention to abolish past rules of construction
which required courts to disregard certain clauses if they contradicted the granting clause
of a deed. Instead, for conveyances executed after 1 January 1968, the courts would, under
N.C.G.S. § 39-1.1, consider equally all clauses in a deed when ascertaining the intent of
the parties. Id. Therefore, N.C.G.S. § 39-1.1(a) provides:

> [i]n construing a conveyance executed after January 1, 1968, in which there are
> inconsistent clauses, the courts shall determine the effect of the instrument on
> the basis of the intent of the parties as it appears from all of the provisions of the
> instrument.N.C.G.S. § 39-1.1(a).

Generally, where there is "no waiver of jury trial or agreement as to facts nor evidence
offered, the court [is] without power to decide a controverted issue of fact raised by the
pleadings." Sullivan v. Johnson, 3 N.C.App. 581, 583, 165 S.E.2d 507, 508 (1969). However, "[a]mbiguous deeds traditionally have been construed by the courts according to
rules of construction, rather than by having juries determine factual questions of intent."
Robinson v. King, 68 N.C.App. 86, 89, 314 S.E.2d 768, 771, disc. rev. denied, 311 N.C.
762, 321 S.E.2d 144 (1984). The meaning of the terms of the deed is a question of law,
not of fact. Brown v. Hodges, 232 N.C. 537, 541, 61 S.E.2d 603, 606 (1950), reh'g denied, 233 N.C. 617, 65 S.E.2d 144 (1951). In light of the purpose of N.C.G.S. § 39-1.1(a),
the statute's requirement that "the courts" interpret the deed did not change the traditional rule that it is the judge's role to determine the intent of the parties. It was not the
legislature's intent to change who interprets the intent of the parties in a deed; rather, the
statute was an effort by the legislature to state how "the courts" should interpret the deed.
Therefore, under the statute it is the judge's role to determine the intent of the parties.

The plaintiffs' basis for their action to quiet title was the alleged fraud of the defendants.
Generally, in actions to quiet title where the plaintiffs rely on fraud to overcome the effect of a deed, they must prove fraud. Ramsey v. Ramsey, 224 N.C. 110, 114, 29 S.E.2d
340, 342 (1944). (citation omitted). Where the cause of action is in fraud, the defendants
would have a basic right to a jury trial. However, Judge Barefoot in this case considered
only the intent of the parties in the deed in question and did not reach the issue of fraud.
Once the intent was determined, "fraud" no longer mattered and no jury trial was necessary. The judge was able to dispose of the case on what appears to be a judgment on the
pleadings.

In Robinson v. King, 68 N.C.App. 86, 314 S.E.2d 768, disc. rev. denied, 311 N.C. 762,
321 S.E.2d 144 (1984), this Court held that in some situations it is necessary to look beyond the four corners of the deed to ascertain the intent of the parties. "[I]ntention, as
a general rule, must be sought in the terms of the instrument; but if the words used leave
the intention in doubt, resort may be had to the circumstances attending the execution
of the instrument and the situation of the parties at that time—the tendency of the modern decisions being to treat all uncertainties in a conveyance as ambiguities to be ex-
plained by ascertaining in the manner indicated the intention of the parties." Robinson
v. King, Id. 68 N.C.App. at 95, 314 S.E.2d at 774, disc. rev. denied, 311 N.C. 762, 321 S.E.2d
144 (1984) (quoting Seawell v. Hall, 185 N.C. 80, 82, 116 S.E. 189, 190 (1923)). In the
present case, the trial judge chose not to hear evidence of "circumstances attending the
execution of the instrument and the situation of the parties at that time." Id. Instead, the
trial judge reasoned that he was able to determine the intent of the parties by considering the entire deed. From the peculiar wording of the deed and the pleadings, the judge

concluded that the parties intended only to convey timber rights. We find no error in the trial judge's ruling.

Affirmed.

Elliott v. Cox, 100 N.C.App. 536, 397 S.E.2d 319 (1990)

WELLS, Judge.

Plaintiffs contend that the court should construe the 1937 deed to pass title to them subject to a life estate interest in Edna if she survived Archie and to declare void the 1988 deed from Edna Buffkin to defendants. Defendants contend that the court should construe the 1937 deed to create a tenancy by the entirety in Archie and Edna Buffkin and give full force and effect to the 1988 deed to defendants.

The materials presented to the court show that the facts in this case are not in dispute, and that only the language in the deed is at issue. "A deed is to be construed by the court, and the meaning of its terms is a question of law, not of fact." Mason v. Andersen, 33 N.C.App. 568, 235 S.E.2d 880 (1977). A deed is to be construed to ascertain the intention of the grantor as expressed in the language used, construed from the four corners of the instrument.

Defendants contend that the introductory recital creates a tenancy by the entirety fee simple and that the following clauses although inconsistent do not affect the tenancy by the entirety. Defendants cite Byrd v. Patterson, 229 N.C. 156, 48 S.E.2d 45 (1948) for the proposition that "... slight inconsistencies in the designation of the grantees in the several provisions of the deed do not affect the nature of the estate conveyed...." Defendants rely on the mistaken premise that the introductory recital in this deed is the granting clause. From this premise, defendants contend that inconsistencies exist in the deed and repugnant clauses should be discarded. We disagree.

The granting, habendum and warranty clauses of the deed are all in accord and clearly express the grantors' intent to limit Edna Buffkin to a life estate should she survive her husband. The estate created in the granting clause is not a tenancy by the entirety fee simple as defendants assert. As stated in Byrd "... in the event of any repugnancy between the granting clause and preceding or succeeding recitals, the granting clause will prevail." The introductory recital that defendants claim creates a tenancy by the entirety is repugnant to the granting clause and must be disregarded.

Defendants also contend that because the introductory recital is first on the deed that it takes priority. Defendants cite Bowden v. Bowden, 264 N.C. 296, 141 S.E.2d 621 (1965) for the proposition that where two clauses in the deed are repugnant, the first in order will be given effect and the latter rejected. Bowden involved a granting clause followed by an inconsistent habendum and warranty clause. We do not agree that Bowden stands for the proposition that an introductory recital, by virtue of being first in the deed, will be given effect over the granting, habendum and warranty clauses all of which are in accord with each other but inconsistent with the introductory recital. Having found the language in the deed to be clear and the clauses free from inconsistency, we hold that the deed did not convey an estate in fee simple to Edna Buffkin.

Finally, defendants contend in the alternative, that if the deed did not create a tenancy by the entirety then the limitation over still should not be given effect because Edna Buffkin was Archie Buffkin's heir at law in 1968 pursuant to N.C.Gen.Stat. § 29-2(3), the Intestate Succession Act.

Assuming arguendo that Edna Buffkin was Archie Buffkin's sole heir when he died, this circumstance is of no avail to defendants. Our Supreme Court has stated and applied the following rule, which is applicable to the facts now before us: Applying the principle, it has been held in several of our decisions construing deeds of similar import that, in case of a limitation over on the death of a grantee or first taker without heir or heirs, and the second or ultimate taker is presumptively or potentially one of the heirs general of the first, the term 'dying without heir or heirs' on the part of the grantee will be construed to mean, not his heirs general, but his issue in the sense of children and grandchildren, etc., living at his death. Under the deed from P.V. and Lucy Buffkin, Archie Buffkin took a fee simple defeasible upon his death without surviving issue. Archie's estate ended when he died without surviving issue, and the limitation over in his deed operated at his death to convey fee simple title to Forest B. Culbreth and Louise White or their heirs.

For the reasons stated, the judgment of the trial court is

Affirmed.

Chapter Summary

Deeds must meet some basic requirements. They must be in writing under the Statute of Frauds and they must have clearly identifiable parties. Deeds must be signed by the grantor, delivered to and accepted by the grantee. The deed must also contain an adequate property description. There are various types of deeds. A quitclaim deed is a deed by the grantor to the grantee where the grantor surrenders any rights that he may have to the real estate. A quitclaim deed makes no promises or warranties of any kind. On the other hand, a general warranty deed contains numerous promises or warranties from the grantor to the grantee. These warranties include the warranty of seizin, quiet enjoyment, the warranty against encumbrances, and the warranty of further assurance. Deeds commonly contain nonessential elements as well. Among these nonessential elements are a seal, which is no longer required under North Carolina law, an acknowledgment of the grantor's signature and a date.

Two of the most important clauses found in a deed consist of the granting clause and the habendum clause. The granting clause contains words that indicate the grantor's intent to transfer the title to the grantee and the habendum clause consists of language showing the nature of the estate transferred to the grantee.

Courts follow specific rules about construing the language found in deeds. When the language is ambiguous, the courts will attempt to give effect to the stated intent of the parties, when that can be gleaned from the document. North Carolina's real property recording statutes give priority to grantees who record their deeds. Generally speaking, the grantee who records his deed before any other claim on the property will have priority.

Review Questions

1. What are the legal minimum requirements for a deed in North Carolina?

2. What is a seal and is it required for deeds?

3. Why is there a requirement that the grantor must sign the deed but not the grantee?

4. What is the difference between a habendum clause and a granting clause?

5. What is the difference between a special warranty deed and a general warranty deed?

6. What is the function of a deed of trust?

7. Provide an example of "words of conveyance" that should be found in a deed.

8. Is the grantee required to sign the deed? Explain your answer.

9. What is the rule in North Carolina regarding property descriptions in deeds?

10. Is consideration required in a deed? Explain your answer.

11. What is a seal and is it a requirement for deeds in this state?

12. What is an acknowledgment in a deed and what purpose does it serve?

13. Explain the rules regarding delivery and acceptance of deeds.

14. What function does a quitclaim deed serve?

15. Explain the covenant of seizin.

16. What is the covenant against encumbrances?

17. What is the purpose of a timber deed?

18. List and explain at least five minimum requirements that any deed in North Carolina should have.

19. What is the covenant of warranty forever?

20. Under what circumstances would a quitclaim deed be used?

Assignment

1. Please research Strong's North Carolina Index and any other treatise on North Carolina Real Property and answer the following questions.

- What are the rules about delivery and acceptance of deeds?

- What is consideration in a deed?

- What is the covenant of seizin?

- What is the covenant of quiet enjoyment?

- What is a "granting" clause in a deed?

2. Go to your local courthouse and locate a deed for someone in your neighborhood or a family member. Get a copy of this deed and locate the following clauses:

- The granting clause

- The abandon clause
- The covenant of seizin
- The grantor's signature
- The property descriptions
- The words of conveyance
- The clause detailing delivery and acceptance of the deed

Terms and Phrases

Deed
Gift deed
Quitclaim deeds
General warranty deed
Seizin
Quiet enjoyment
Encumbrances
Further assurance
Special warranty deed
Deed of trust
Timber deed
Deed of correction
Sheriff's deed

Tax deed
Grantor
Grantee
Delivery
Acceptance
Escrow
Consideration
Acknowledgment
Seal
Granting clause
Habendum clause
Recording statute
Connor Act

Chapter 7

Property Descriptions, Boundaries, Rights and Liabilities Arising from Land Ownership

Chapter Objectives

At the conclusion of this chapter, you should be able to:

- Draw a metes and bounds description
- Explain the water rights available to a land owner
- Describe the rights that a land owner has in the air above the real estate and in the soil below it
- Explain premises liability
- Describe how property boundaries change when they are bordered by water

I. Introduction

"Land" or "real property" is traditionally described as the actual earth and anything permanently attached to it, such as trees, grass, shrubs or structures. In this chapter, we will examine the rights that owners in real estate have, including lateral support, water rights, the rules regarding boundaries and the liabilities that also arise from possession and/or ownership of real property. We will begin our discussion by explaining how real property is described in a deed, how this description can vary according to the rules of determining boundaries, including how water affects a property's boundaries, then proceed to a discussion of air and mineral rights and conclude with a discussion of premises liability.

II. Property Descriptions in Deeds

One of the requirements of a legally sufficient deed is an adequate description of the property being conveyed. (The remaining legal requirements of deeds are discussed in chapter 6). Property descriptions must be either a) sufficient in themselves or b) sufficient by reference to some other source, such as a plat or another deed.[1]

A property description is sufficient in itself when it:

- Has a definite beginning and ending point; and
- Makes specific references to property lines and roadways and other landmarks.[2]

Among the other requirements for valid property descriptions is that the description must be sufficient at the time that the deed is recorded. It cannot be 'fixed' by recording other documents at a later time. The description must stand on its own, giving specific reference points for the boundary lines and making reference to other natural or artificial boundary landmarks. The property description can refer to another document not included in the deed, but that other document must make the property description complete. When a plat, survey or map is referred to in a deed as part of the property description, it becomes a part of the deed. As far as North Carolina law is concerned, a plat referenced in this way is as much a part of the deed as any other provision, even though it is not recorded with the deed.[3]

> Sidebar: "A map or plat, referred to in a deed, becomes part of the deed, as if it were written therein."[4]

Consider the following example of an insufficient property description (from *Brooks v. Hackney*[5]):

> "Thence with the Whitehead line. Thence straight to the road that goes by Plainfield Church and with the road to the church to include 25 acres in all."

> According to the North Carolina Supreme Court: "When one attempts to connect these points, this language fails adequately to specify where the parties intended the property line to divert from the Whitehead line, and thus the last call could be in any number of locations in order to include twenty-five acres. The last boundary line is therefore subject to a number of constructions, each with significant variations. The writings at issue here do not refer to anything extrinsic from which the description can be made more certain, and the description is patently ambiguous."[6]

When a property description is the subject of litigation, how does a party prove that the description is legally valid? At a minimum, the party should be able to prove that the description covers the boundaries of the property; that the description fits the land in question; that the metes and bounds description is accurate and that the property description refers to natural boundaries and formations, where appropriate.[7]

When a property description is insufficient, it is referred to as ambiguous. There are two legal classifications of ambiguous property descriptions: patent ambiguities and latent ambiguities.

---

1. *Foreman v. Sholl*, 113 N.C. App. 282, 439 S.E.2d 169 (1994).
2. *Blackwell v. City of Reidsville*, 129 N.C.App. 759, 502 S.E.2d 371 (1998).
3. *Parrish v. Hayworth*, 138 N.C.App. 637, 532 S.E.2d 202 (2000).
4. *Stines v. Willyng, Inc.*, 81 N.C.App. 98, 101, 344 S.E.2d 546, 548 (1986).
5. 329 N.C. 166, 404 S.E.2d 854 (1991).
6. *Brooks v. Hackney*, 329 N.C. 166, 404 S.E.2d 854 (1991).
7. *Powell v. Mills*, 237 N.C. 582, 75 S.E.2d 759 (1953).

Figure 7-1. Proving a Property Description

The description must
    Apply to the land in question
    Describe the boundaries of the property
    Be an accurate metes and bounds description
    Refer to natural boundaries or landmarks where appropriate

---

A. Patent Ambiguities

When a description is so vague that the property cannot be identified, or its boundaries specified with clarity, it is patently ambiguous. This designation authorizes the court to invalidate the deed. According to the North Carolina Supreme Court, "A patent ambiguity exists when the description leaves the land to be conveyed in a state of absolute uncertainty and which refers to nothing extrinsic by which it might possibly be identified with certainty."[8] A patently ambiguous deed gives the reader no certainty about where the property is located or what its boundaries are. When a party is attempting to enforce a deed containing a patently ambiguous description, there is very little that the party can do to keep the deed from being invalidated. Parole evidence, for instance, is inadmissible in such a situation.

1. Parol Evidence Not Allowed to Correct Patently Ambiguous Description

Faced with an inadequate property description, the parties cannot attempt to resolve the situation by offering testimony about what the property description actually means. This is referred to as parol evidence. Parol evidence is not permitted to interpret the property description. The property description must stand on its own; courts will not consider evidence or testimony that seeks to explain or expand on a patently ambiguous property description. Given this situation, a party cannot take the stand and attempt to explain the description.

Parol Evidence: Oral testimony offered to explain or interpret the provisions of a written document.

Sidebar: When (a description is patently ambiguous) parol evidence is not admissible to explain the description and the deed is void.[9]

Figure 7-2. Defining Patently Ambiguous Property Descriptions

A property description is patently ambiguous when:
- It leaves the land in a state of absolute uncertainty and
- Refers to nothing extrinsic by which it might be identified with certainty.*

* *Lane v. Coe*, 262 N.C. 8, 136 S.E.2d 269 (1964).

---

8. *Lane v. Coe*, 262 N.C. 8, 136 S.E.2d 269 (1964).
9. *Kidd v. Early*, 289 N.C. 343, 353, 222 S.E.2d 392, 400 (1976).

However, a description will not be ruled to be patently ambiguous even when the description is uncertain in one document, but is made specific in another. In this situation, the description would be described as latently ambiguous.

B. Latent Ambiguities

A latently ambiguous property description is insufficient when viewed by itself, but does refer to some other document through which a more precise identification can be made. Examples of latently ambiguous descriptions include the following situation: "I hereby sell to X all of my land in Hemphil County." Such a description would be patently ambiguous. However, if this same wording includes a reference to "as set out in deed book, 1019, page 123," a patently ambiguous description is converted into a latently ambiguous description. Latently ambiguous descriptions are not void and parol evidence can be used to explain or interpret the provisions.[10]

C. Metes and Bounds Descriptions

The most commonly accepted, and perhaps the most accurate, method of describing property is by a metes and bounds description. A metes and bounds description sets out the distance and direction of the property's boundaries. Metes (distance) and bounds (direction) follow the course of the property lines from a point of beginning (P.O.B.) in a clockwise description, from border to border until returning to the P.O.B. In many ways, a metes and bounds description is similar to the way treasure maps describe the location of the prize. However, instead of "twelve paces west to an old stump, then twenty paces east to the mouth of a cave" and thus to the buried treasure, a metes and bounds description is actually a step by step tour of the entire property line. Instead of treasure, the end of a metes and bounds description brings you back to where you started. Along the way, it describes every twist and turn of the property so that there can be no doubt about the exact location and boundary line of the property.

Here is an example of a metes and bounds description:

> Starting from the northwestern most point of lot 9 Plat Book 28 page 30 thence N. 85 degrees 07' 20" W. 37.40 feet to the point and place of beginning; thence N. 85 degrees 07' 20" W. 102.46 feet; thence N. 11 degrees 18' 10" W. 36.37 feet to a point which is the northeastern most point of the Smith property thence S. 70 degrees 38' 18" E. 139.66 feet to the point and place of beginning (P.O.B.).

As you can see from this example, a metes and bounds description is extremely precise. Distances are given to 1/100 of a foot and direction is given not only in degrees, but also in finer gradations of minutes and seconds. The degrees refer to the hash marks on a typical drawing compass. For instance, "N. 85 degrees 07' 20" W. 37.40 feet," directs the reader directly North, and then 7 degrees to the West (ignoring the 20", which is difficult to locate on a typical compass). If you were drawing this line, and north was the top of the page, then your line would be at a slight angle toward the upper left corner of the page. We will draw out metes and bounds descriptions in the next section of this chapter.

---

10. *Bradshaw v. McElroy*, 62 N.C.App. 515, 302 S.E.2d 908 (1983).

Although metes and bounds descriptions are precise, they do present problems for the legal professional. When inserting a property description in a deed or real estate contract, you should pay careful attention to the metes and bounds description, ensuring that it is word-for-word correct. When transcribing a long metes and bounds description, it is easy to leave out a line and create a legally insufficient description.

Older metes and bounds descriptions do not use the same type of terminology or measuring units. Consider the following example:

> BEING Grant No. 97 by the State of North Carolina to John Guerard, dated April 13, 1870, recorded in Book L-2 page 644, New Hanover County Registry, and more particularly described by metes and bounds as follows:

> BEGINNING at a stake in the southwest corner of your new survey in your old line; running thence south 72 degrees east 150 poles to your corner on the Sea Banks; thence along the sea shore South 18 degrees West 384 poles to a stake at the end of the bank near a small inlet; thence across the sound South 72 degrees west 115 poles to your old line; thence along said line to the place and point of BEGINNING; containing three hundred acres, more or less.[11]

Notice that this description does not describe the directions in finer gradations of degrees. Instead of presenting direction in degrees/minutes/seconds, this description simply provides "South 72 degrees west." However, that is not the real problem presented by this property description. What are "poles?"

Older property descriptions, such as those found in deeds from the 1960s and earlier, often measure distances in terms of 'poles,' 'rods' and 'chains.' These are all units of distance, in the same way that miles and yards are units of distance. When deciphering these older property descriptions, you must first convert poles and chains into feet and then draw the description based on the conversion. See Figure 7-3 for a conversion chart.

Figure 7-3. Conversion Chart for Old Metes and Bounds Descriptors

1 Chain = 66 feet
1 Rod = 16.5 feet
1 Pole = 16.5 feet
1 Perch = 16.5 feet
1 link = 7.92 inches
1 Acre = 43,560 square feet, or
Square acre = 208.71 feet on each side
1 mile = 5280 feet

---

1. Drawing Metes and Bounds Descriptions

Before we explain how to draw metes and bounds descriptions, we should first address the question of why acquiring this skill is helpful. Being able to draw metes and bounds descriptions helps you visualize the property descriptions in a way that simply reading distances and directions never can. Drawing out the description also allows you to compare your drawing with other, known drawings of the same property. You can compare your drawing to plats, tax maps and other drawings of the property. A drawing

---

11. *Resort Development Co. v. Phillips*, 278 N.C. 69, 178 S.E.2d 813 (1971).

will help you immediately identify when the property description is in error (or is actually the description for an entirely different parcel).

In order to draw metes and bounds descriptions, you will need a circular, Land Measure Compass, or a semi-circular protractor. Land Measure Compasses can be obtained from a wide variety of sources, although one of the easiest ways is to obtain one given out as promotional items advertising a Title Insurance or Surveying Company. You will also need a regular, straight ruler.

To draw a metes and bounds description, get a blank piece of paper and then locate a point on the paper to serve as your point of beginning (P.O.B.) One way of deciding where your P.O.B. will be is by reading through the entire description and locating the longest boundary line. If the longest described line is on the North-South axis, then your P.O.B. should be towards the bottom of your blank page. If the longest line in on the East-West axis, then your P.O.B. should be closer to the left hand margin of your page. The reason we specify the left hand margin of your blank page is that metes and bounds descriptions are written in a clockwise fashion, meaning that they usually start on the left hand side of the page and progress in a clockwise manner from there.

We'll start with a very basic example.

"From P.O.B., N 30 degrees E, 100 feet, then S 30 degrees E, 100 feet, then S 30 degrees West, 100 feet, then N 30 degrees W, 100 feet to P.O.B."

We can start to draw this description by first locating a spot towards the lower, left hand corner of your blank page. Draw a dot there. Place the center of your compass on this point, with North on the compass pointing directly towards the top of the page. A direction such as "N 30 degrees E," means 'North 30 degrees towards the East." Locate north, and then go 30 degrees towards the East. In this situation, you will go right down the curve of your compass or protractor until you locate 30 degrees. Mark that point and then remove your compass. You should know have two points: your original P.O.B. and the mark indicating North 30 degrees East from that point. You can now draw a line connecting these lines, but before you do, we have one other matter to decipher.

How long should this line be?

The description says that the line is "N 30 degrees E, 100 feet." Obviously, we must scale down 100 feet to some distance that would actually fit on a blank sheet of paper. One way of doing this is create a scale in which 100 feet = 1 inch. Most attorneys use a scale closer to 1 inch = 200 feet, in order to make sure that the drawing actually fits on the page. We'll use the 1-inch = 100 feet scale just to keep things nice and simple. Under that scale, your line connecting your P.O.B. and the new N 30 degrees East mark would measure 1 inch. Place your rule along the axis of these two lines and measure 1 inch from the P.O.B. You may find that the line doesn't reach your new mark. No problem. That mark was just there to give you a direction. In fact, as soon as you draw your 1-inch line, you should probably erase that N 30 degrees East mark so that it won't cause any later confusion.

You now have a 1-inch line that starts at the left hand bottom corner of your blank sheet and aims roughly at the upper, right corner of your page. Now what? Move your compass to the end of this new line and dial in your new direction. According to our sample, this new direction is "S 30 degrees E, 100 feet." Following the same process that we outlined above, your line should point in the general direction of the lower, right corner of your page and will be 1 inch long.

Draw this metes and bounds description. You should end up with a square, with one corner of the square pointing towards the top of your page.

Sometimes, a metes and bounds description will give you a direction such as "directly north," or "due North" or simple N 100 feet. In this case, the description simply means directly north, with no angling off on either side.

If you are ready to try your hand at drawing some metes and bounds descriptions, go to the end of this chapter and draw the descriptions that you will find there.

D. Other Methods to Describe Property: Government Survey System

As part of the Pubic Land Act of 1785, the federal government created a system for surveying, and giving away, parcels of land in new territories west of the original colony states. Because North Carolina is an original colony state, this system does not apply.

E. Other Methods to Describe Property: Reference to a Plat   *TQ*

A plat is a drawing of the property, prepared by a surveyor. A plat can be recorded in the Registrar of Deeds office and often contains all of the same information provided in a metes and bounds property description. A statute in North Carolina gives plats the status of official, recorded documents, provided that they meet certain requirements. Once recorded, a plat can be one of the documents referred to in a legally valid property description. See Figure 7-4.

F. Other Methods to Describe Property: Torrens Registration

The Torrens System is a system of land registration invented by Sir Robert Torrens. The Torrens' method greatly simplified the rules regarding registration of English deeds by gathering together all information about a particular parcel into a single document. The appealing aspect of a Torrens registration scheme is that when a person wishes to know whether an encumbrance, such as a lien, has been filed against the property, he or she can simply pull the registration card and read what has been printed there. Such a system almost completely eliminates the need for a title search and greatly simplifies other aspects of real property titles.

Torrens registration has been in effect in North Carolina since 1913, but never really caught on. The logical premise behind Torrens was not enough to overcome centuries of practice. These days it is rare to find a property that is still registered under Torrens. Most attorneys who come across such property immediately move to take the listing out from under the Torrens system and return it to the more common system of recording the chain of title in the Registrar of Deeds office.

> Sidebar: When an owner registrars a parcel under the Torrens system, he or she is protected against all claims that the title has a cloud or other legal problem.[12]

---

12. *State v. Johnson*, 278 N.C. 126, 144, 179 S.E.2d 371, 383 (1971).

Figure 7-4. North Carolina General Statute § 47-30. Plats and Subdivisions; Mapping Requirements

(a) Size Requirements.—All land plats presented to the register of deeds for recording in the registry of a county in North Carolina after September 30, 1991, having an outside marginal size of either 18 inches by 24 inches, 21 inches by 30 inches, or 24 inches by 36 inches, and having a minimum one and one-half inch border on the left side and a minimum one-half inch border on the other sides shall be deemed to meet the size requirements for recording under this section. Where size of land areas, or suitable scale to assure legibility require, plats may be placed on two or more sheets with appropriate match lines. Counties may specify either:

(1) Only 18 inches by 24 inches;

(2) A combination of 18 inches by 24 inches and 21 inches by 30 inches;

(3) A combination of 18 inches by 24 inches and 24 inches by 36 inches; or

(4) A combination of all three sizes.

For purposes of this section, the terms "plat" and "map" are synonymous.

(b) Plats to Be Reproducible.—Each plat presented for recording shall be a reproducible plat, either original ink on polyester film (mylar), or a reproduced drawing, transparent and archival (as defined by the American National Standards Institute), and submitted in this form.

(c) Information Contained in Title of Plat.—The title of each plat shall contain the following information: property designation, name of owner (the name of owner shall be shown for indexing purposes only and is not to be construed as title certification), location to include township, county and state, the date or dates the survey was made; scale or scale ratio in words or figures and bar graph; name and address of surveyor or firm preparing the plat ...

(f) Plat to Contain Specific Information.—Every plat shall contain the following specific information:

(1) An accurately positioned north arrow coordinated with any bearings shown on the plat. Indication shall be made as to whether the north index is true, magnetic, North Carolina grid ("NAD 83" or "NAD 27"), or is referenced to old deed or plat bearings. If the north index is magnetic or referenced to old deed or plat bearings, the date and the source (if known) the index was originally determined shall be clearly indicated ...

(8) All visible and apparent rights-of-way, watercourses, utilities, roadways, and other such improvements shall be accurately located where crossing or forming any boundary line of the property shown ...

(11) Notwithstanding any other provision contained in this section, it is the duty of the surveyor, by a certificate on the face of the plat, to certify to one of the following:

a. That the survey creates a subdivision of land within the area of a county or municipality that has an ordinance that regulates parcels of land;

b. That the survey is located in a portion of a county or municipality that is unregulated as to an ordinance that regulates parcels of land;

A plat, when certified pursuant to G.S. 47-30.2 and presented for recording, shall be recorded in the plat book or plat file and when so recorded shall be duly indexed. Reference in any instrument hereafter executed to the record of any plat herein authorized shall have the same effect as if the description of the lands as indicated on the record of the plat were set out in the instrument.

Sidebar: "The general purpose of the Torrens system is ... to secure by a decree of court, or other similar proceeding, a title impregnable against attack ... and to protect the registered owner against all claims or demands not noted on the book for the registration of titles."[13]

---

13. *Beck v. Beck*, 125 N.C.App. 402, 481 S.E.2d 317 (1997); *State v. Johnson*, 278 N.C. 126, 144, 179 S.E.2d 371, 383 (1971) (quoting Frederick B. McCall, *The Torrens System—After Thirty-Five Years,* 10 N.C.L.Rev. 329, 330 (1932)).

III. Water Rights

Water, or riparian rights, can be a complex issue that could easily take up an entire volume of its own. Although water rights can be broken down into three categories: water rights for land owners, water rights of the public and water rights of the government, we will limit our discussion to the water rights of land owners, primarily because this is the one area where a legal professional is likely to encounter them.

A. Right to Draw Water

Owners of land that border on water have certain inherent rights to use that water. The rule in North Carolina is simple: when an owner's land is in contact with water, he or she has the right to make reasonable use of it. Under ordinary circumstances, all owners whose land borders on the body of water, including rivers and streams have the right to take water from the source. Obviously, this right is limited to the extent that the owner cannot use so much of the water that it prevents others from doing so. Other limitations on owners are the prohibition against altering the course of the river or polluting it to such an extent that the water becomes unusable for other owners who also border the stream.

1. Reasonable Use Test

Our state has adopted the "reasonable use" test to determine when an owner's use of water is excessive or injurious to others. Under this rule, the owner may use the water to an extent considered reasonable under the circumstances. The factors that determine reasonableness will vary from case to case. Whether a particular owner's water use is reasonable is a question to be determined by a jury.[14]

B. Natural Forces That Affect Property Descriptions

When one or more boundary lines of a parcel border on water, the question often becomes: where exactly does one draw the property line? Water levels tend to rise and lower not only through the course of a year, but sometimes during the course of a single day. Property boundaries can be affected not only by tides, but also by the more gradual natural actions that affect boundary lines. Among these natural forces are:

- Accretion
- Erosion
- Avulsion
- Reliction

1. Accretion

Accretion is the gradual deposit of soil on an owner's property that expands the total size of the parcel. In this situation, the boundary line shifts to reflect the new expansion

---

14. *City of Durham v. Eno Cotton Mills,* 141 N.C. 615, 54 S.E. 453 (1906); *Pine Knoll Association, Inc. v. Cardon,* 126 N.C.App. 155, 484 S.E.2d 446 (1997).

of dry land. When accretion occurs by natural forces, it gives the landowner a windfall. Without paying for any additional property, he or she has gradually acquired more land.

In defining the natural processes that can affect property boundaries, "our Supreme Court has stated that when the location of a body of water constituting the boundary of a tract of land, is gradually and imperceptibly changed or shifted by accretion, reliction, or erosion, the margin or bed of the stream or body, as so changed, remains the boundary line of the tract, which is extended or restricted accordingly. The owner of the riparian land thus loses title to such portions as are so worn or washed away or encroached upon by the water. Thus the lots of the plaintiff were gradually worn away by the churning of the ocean on the shore and thereby lost. Its title was divested by 'the sledge-hammering seas the inscrutable tides of God.'"[15]

2. Erosion

Erosion is the opposite of accretion. When the action of water slowly takes away soil from a parcel, the owner's overall lot size gradually decreases. The owner is not permitted to adjust his boundaries to reflect the slow loss of acreage.

3. Avulsion

Avulsion is a lesser known process where dry land is suddenly added or lost by the action of water. Rivers can sometimes shift their courses dramatically, and when this shift results in a sudden change in a property's boundaries, the process is accurately described as avulsion, not accretion or erosion.

4. Reliction

Reliction is the gradual exposure of dry land by receding waters. Although this process is not common, it can affect a property's boundaries, or even an entire parcel.

C. Determining Water Boundaries

Although a metes and bounds description is one of the best ways to describe property, we have already seen situations where such a description is inadequate. Metes and bounds descriptions do not assist a real estate professional in determining the air rights above the property, or the mineral rights under the surface. Property descriptions also run into practical difficulties. When one line of the property is bordered by a river, lake or stream, exactly where should the property line be located? If the water level varies, as they usually do, doesn't this mean that the property line also varies, sometimes several times a day? North Carolina follows a two-prong approach to this issue. The first prong is to determine the classification of the body of water in question. That classification will then determine the rules applicable to boundary lines and water courses. The first question that must be asked when dealing with water is whether the water is navigable?

---

15. *Carolina Beach Fishing Pier, Inc. v. Town of Carolina Beach,* 277 N.C. 297, 304, 177 S.E.2d 513, 517 (1970).

1. Navigable Waters

North Carolina defines a "navigable" body of water as one that is capable of supporting commercial navigation. This means, in essence, a river, lake or other body of water that a boat could cross. Here a "boat" includes pleasure craft. Under the public trust doctrine that is a feature of most state's policies regarding water, when rivers or lakes are navigable and thus capable of use for commercial purposes, these bodies are the property of the state, not individual land owners. The state retains title to these bodies of water as a way of furthering commerce.

Courts have wrestled with the definition of navigable waters for years. In a particularly well written opinion, the North Carolina Supreme Court created a straightforward and practical definition of what has often been a complicated topic.

In *Gwathmey v. Dept. of Environment* the court wrote:

> "We hold that any waters, whether sounds, bays, rivers, or creeks, which are wide enough and deep enough for the navigation of sea vessels, are navigable waters, the soil under which is not the subject of entry and grant under our entry law, and the rights of fishing in which are, under our common and statute law, open and common to all the citizens of the State."[16]

Figure 7-5. N.C.G.S. § 146-6. Title to Land Raised from Navigable Water

(a) If any land is, by any process of nature or as a result of the erection of any pier, jetty or breakwater, raised above the high watermark of any navigable water, title thereto shall vest in the owner of that land which, immediately prior to the raising of the land in question, directly adjoined the navigable water. The tract, title to which is thus vested in a riparian owner, shall include only the front of his formerly riparian tract and shall be confined within extensions of his property lines, which extensions shall be perpendicular to the channel, or main watercourses.

---

a. Boundary Lines along Navigable Bodies of Water

When property borders on a navigable body of water, the boundary line is the bank, or the mid-distance between low and high water marks (if the property borders the ocean).

2. Non-Navigable Water

When water is classified as non-navigable, the rules about boundaries change. When a property is bordered by a non-navigable body of water, the owner's property line runs to the middle of the stream. The opposite owner's boundary line also runs to the middle, effectively dividing the stream in half. If the course of the stream changes, then the property boundaries will also change. Obviously, these rules are not a factor when the stream passes through the middle of a parcel. In that case, the only concern for the property owner is the reasonable use of the water itself.

---

16. *Gwathmey v. State Through Dept. of Environment, Health, and Natural Resources Through Cobey*, 342 N.C. 287, 299, 464 S.E.2d 674, 681 (1995).

IV. Lateral Support

Property owners have an absolute right to lateral support of their property. This means that adjoining landowners can be enjoined from taking action that would make the property owner's land unstable. Suppose, for instance, that Frank owns a one acre tract. Lizzie, who lives next door, begins digging a large pit on her property, slicing down through the earth directly on the property line. If she digs down far enough, and fails to support the hole, the sides will collapse and part of Frank's property will crumble into Lizzie's hole. Frank's ownership and enjoyment of his property would be meaningless without some ability to protect the structure of the soil from collapse.

In North Carolina, the rules about lateral support give a landowner an absolute, inherent right to soil support when the land is in its natural state. If, on the other hand, the land is not in its natural state and has been modified, such as with structures or construction, the owner no longer has an absolute, inherent right. Instead, the owner may sue the adjoining landowner under a negligence theory, not a real property principle. In the next section, we will see how negligence law has a profound impact on property issues again in the context of premises liability.

V. Premises Liability

In addition to air, mineral and water rights, property owners also have obligations imposed on them. One such area is the topic of premises liability and unlike the other topics we have discussed in this chapter, it is based on negligence law, not property law. When a person possesses property, he or she owes visitors a special duty to keep the area safe. You will notice that in this section, unlike the others presented in this chapter, we do not speak about the property owner, but the property possessor. Obligations under premises liability are imposed on the person who possesses the property, whether that person is the owner or tenant. One reason for this variation is that the person in possession of the property is always in a better position to know about defects or dangerous conditions on the property that might injure other people.

A. Classifying Visitors to the Property

In the past, North Carolina had three separate classifications of visitors to real property. The possessor's duty varied depending on the visitor's category. The three classifications were:

- Trespassers
- Licensees
- Invitees

1. Trespassers

The general rule under North Carolina law is that there is no duty to trespassers. Possessors of land have no obligation to make their property safe or to take other actions that would ensure the safety of persons who are on the land without permission. Although there are some exceptions to this rule, such as the attractive nuisance doctrine, the general rule still holds in this state.

Trespasser: A person who is on the property of another without permission.

a. Exceptions to the General Rule of No Duty to Trespassers

Over time, the rather harsh rule that a land possessor owed no duty to a trespasser was gradually modified. One of the biggest problems with the rule involved children. Under the law, children always receive special protection. Their inexperience with the world and their lack of maturity require adults to look after them. When a child trespasses on property and is injured, should the same 'no duty to trespassers' rule apply? What if the land possessor had good reason to know that children would attempt to trespass? What if the land possessor has a swimming pool or a junkyard or a closed playground? Shouldn't he be forced to take some precautions to protect children, even if he is under no obligation to protect against adult trespassers?

i. The Attractive Nuisance Doctrine

Under the attractive nuisance doctrine, a person who possesses property to which children would naturally be drawn, such as railroad yards, closed playgrounds, etc., must take reasonable steps to secure the premises from danger by trespassing children. "A landowner ordinarily owes a duty to exercise ordinary care for the protection of one of tender years, after his presence in a dangerous situation is or should have been known."[17]

2. Licensees

When someone is invited on to the property, that person is not a trespasser. In many jurisdictions, this invited person can fall into one of two categories: licensee or invitee. The defendant's duty to a licensee is different than his duty to an invitee.

The term "licensee" refers to a guest. This is a person who has come to the premises for personal or social reasons, not business. The duty of a possessor to a licensee is simply to warn of a dangerous condition.

> **Licensee:** A person who enters another person's premises by invitation for friendship, convenience, curiosity or entertainment.

3. Invitees

An invitee is a customer or a client. This person has come to the premises for a business reason. In most jurisdictions, the property possessor owes the highest duty to an invitee. He must not only warn of dangerous conditions, but also take reasonable actions to make the premises safe.

> **Invitee:** A person who comes onto the property with a business purpose.

---

17. *Freeze v. Congleton*, 276 N.C. 178, 182, 171 S.E.2d 424, 426 (1970).

4. *North Carolina Has Abolished the Distinctions between Invitees and Licensees*

In 1998, the North Carolina Supreme Court abolished the distinctions between, and the different duties owed to, licensees and invitees. The Court's primary motivation is the confusion that had resulted after decades of cases that attempted to classify a wide range of visitors. The Court did not change the owner's duty to trespassers. North Carolina now requires a standard of reasonable care for all lawful visitors.

Relevant Case

Carolina Beach Fishing Pier, Inc. v. Town of Carolina Beach[18]

HUSKINS, Justice.

The first question for decision here is whether plaintiff's lots, or any portion thereof, were 'taken' by the Town of Carolina Beach for the construction of the berm erected to control tidal erosion. Resolution of this problem requires a discussion of the general principles of ownership applicable to tidal lands.

It has been settled since the passage of the Submerged Lands Act of 1953 by the United States Congress that the lands beneath coastal waters belong to the states, and not the federal government. 'The seaward boundary of each original coastal State is approved and confirmed as a line three geographical miles distant from its coast line Nothing in this section is to be construed as questioning or in any manner prejudicing the existence of any State's seaward boundary beyond three geographical miles if it was so provided by its constitution or laws prior to or at the time such State became a member of the Union, or if it has been heretofore approved by Congress.' 43 U.S.C. § 1312. This concession is subject to specific reservations for use of such waters for navigation, flood control, or the production of power by the federal government. 43 U.S.C. § 1311; 67 Stat. 30. The authority of the State is further restricted by the Commerce Clause of the United States Constitution. '(T)he federal government, by virtue of its constitutional authority to regulate interstate and foreign commerce, has paramount power to control all navigable waters of the United States to the extent necessary for that purpose, and both the state and the riparian owners hold such waters and the lands under them subject to that power.' Annotation, Rights to land created at water's edge by filling or dredging, 91 A.L.R.2d 857 (1963). See generally, Aaron L. Shalowitz, Boundary Problems Raised by the Submerged Lands Act, 54 Colum.L.Rev. 1021 (1954). There is no ascertainable federal interest here, and we therefore direct our comments to the interests of the State and its property owners.

Where is the dividing line between the property of the State and that of the littoral private owner? There is a division among the States on that question, and the groups may be conveniently labeled 'high-tide' states and 'low-tide' states.

The 'strip of land between the high- and low-tide lines' is called the foreshore. The high-tide states hold that private property ends at the high-water mark, and that the foreshore is the property of the state. The low-tide states, on the other hand, fix the boundary at the low-water mark, and the foreshore is said to belong to the littoral

---

18. 277 N.C. 297, 177 S.E.2d 513 (1970).

landowner unless it has been otherwise alienated. Powell on Real Property, supra; Annotation, supra, 91 A.L.R.2d 857; 6 Thompson on Real Property § 3084 (1962); 56 Am.Jur., Waters § 458.

Although the North Carolina position is somewhat obscured by the vagaries of ancient cases, See David A. Rice, Estuarine Land of North Carolina: Legal Aspect of Ownership, Use and Control, 46 N.C.L.Rev. 779 (1968), North Carolina is a high-tide state. Under the old 'entry and grant' statutes (which were replaced in 1959 by the State Land Act, Session Laws, 1959, c. 683, codified as Gen.Stat., c. 146), only land under non-navigable waters could be entered. Ownership which might interfere with navigation was not allowed. Therefore, littoral rights in ocean-front property did not include the title to the foreshore, which remained in the State.

The State Land Act of 1959, supra, carries forward the distinction between navigable and non-navigable waters and provides that land under navigable waters cannot be 'conveyed in fee', but that easements may be granted. G.S. § 146-3. More importantly, the act creates a new subclassification for lands 'which lie beneath. The Atlantic Ocean to a distance of three geographical miles seaward from the coastline of this State,' and provides that no such lands can be 'conveyed in fee.' G.S. §§ 46-3 and 146-64. There is nothing in the new act to change the general rule that ownership of the foreshore remains in the State. On the contrary, it is noteworthy that a special class was created for the protection of the foreshore and the marginal seas. We therefore adhere to our long established rule that littoral rights do not include ownership of the foreshore.

The littoral owner may, however, in exercise of his right of access, construct a pier in order to provide passage from the upland to the sea. "But the passage under the pier must be free and substantially unobstructed over the entire width of the foreshore. This means that from low to high water mark it must be at such a height that the public will have no difficulty in walking under it when the tide is low or in going under it in boats when the tide is high." This language is consistent with the view we take here that the foreshore is reserved for the use of the public.

Applying the foregoing principles, we hold that the seaward boundary of plaintiff's lots is fixed at the high-water mark. The high-water mark is generally computed as a mean or average high-tide, and not as the extreme height of the water.

Chapter 511 of the 1963 Session Laws relating to erosion control work in the Town of Carolina Beach was ratified 22 May 1963. Section 1 of the Act provides that so much of the lands to be filled in and restored which lie east of the 'building line' (to be established as provided in said Act) is granted and conveyed in fee simple to the Town of Carolina Beach. Plaintiff's Exhibit 'U' is a map of the 'building line' established by the Town along the ocean front pursuant to said Act. This map, offered in evidence by plaintiff, shows that in January 1964 Lots 1 through 10 of Block 216 were completely submerged and the mean high-water mark of the Atlantic Ocean was in approximately the center of Carolina. Beach Avenue north. The building line at this point was accordingly established along the western margin of Carolina Beach Avenue north. Thus, twelve months before the berm was built, plaintiff's lots had been taken by the sea and title thereto had vested in the State of North Carolina. This condition is confirmed by the following testimony of plaintiff's principal stockholder and witness Sam H. Blake: 'By the fall of 1963 I had to extend the entrance of the ramp across the western side of Carolina Beach Avenue, and that was because one would have had to walk through water to get to the ramp at times. That street is approximately 40 feet wide, and our extension was 40 feet to the west in the fall of 1963, which was because the water had moved up into the street, but not all the time.'

'It is a general rule that where the location of the margin or bed of a stream or other body of water which constitutes the boundary of a tract of land is gradually and imperceptibly changed or shifted by accretion, reliction, or erosion, the margin or bed of the stream or body, as so changed, remains the boundary line of the tract, which is extended or restricted accordingly. The owner of the riparian land thus ... loses title to such portions as are so worn or washed away or encroached upon by the water.' 56 Am.Jur., Waters §477; Jones v. Turlington, 243 N.C. 681, 92 S.E.2d 75 (1956). Thus the lots of the plaintiff were gradually worn away by the churning of the ocean on the shore and thereby lost. Its title was divested by 'the sledge-hammering seas ... the inscrutable tides of God.' Herman Melville, Moby Dick.

G.S. §146-6, which governs the title to land raised from navigable waters, permits vesting of title to such lands in the littoral landowner (1) where he does the filling himself by permission of the State and under approved procedures or (2) where the purpose of the filling is 'to reclaim lands theretofore lost to the owner by natural causes.' G.S. §146-6(b), (c). Manifestly, the purpose here was the preservation and protection of the Town of Carolina Beach from the fury of the sea rather than the reclamation of the lands of private owners along the beach. Accordingly, we conclude that the purpose to be served by construction of the berm was not to reclaim lands theretofore lost to the owner by natural causes, and when Lots 1 through 6 and Lot 9 of Block 216 were raised above sea level by the sand berm title to the land so created which was located east of the building line vested in fee in the Town of Carolina Beach as provided in Chapter 511 of the 1963 Session Laws. This legislative grant to the Town of title to property east of the building line and extending to the Low water mark of the Atlantic Ocean is inconsistent with G.S. §146-3(1). Even so, the 1963 Act repeals all laws in conflict with it and must be regarded as controlling in this instance. The Legislature has the power to abrogate, amend or make exceptions to its own acts. In this instance it has done so. Therefore, by virtue of Chapter 511 of the 1963 Session Laws, the Town of Carolina Beach owned the lots in question when the sand berm was built.

Plaintiff did not sue for damages to its fishing pier. Rather, plaintiff alleged that construction of the berm resulted in a total loss of the seven lots described in the complaint upon which was located a commercial fishing pier extending into the Atlantic Ocean approximately 900 feet from the mean high water mark. Plaintiff sought recovery of $41,000 as the fair market value of said property at the time it was allegedly taken by defendant for a public purpose. Such is the theory of plaintiff's case, and it must be tried upon that theory. It cannot be submitted to the jury on a theory of liability not supported by allegation and evidence. Moody v. Kersey, 270 N.C. 614, 155 S.E.2d 215 (1967); Calloway v. Wyatt, 246 N.C. 129, 97 S.E.2d 881 (1957); Herring v. Creech, 241 N.C. 233, 84 S.E.2d 886 (1954); Morgan v. High Penn. Oil Company, 238 N.C. 185, 77 S.E.2d 682 (1953). Plaintiff cannot avail itself of evidence contrary to the allegations of its complaint. Davis v. Rigsby, 261 N.C. 684, 136 S.E.2d 33 (1964); Watson v. Clutts, 262 N.C. 153, 136 S.E.2d 617 (1964); Faison v. T. & S. Trucking Co., 266 N.C. 383, 146 S.E.2d 450 (1966). Thus the trial court properly rejected plaintiff's proffered evidence of the cost of a 180-foot extension to the fishing pier and the cost of replacing the ramp. That was not the theory of the case, and the complaint understandably contains no allegation which would render such evidence admissible. Had a taking been shown there was no competent evidence upon which the jury could have based its answer to the damages issue.

Plaintiff having failed to show either a taking or damages under applicable rules of law, the judgment of nonsuit is

Affirmed.

Chapter Summary

One skill that a real estate professional must possess is the ability to draw metes and bounds descriptions. A metes and bounds description is the distance and direction of each of the boundary lines so that any described parcel may be drawn precisely.

There are many rights and obligations that arise directly from ownership of real estate. Among the rights conferred by this ownership are air and mineral rights. The owner has the right not only to the surface and anything permanently attached to the surface of his real estate parcel, but also the right to use the airspace above the parcel to a reasonable distance. Similarly, an owner also has rights in the soil located below the surface of his real estate tract. When a person possesses mineral rights to the soil, it means that he or she is allowed to remove minerals and other substances from below the surface of the soil. Mineral rights are often transferred separately from the transactions involving the rights in the parcel itself.

Other important rights that arise directly from ownership in real estate are water rights. Water rights include not only the ability to draw water for use, but also define how a property's boundaries may change over time by the natural forces that water may apply to the land. Through erosion or accretion, a landowner's property boundaries may change. Accretion is the process of adding additional square footage to the parcel, while erosion is the process of slowly removing area from the parcel. Real estate owners also have the right of lateral support, which refers to the inherent right of all landowners to have their soil supported to keep it from crumbling. Under the right of lateral support, an owner may bring action against another landowner to enjoin specific actions that will destroy his or her lateral support.

Among the liabilities that a real estate owner or possessor may suffer include the broad topic of premises liability. Possessors of real estate are under legal obligation to keep their premises safe for visitors. There is no obligation to keep the premises safe for trespassers.

Review Questions

1. Explain the process used to draw a metes and bounds description.
2. What are some of the elements necessary to prove the sufficiency of a property description?
3. What is a patent ambiguity in a property description?
4. What is a latent ambiguity in a property description?
5. What is parol evidence?
6. What are "rods", "poles" and "chains?"
7. What is the Torrens system of registration?
8. How far above the surface of real estate does an owner have air rights?
9. How do mineral rights compare to air rights?
10. What rights does an owner have to draw water from an adjoining stream, river or lake?
11. What is the "reasonable use" test in regard to water rights?
12. Compare and contrast accretion and erosion.
13. What is the difference between avulsion and reliction?
14. How do an owner's property boundaries change when the water level of the course of the body of water changes in a navigable river or ocean?
15. According to North Carolina law, what is the difference between a navigable body of water and a non-navigable body of water?
16. What is the public trust doctrine as it applies to water rights?
17. What is the right of lateral support in real estate?
18. What is the definition of a trespasser?
19. What is the attractive nuisance doctrine?
20. Prior to 1998, how did North Carolina define licensees and invitees?
21. Explain the ruling in this chapter's relevant case.

Assignment

Draw the following metes and bounds descriptions:

For the following exercises, you will need a circular, Land Measure Compass. You will also need a regular, straight ruler. Place the compass center point over the point of beginning, with North always facing the top of the page. Turn the dial to the desired direction and mark that point with a pencil. Using your straight ruler, measure from the beginning point along the direction indicated to the corresponding inches. Remember, for purposes of this exercise, our conversion is 100 ft = 1 inch.

1. Beginning at a point on the southwest corner of the lot, then proceeding due North 400 feet to a point, then due East 400 feet to a point, then due South 400 feet to a point, then due West 400 feet to the point of beginning.

2. Beginning at a point on the southwest corner of the lot, then North 60 degrees East 200 feet to a point, then South 85 degrees East 300 feet to a point, then South 25 degrees East, 300 feet to a point, then South 60 degrees West 200 feet to a point, then North 50 degrees West, 550 feet to the point of beginning.

3. Beginning at a point on the North side of the property, South 52 degrees East, 250 feet to a point, then South 30 degrees West, 250 feet, then South 68 degrees West, 300 feet, then North 90 degrees, 40 feet to a point, then North 65 degrees East, 200 feet, to a point, then North 9 degrees West, 150 feet to a point, then North 52 degrees West 100 feet, to a point, then North 41 degrees East 200 feet to the point of beginning.

Terms and Phrases

Patent ambiguity	Accretion
Latent ambiguity	Erosion
Parol evidence	Avulsion
Chain	Reliction
Rod	Navigable waters
Pole	Non-navigable waters
Plat	Lateral support
Torrens Registration	Premises Liability
Air rights	Trespasser
Mineral rights	Invitee
Water rights	Licensee
Reasonable Use Test	Attractive Nuisance Doctrine

Chapter 8

Real Estate Contracts

Chapter Objectives

At the conclusion of this chapter, you should be able to:

- Define the basic components of any contract
- Explain the basic prerequisites of a legally valid offer
- Describe the law of acceptance
- Explain the importance of capacity and competency of the parties to a contract
- Explain the various types of contracts that are important in real estate practice

I. Introduction to Contract Law

In this chapter, we will explore the topic of contract law as it is set out in North Carolina case law and statutes. There is a close affinity between real property law and contract law that arises directly from everyday practice. Contracts are important in a wide variety of real estate transactions, from landlord-tenant relationships, brokerage agreements, to offers of purchase and contracts for sale of real estate. We will begin our discussion of contract law by examining the basic elements of any contract and then proceed to the more specialized types of real estate contracts.

A. Defining a Contract

A contract is an agreement between two or more parties who have legal capacity to do some act. When a contract is created, it gives the parties specific rights and obligations. If a party breaches the terms of the contract, the other party has the right to sue for damages or seek equitable relief. Although we will be discussing real property contracts in this chapter, the general law of contracts applies to all types of agreements, whether they involve real property transactions or not.

> **Contract:** An agreement that gives the parties the right to enforce an obligation through the law.

A valid contract has basic components, consisting of a valid offer and an acceptance, mutual assent, capacity of the parties, legality of subject and consideration. The basic elements of a contract are set out in Figure 8-1.

Figure 8-1. The Legal Components of a Contract
- Offer
- Acceptance
- Consideration
- Legality
- Capacity

---

1. Offer

An offer is one party's indication of a willingness to enter into a contract. Offers are specific about their terms. They invite another person to enter into a legally-binding agreement. The details that must be present in an offer include: who will be bound by the contract and what exactly will be exchanged, on what terms and how the contract will be performed. Although offers must be specific, there are no rules that require inordinate specificity.[1] An offer must answer some basic questions, such as:

- Who will be bound?
- What will be exchanged?
- What are the terms?
- How can a party successfully perform under the contract?

If these general questions can be answered by reviewing the terms of the offer, then the offer is considered to be legally sufficient. Consider the next scenario and answer the question: Is this a valid offer?

Scenario #1.

Juan has decided to sell his home. He doesn't want to use a real estate broker, so he puts a "For Sale" sign in his yard and waits for a response. Is the sign an offer?

Answer: No. Juan's "For Sale" sign is not an offer. How can we be sure? Examine Juan's actions in light of the basic requirements for an offer. Does the "For Sale" sign indicate who will be bound by the offer? Does it indicate what the terms of the offer are? Does it state how a party can successfully perform under the contract? The answers to all of these questions are no. Therefore, Juan's sign is not an offer. What is it?

Juan's sign, like most "For Sale" signs, is an invitation to other people to make an offer.

Scenario #2.

In answer to Juan's "For Sale" sign, Mary calls Juan. She asks, "What is the sale price?"

Juan replies, "Make me an offer."

"How about $100,000?"

Is Mary's question an offer? Does it answer the basic questions that we ask for all offers? Although there isn't much detail in Mary's statement, we could argue that it is an

---

1. *Scott v. Foppe*, 247 N.C. 67, 100 S.E.2d 238 (1957).

offer. Who will be bound? Implied in Mary's question is that she will be bound. It is a given that the real estate will be exchanged between the parties. We can also answer the question about terms. The last question, dealing with successful performance is a little vague, but we seem to have something that we could arguably refer to as an offer.

Under North Carolina law, there is no requirement that an offer specify all possible contingencies, or that it must be phrased in legal terms. A valid offer can be couched in everyday language and the words used will be given their ordinary meaning. Another test that we can apply to an offer is even more basic. Does the offer create something that another person could accept?

> Sidebar: An offer indicates a person's willingness to enter into a contract; it is also specific about what is being offered and how a person can accept.

2. Acceptance

When a valid offer has been made, the party to whom it is made has three possible options. He can reject the offer, accept it or make a counter-offer. When a party rejects an offer, there is no longer a possibility of a contract, unless a new offer is made. In the next section, we will examine how and when an acceptance is considered legally sufficient and then discuss the legal significance of counter-offers.

If an offer meets the minimum requirements set out above, then it creates the "power of acceptance" in the offeree.

> Sidebar: In order to have a binding contract under North Carolina law, there must be an offer, an acceptance and consideration.[2]

a. The Power of Acceptance

A legally valid offer gives another person the power of acceptance. Simply put, the power of acceptance is the ability of a person to accept an offer and create a legally binding contract between the two parties. Let's continue with our example of Juan's desire to sell his house.

Scenario #3. Mary's Offer.

Mary has decided to make an offer on Juan's house. She details her offer as follows:

"Offer price: $100,000, contingent on obtaining financing:

On condition that the house pass an inspection

On condition that the closing occur within sixty (60) days."

Is this offer sufficiently detailed to create the power of acceptance for Juan?

Answer: yes.

Mary's offer meets the minimum requirements of specificity and creates the power of acceptance in Juan. If he accepts, a binding contract will be created between them.

> **The Power of Acceptance:** The ability of a person to create a binding, legal contract by accepting a valid offer.

---

2. *Cap Care Group, Inc. v. McDonald*, 561 S.E.2d 578 (2002).

i. Communicating the Acceptance

When an offer is accepted, the acceptance must be communicated to the offeror. Without this critical step, there is no valid acceptance and therefore no contract. Unless the offer specifically limits the method used to communicate the acceptance, it can be sent through any means.[3]

ii. Mailbox Rule

The so-called "Mailbox Rule" is a rule that states that an acceptance is legally effective when it is deposited in the U.S. postal system. All states have some version of the mailbox rule. The reason for the rule is simple: without it, any offer accepted by mail would not be effective until received. A mailed acceptance could take one to three days to reach the person addressed. In those three days, many things could happen, all of which could cause confusion without some rule dictating when the acceptance becomes effective.

b. Counter-Offers

Scenario #4.

Juan likes Mary's offer except for the price. He wants more for his house. He answers Mary's offer with the following:

"I like your offer, but I want $120,000."

What is the significance of this statement?

This is a counter-offer. People make counter-offers all the time without realizing what this does to the underlying dynamic of a legally binding offer. A counter-offer rejects the original offer. Essentially, what has happened is that Juan has rejected Mary's offer and made his own offer. Now, the power of acceptance shifts back to Mary. If she accepts the new offer, a valid contract will come into existence.

3. Mutual Assent

Mutual assent is the final product of a valid offer and acceptance. Also known as the "meeting of the minds," it is the manifestation of the agreement between the parties. Each party understands the nature and consequences of the agreement and is legally able to carry the agreement through. Later in this chapter, we will see that fraud, coercion and other actions can result in a void contract. This is because all of these actions destroy the concept of mutual assent. For instance, if a person is forced to enter into a contract, there can be no mutual assent and therefore no enforceable contract.

4. Consideration

The requirement of **consideration** in a contract has been a feature of contract law for centuries. Consideration is bargained-for-exchange between the parties. In order to create an enforceable contract, contract law requires that both parties surrender something of value in exchange for something else of value. No valid contract can be created when one party incurs no legal obligation. For instance, there would no consideration for a

---

3. *Albemarle Educational Foundation, Inc. v. Basnight*, 4 N.C. App. 652, 167 S.E.2d 486 (1969).

contract to require a parent to feed her child. Parents are already under that obligation and there is not contractual promise that will substitute for that obligation.

Consideration is usually not a major inquiry in real estate contracts. It can be an important feature of gift transactions, but for most real estate transactions, the validity of the consideration is not an issue.

> **Consideration**: a requirement of contract law that all parties bound to the contract incur some form of legal detriment or obligation under the agreement.

5. *Legality of Contracts*

One important aspect of any contract is the action that is contemplated by the parties. When the action involves an illegal activity, the contract is not enforceable. Because the courts use the court system to enforce the contract, allowing the parties to enforce a policy that runs counter to statutes or public policy would cause an untenable situation. In order to avoid this problem, any contract that has an illegal subject is not enforceable. Examples of contracts with illegal subjects include contracts to carry out crimes or to charge a usurious interest rate.

When a contract contains an illegal provision, courts and the state will attempt to enforce the rest of the contract, ignoring the illegal provision. When that is impossible, the entire contract will be voided.[4]

6. *Capacity*

We have already dealt with the concept of capacity in the previous chapter. When we discussed deeds, we saw that a party's capacity, at least the grantor's, was essential to a valid conveyance. A similar rule applies to contracts, except that both parties must have legal capacity before a contract will be enforced. A person who has legal capacity is competent and does not suffer from any impediment that would prevent her from entering legally binding agreements. Persons who lack capacity include those who have been ruled to be mentally incompetent and anyone suffering from a mental disease or operating under the effects of alcohol or other drugs. Children (those under the age of 18) also lack capacity to enter into contracts. When a contracting party lacks capacity, the contract will not be enforced against her.

> **Capacity**: The requirement that a party to a contract have the mental ability to understand the nature and consequences of a contractual relationship.

II. The Statute of Frauds

The statute of frauds was originally developed in England in the 1600s. The purpose of the statute was to prevent fraud by requiring certain types of contracts to be in writing before they could be enforceable through the court system. Examples of contracts that fall under the jurisdiction of the Statute of Frauds include:

- Wills
- Contracts to answer for the debt of another

---

4. *Rose v. Vulcan Materials Co.*, 282 N.C. 643, 194 S.E.2d 521 (1973).

- Contracts in anticipation of marriage (pre-nuptial/ante-nuptial agreements)
- Contracts for the sale of land
- Contracts that cannot be performed within one year of the date of their creation
- Contracts for the sale of goods exceeding $500 in value
- Contracts for the sale of securities (stocks, bonds)

Although many of these classifications are interesting, we will limit our discussion to the Statute of Frauds as it applies to real estate transactions.

North Carolina Statute of Frauds is embodied in General Statute § 22-2. This statute requires that any contract that conveys an interest in real estate must be in writing in order to be enforced. See Figure 8-2 for the complete text of the statute.

Figure 8-2. § 22-2. Contract for Sale of Land; Leases

All contracts to sell or convey any lands, tenements or hereditaments, or any interest in or concerning them, and all leases and contracts for leasing land for the purpose of digging for gold or other minerals, or for mining generally, of whatever duration; and all other leases and contracts for leasing lands exceeding in duration three years from the making thereof, shall be void unless said contract, or some memorandum or note thereof, be put in writing and signed by the party to be charged therewith, or by some other person by him thereto lawfully authorized.

This statute applies not only to contracts for sale of real property, but also to any transaction involving mineral rights or options to purchase land. Under this statute, contracts that transfer interest in real estate must be in writing, as well as any modification of these contracts.

III. Formation Issues in Contract Law

Courts are constantly called upon to interpret the language used and intention of the parties to a contract. This interpretation involves a review of the basic formational issues involved in creating the contract in the first place. In certain situations, the contract may be rescinded or voided when there is a legitimate claim of mistake, fraud or undue influence in the creation of the contract. Unless these situations are present, the contract as negotiated will continue in existence.

A. Mistake

Under North Carolina contract law, "mistake" has a very particular meaning. A mistake is a misunderstanding shared by both sides to the contract. If only one party is operating under an incorrect version of the facts, this does not qualify as a contractual mistake. When both parties are under a mistaken impression about a material element of the contract, courts may intercede and rescind the contract.[5] You'll find an example of the law of mistake in this chapter's "Relevant Case."

---

5. *Lancaster v. Lancaster*, 138 N.C. App. 459, 530 S.E.2d 82 (2000).

B. Interpreting Contract Language

In situations where the contract has plain and unambiguous language, the courts must interpret the contract as it is set out. However, plain and unambiguous contracts are usually not litigated. Instead, it is the ambiguous and confusing contracts that often challenge North Carolina judges.[6]

C. Fraud and Misrepresentation

If a party can show that a contract was obtained under fraudulent circumstances, the court is authorized to rescind or void that contract. However, in order to prove fraud, a party must show that the other party deliberately made a false statement about a material fact. A material fact, in this context, refers to any of the important terms of the contract, such as price, terms, or parties.[7]

1. Two Types of Fraud Involved in Contracts

Fraud can be classified in two different ways. First, there is fraud in the execution of contract and then fraud in the inducement.

a. Fraud in the Execution of a Contract

Fraud in the execution of the contract refers to a factual misrepresentation in creating the contractual obligation between the parties. Examples of fraud in the execution of a contract would be misrepresentations or outright forgeries in the actual contract.

b. Fraud in the Inducement

Fraud in the inducement of the contract refers to a factual misrepresentation that induces or encourages a party to enter into a contract under an impression of the facts that is not true.

2. The Effect of Fraud on a Contract

When a party proves fraud, the court is authorized to rescind the contract and place the parties back into their original positions. The defrauded party may also be entitled to damages.

3. Statements That Are Not Fraudulent

In most situations, only statements that relate to direct misrepresentations of material facts are considered to be fraudulent. Other statements, such as opinions and "puffing," are not considered to be misrepresentations.

---

6. *State ex rel. Utilities Com'n v. Thrifty Call, Inc.*, 571 S.E.2d 622 (N.C. Ct. App. 2002).
7. *Massey v. Duke University*, 130 N.C. App. 461, 503 S.E.2d 155 (1998).

a. Opinions

When a party offers an opinion, it is usually not considered to be a material misrepresentation of the facts. After all, most people assume that an opinion is based more on feelings than on facts.

b. Sales Statements or "Puffing"

Puffing refers to the type of statements commonly associated with salespersons. Such statements, such as "this is the finest house you'll ever see" or "This is the finest quality workmanship," are considered to be typical sales statements and not be taken literally.

D. Duress, Coercion and Undue Influence

Duress, coercion and undue influence all refer to overcoming a party's will and forcing her to engage in a contract that she ordinarily would never have agreed to. It is one of the basic principles of contract law that persons cannot have contracts forced upon them. A person must enter into a contract voluntarily. The principle of mutual assent requires that parties act voluntarily and when force, threats or coercion are used free will is destroyed.

1. Duress

Duress is the threat or the actual application of physical force to make a person enter into a contract. An example of duress is threatening someone with violence unless he signs a contract.

2. Coercion

Coercion is the application of psychological pressure on a party to force him to enter into a contract. Examples of coercion include blackmail or other psychological threats. When coercion is proved, the court is authorized to rescind or void the contract.

3. Undue Influence

Undue influence is the use of a position of trust or family relationship to overcome a person's objections to enter into a contract. Undue influence can arise when a person's caretaker uses psychological manipulation to overcome a party's will and bind her in a contract

E. Unfair and Deceptive Trade Practices

In addition to concerns about duress or coercion, North Carolina's Unfair and Deceptive Trade practice laws must also be considered. By its own terms, NCGS § 75-1.1 applies to "all business activities," including landlord-tenant relationships. Under this statute, a person who has been the victim of unfair trade practices may sue to rescind the contract.

Figure 8-3. § 75-1.1. Methods of Competition, Acts and Practices Regulated; Legislative Policy

(a) Unfair methods of competition in or affecting commerce, and unfair or deceptive acts or practices in or affecting commerce, are declared unlawful.

(b) For purposes of this section, "commerce" includes all business activities, however denominated, but does not include professional services rendered by a member of a learned profession.

IV. Types of Contracts

Contracts can be classified in a wide variety of ways. Two broad categories of contracts include unilateral contracts and bilateral contracts.

A. Unilateral and Bilateral Contracts

A unilateral contract is one in which a person makes a promise in exchange for an action. The most common example of a unilateral contract is a reward poster. In a unilateral contract, a person is exchanging action for a promise. Unilateral contracts are not common in real estate transactions. On the other hand, bilateral contracts are very common and are the usual means to transfer interest in real estate.

> **Unilateral Contract:** A contract where the parties exchange an action for a promise.

1. Bilateral Contracts

Bilateral contracts are the most common type of contract. In a bilateral contract, both parties make reciprocal promises to one another. In a typical real estate transaction, the seller is promising to deliver possession and title to the real estate in exchange for money. The buyer is promising to produce money on a specific day in exchange for possession and title to the real estate. This is a bilateral contract, or an exchange of promises.

> **Bilateral Contract:** A contract in which the parties exchange promises.

Classifying the type of contract created by a valid offer and acceptance is important when it comes to enforcing the contract or assessing damages for breach. Unilateral and bilateral contracts are enforced in different ways. We will discuss contract damages later in this chapter.

V. Real Estate Contracts

There are a wide variety of real estate contracts. These contracts range from brokerage agreements, listing agreements, and options to purchase, as well as offers to purchase real estate. We will examine the specific features in each of these types of contracts in the following sections.

A. Listing Agreement

A listing agreement is the contract between a real estate broker and the seller. In the listing agreement, the seller agrees to pay the real estate broker a commission when the broker produces a buyer who is ready, willing and able to meet the purchase price. The contract is referred to as a "listing contract" because it sets the stage for the manner in which the property will be advertised by the real estate agency. The listing refers not only to how the property will be advertised for sale, but also how the commission will ultimately be shared. There are three general types of listings:

- Open listing
- Exclusive listing
- Multiple listing

1. Open Listing

An open listing allows the property to be sold through any broker. The owner may even secure a buyer and avoid paying the commission. The seller would be obligated to pay a commission to any broker who produces a buyer capable of purchasing the property. If the seller locates a buyer, he or she is not liable to pay a commission. Open listings are not very common.

2. Exclusive Listing

Under an exclusive listing agreement, the seller employs only one individual who has legal authority to close the sale. No other broker will obtain a commission by producing a buyer other than the one with whom the seller has a contract.

3. Multiple Listing

Multiple listings are the most common type of real estate listing because they offer several advantages over open listings and exclusive listings. Under a multiple listing, the listing agent shares a commission with any broker who produces a buyer. This gives all brokers in the area a vested interest in working to sell any property listed in the Multiple Listing Service. The various brokers will share the commission between them. Under a multiple listing, a seller theoretically has every broker in the area working for him.

B. Offer of Purchase and Contract

An offer of purchase and contract is a written document that presents the details of the buyer's offer to the seller to purchase real estate. This contract reflects the negotiations between the buyer and seller and the final terms of their agreement. Among the specifics set out in an offer of purchase and contract are:

- A description of the real estate involved
- A provision for the purchase of any personal property located on the premises
- Purchase price details, including earnest money deposit.

- Conditions, including the buyer's financing condition and loan commitment letter
- Evidence of title
- Property disclosures
- Risk of loss provisions
- Signature provisions

1. Property Description

The property in question should be adequately described. An adequate description must be something beyond the simple mailing address. Standard Form Two, approved by both the North Carolina Bar Association and the North Carolina Association of Realtors, provides blanks not only for street address of the property, but also for city and town location, as well as legal description.

2. Purchase of Personal Property

The buyer and seller may, in addition to purchasing real property, also negotiate the purchase of certain items of personal property located on the premises. Because personal property is a separate and distinct class from real property, any personal property items that are purchased along with the real estate must be listed separately.

3. Purchase Price Details

The offer of purchase and contract will set out not only the purchase price but will also make provisions for earnest money deposit. Earnest money is the money put down by the buyer early on in the negotiation process as proof of good faith to the contract. This money must be accounted for later on in the sale process.

4. Conditions

The buyer will usually make his or her offer contingent upon certain events, particularly financing. The buyer's offer usually contains a condition revoking the offer in the event that the buyer is unable to obtain suitable financing. Other conditions may include the buyer's express condition of sale of his current home prior to concluding the purchase of the new home.

5. Evidence of Title

The evidence of title provision in the offer to purchase and contract is the seller's promise to use his or her best efforts, including hiring attorneys and conducting title searches on the property, to ensure that the buyer receives marketable title to the property in question.

6. Property Disclosures

North Carolina law requires that the buyer receive a copy of the North Carolina Residential Property Disclosures prior to the signing of the offer to purchase and contract. This provision also allows the buyer to conduct a property inspection within a specific time period after the signing of the contract.

7. Risk of Loss Provisions

The offer of purchase and contract provides that the risk of loss, specifically whose insurance company will pay for any damages to the property, rests squarely on the seller prior to closing. After the closing, however, risk of loss shifts to the new owner and his insurance company.

8. Closing Provisions

The offer of purchase and contract will also contain provisions concerning the actual closing. In some cases, the buyers may elect to include a "time is of the essence" contract clause provision. This is a clause that requires the closing to occur at a specific date, otherwise the contract will be considered null and void.

9. Signature Provisions

In Chapter 6, we saw that for a deed to be legally effective, the only signature required was that of the grantor. That is not the case in offers to purchase and contract of sale. This contract has signature provisions for all parties concerned and must be signed. Without the signatures, the contract is legally insufficient and cannot be enforced.

10. Particular Clauses: Time Is of the Essence

When a contract contains a "time is of the essence" clause, it means that the closing must occur on the day specified in the contract. If it does not, the contract is considered null and void and cannot be enforced. For an example of the wording used to create such a clause see paragraph number 12 in Figure 8-4.

C. Options

An option is a contract between a seller and a prospective buyer, where the seller agrees that he will not sell the property to some other person, but only for a stated period of time. A prospective buyer might seek an option on property instead of simply buying the property when he is attempting to negotiate contracts with other vendors and is not sure about the ultimate prospects of success. Negotiating an option with a potential seller involves only a tiny fraction of the money that it would take to actually purchase the property. In this case, the terms of the contract are simply that the seller will not sell or will hold the buyer's offer for a specific period of time. If the buyer does not close the transaction within the prescribed period, or the time expires, the contract is canceled and the seller is free to sell the property to anyone else he chooses.

VI. Breach of Contract

When one party refuses to live up to his obligations under the contract, the other party is relieved of any further obligation in the contract and may sue for breach of contract.

Figure 8-4. Offer of Purchase and Contract of Sale

THIS OFFER OF PURCHASE AND CONTRACT OF SALE, dated the _____ day of _____, 19__, between _____ and _____ (collectively referred to herein as the "Seller") whose address is _____ and _____ and _____ (collectively referred to herein as the "Buyer") whose address is _____.

1. The Property. The Seller agrees to sell to the Buyer, and the Buyer agrees to purchase from the Seller the fee simple real property located in _____, North Carolina, who legal description is as follows:

Included in the property hereby sold are all permanently attached fixtures, and the following items, if any, now on the property: kitchen stove and oven, refrigerator, alarm systems, water filters, carpet, fire place screens, draperies, shades, screens, storm doors and windows, venetian blinds, curtain rods, awnings, shrubbery, light fixtures, television aerial, dishwasher, garbage disposal, clothes washer, clothes dryer, window air conditioning units and _____ _____

2. Purchase Price. The purchase price for the property is _____ Dollars ($), of which the Buyer has paid _____ Dollars ($) as Earnest Money, The balance of the purchase price shall be paid by the Buyer to the Seller in cash at settlement.

3. Time and Place of Settlement. Unless the parties agree otherwise, settlement shall take place at _____ a.m./p.m., at _____

4. Financing Contingency. The Buyer's obligation to purchase the property is contingent upon the Buyer obtaining, from a lending institution, a commitment for a mortgage loan, secured by the property, in the principal amount of not less than _____ Dollars ($), at an interest rate not to exceed _____ percent (__%) per annum, repayable in equal monthly installments of principal and interest over a period of not less than thirty (30) years, and requiring the payment of _____ of points/fees of not more than _____ (__%) percent of the total loan amount. The Buyer shall apply for and receive a commitment of financing from a suitable lending institution within 10 days of the date of this contract.

5. Termite Infestation or Damage.

(a) The Buyer shall have the right to have the dwelling on the property inspected by a licensed pest control operator within ten (10) days of the date of this Contract. The fees for this inspection will be borne exclusively by the Buyer. If the inspecting company should report an infestation by termites or other wood boring insects, the Buyer shall notify the Seller of this fact, in writing, including a written report prepared by the inspecting company. Seller shall have _____ days to correct, repair or take other suitable action to repair the damage and shall certify this action to the Buyer, in writing.

6. Home Inspection. The Buyer shall have the right at Buyer's expense to have the dwelling on the property inspected by a home inspection service or engineer within ten (10) business days of the date of this contract. This inspection will involve a visual inspection of the mechanical, electrical, plumbing and structure elements of the premises. Neither Buyer, nor inspector shall damage the property during the inspection process. The Buyer shall provide the Seller with a copy of the inspector's written report, within a reasonable period of time after the inspection. The failure of the seller to provide the buyer or the buyer's inspector access to said premises will be deemed a violation of this contract and in that event, seller shall return the buyer's earnest money deposit.

7. Evidence of title. At the closing or settlement of this contract, upon the buyer's complete payment of all outstanding purchase monies, seller shall provide the buyer evidence of title through a general warranty deed, in fee simple absolute, detailing the seller's title to the property, free and clear from any encumbrances. Seller will convey title to the buyer at the closing. The seller is responsible for paying any transfer taxes, conveyance fees or other sales taxes based on this transaction.

8. Risk of Loss. The property shall be held at the risk of the Seller until the settlement occurs. Upon receipt of all closing documents, risk of loss shall vest in the buyer.

9. Default by the buyer. In the event of the buyer's default under this contract, the seller shall have the right to retain all deposits and earnest money paid by the buyer as liquidated damages under this contract. Seller reserves the right to seek additional damages and equitable remedies against the buyer for a willful breach of this contract.

10. Real Estate Commission. The seller agrees, that at the time and place of closing, he will pay a commission on 6% to the real estate brokers who have produced a buyer who is ready willing and able to conclude the transaction.

11. Entire agreement. This contract contains the entire agreement of the parties. This contract will not be modified by any parole evidence or other communications not contained herein.

12. Contract addendum. Time is of the essence in this contract. The closing date for this transaction is set for the 15th day of May, 2005.

   This contract shall be governed by the laws of the State of North Carolina.

WITNESS the hands and seals of the parties.

Seller	Buyer
Date	Date

Contract law provides several different remedies and damages for the non-breaching party. The remedy sought often depends on the identity of the party seeking the damages. Sellers might well seek a different remedy for a breach than the buyers would.

A. Remedies for Breach

Breach of contract gives the non-breaching party the right to sue for damages or equitable relief. A court can exercise its equity power to order an injunction, specific performance or other action that is separate and distinct from the court's power to award monetary damages.

1. Remedies for the Seller

When the buyer breaches the contract, the seller might well retain the Earnest Money Deposit, which was originally offered as the buyer's good faith and is made on condition that it will be forfeited on the buyer's failure to conclude the contract. However, the seller might well seek other remedies. For instance, the seller might decide to sue for monetary damages. Suppose that the seller sold the house to another buyer later on, but at a lower price. The seller would be authorized to sue the breaching buyer for the difference in the original contract price and the reduced price he later obtained.

2. Remedies for the Buyer

Although a buyer might also be authorized to sue for monetary damages from a breaching seller, the buyer's main concern is probably concluding the contract. In this situation, the buyer might sue under the equitable remedy of specific performance. Under this doctrine, a court would be authorized to force the seller to comply with the terms of the original contract and sell the house to the buyer.

3. Remedies for the Broker

When a seller refuses to go through with a sale and the broker has completed all of his or her contractual duties, the broker has a cause of action against the seller for the real estate commission. This commission becomes due when the broker produces a buyer who is ready, willing and able to conclude the transaction and the sale fails to occur because of the seller's actions. In this situation, the broker would be entitled to the commission even though the sale did not occur.

Relevant Case

Taylor v. Gore, 161 N.C.App. 300, 588 S.E.2d 51 (N.C.App.2003)

CALABRIA, Judge.

Robert Taylor and Serina A. Taylor ("plaintiffs") appeal the 16 and 17 September 2002 orders granting summary judgment for defendants Bay Circle Realty, Wilma Murphy ("Murphy") and L.R. Gore ("Gore") (collectively "defendants"). Plaintiffs assert defendants failed to show there is no genuine issue of material fact, and therefore the trial court erred in granting their motions for summary judgment. We affirm the summary judgment for defendants Bay Circle Realty and Murphy, and reverse as to defendant Gore.

In April 1999, plaintiffs purchased a 15.26 acre plot of land from Gore. Murphy, on behalf of Bay Circle Realty, served as Gore's real estate agent. Prior to the sale, Murphy gave plaintiffs a survey of the property that stated "SUBJECT PROPERTY IS NOT IN A FEDERAL (HUD) DESIGNATED FLOOD HAZARD AREA." In July 2001, plaintiffs sought to develop the land and discovered it was not suitable because a portion of the property was, in fact, located in a flood zone.

In February 2002, plaintiffs filed suit against defendants. Plaintiffs alleged the contract was based on a mistake of fact that the property was not located in a flood zone, and since this mistake is substantial and affects the essence of the contract, the contract should be rescinded. Plaintiffs further alleged defendants Murphy and Bay Circle Realty breached their duty to communicate truthful information by providing plaintiffs with an incorrect survey indicating the property was not in a flood zone, and by failing to advise plaintiffs to acquire their own survey because of the hazards of relying on any survey supplied by a seller. Finally, plaintiffs alleged defendants failed to disclose that the property was in a flood zone and misrepresented that it was not in a flood zone.

I. Misrepresentation Claims

First, we note that Gore, as Murphy's principal, is liable for Murphy's actions. MacKay v. McIntosh, 270 N.C. 69, 72–73, 153 S.E.2d 800, 803 (1967) ("'[a principal] is bound by the agent's material representations of fact to the same extent as if he had made them himself.'"). Accordingly, although the claims stem from Murphy's delivery of the survey to plaintiffs, Gore is liable for Murphy's actions and representations. Therefore, we address these defendants jointly.

To prove a claim of fraudulent misrepresentation, "the party asserting it must show (i) false representation or concealment of a material fact, (ii) reasonably calculated to deceive, (iii) made with intent to deceive, (iv) which does in fact deceive, (v) resulting in damage to the injured party." Deans v. Layton, 89 N.C.App. 358, 366–67, 366 S.E.2d 560,

565–66 (1988). "A defendant cannot 'be liable for concealing [or falsely representing] a fact of which it was unaware.'" Forbes v. Par Ten Group, Inc., 99 N.C.App. 587, 594, 394 S.E.2d 643, 647 (1990) (quoting Ramsey v. Keever's Used Cars, 92 N.C.App. 187, 190, 374 S.E.2d 135, 137 (1988)). "If a defendant presents evidence that it did not know of the fact in issue, 'the burden shifts to plaintiff to prove that defendant knew or had reason to know' the fact." Id., (quoting Ramsey, 92 N.C.App. at 191, 374 S.E.2d at 137). Plaintiffs' claim fails because defendants' affidavits negate the element of "intent to deceive" by providing "[i]f part of the property is in a special flood zone, this information was not known to me nor was the possibility that any part of the property was located in a special flood zone even suggested to me...." Plaintiffs did not produce conflicting evidence and failed to meet their burden of showing defendants "knew or had reason to know" the survey was incorrect.

To prove a claim of negligent misrepresentation, plaintiffs must show: (1) "'in the course of a business or other transaction in which an individual has a pecuniary interest,'" (2) defendants "'supplie[d] false information for the guidance of others[,]'" (3) "'without exercising reasonable care in obtaining or communicating the information.'" Everts v. Parkinson, 147 N.C.App. 315, 328, 555 S.E.2d 667, 676 (2001) (quoting Fulton v. Vickery, 73 N.C.App. 382, 388, 326 S.E.2d 354, 358 (1985)). Defendants' affidavits demonstrate they relied on the validity of the survey, believing it accurately stated the property was not in a flood zone. Plaintiffs did not allege such reliance was unreasonable. Moreover, we have previously held a seller's agent not liable because she had "no reason to question [the surveyor's] affirmative representation and make her own independent investigation when [the surveyor's] expertise was specifically in the area of conducting surveys and when he was paid to specifically conduct such survey." Clouse v. Gordon, 115 N.C.App. 500, 509, 445 S.E.2d 428, 433 (1994). We apply this same rule to the seller. Accordingly, we hold the trial court properly granted defendants' motion for summary judgment on the basis of misrepresentation.

II. Mistake Claim

Plaintiffs also assert the trial court erred in granting defendant Gore's motion for summary judgment of plaintiffs' claim that the contract was based on a substantial mistake of fact affecting the essence of the contract. We agree.

"'[I]t is well established that the existence of a mutual mistake as to a material fact comprising the essence of the agreement will provide grounds to rescind a contract.'" Monroe Constr. Co. v. State, 155 N.C.App. 320, 330, 574 S.E.2d 482, 489 (2002), disc. rev. denied, 357 N.C. 165, 580 S.E.2d 370 (2003) (quoting Lancaster v. Lancaster, 138 N.C.App. 459, 465, 530 S.E.2d 82, 86 (2000)). It is also established that "'[t]he mistake of one party is sufficient to avoid a contract when the other party had reason to know of the mistake or caused the mistake.'" Creech v. Melnik, 347 N.C. 520, 528, 495 S.E.2d 907, 912 (1998) (quoting Howell v. Waters, 82 N.C.App. 481, 487–88, 347 S.E.2d 65, 69 (1986)). Accordingly, despite defendant Gore's assertion to the contrary, plaintiffs may assert a claim of mutual mistake as well as a claim of unilateral mistake because Gore supplied the flawed survey.

We note there are genuine issues of material fact regarding the claim of mistake, including, inter alia, whether the mistake was mutual or unilateral and whether the mistake affected the essence of the contract. Despite these issues, we consider that "[North Carolina] Supreme Court decisions have raised questions regarding application of the doctrine of mutual mistake to executed real estate contracts." Howell, 82 N.C.App. at 489, 347 S.E.2d at 70 (citing Hinson v. Jefferson, 287 N.C. 422, 215 S.E.2d 102 (1975); Financial Services v. Capitol Funds, 288 N.C. 122, 217 S.E.2d 551 (1975)). However, the Supreme

Court recognized "certain mistakes will justify the rescission of an executed real estate contract; [and, this Court reasoned,] a mistake induced by a misrepresentation is as persuasive a case for rescission as any." Id., 82 N.C.App. at 491, 347 S.E.2d at 71. Accordingly, this Court held "dispositive" the distinction that the mistake in Hinson and Financial Services was premised upon mistaken assumptions of the parties, and the mistake in Howell was based upon misrepresentation by the seller. Id. Therefore, although some uncertainty exists regarding the applicability of mistake to real estate contracts because "we jealously guard the stability of real estate transactions," precedent permits plaintiffs' claim against defendant Gore because it is based upon a mistake caused by a misrepresentation and not a mutual mistaken assumption. Financial Services, 288 N.C. at 139, 217 S.E.2d at 562.

Defendant Gore asserts he is entitled to summary judgment on the claim of mutual mistake because "[n]owhere in their pleadings have they alleged that there was a mutual mistake." However, "[t]he most fundamental tenet of modern pleading rules is that the pleadings should give 'sufficient notice of the claim asserted "to enable the adverse party to answer and prepare for trial ... and to show the type of case brought.'"" Holloway v. Wachovia Bank & Trust Co., 339 N.C. 338, 347, 452 S.E.2d 233, 238 (1994) (quoting Sutton v. Duke, 277 N.C. 94, 102, 176 S.E.2d 161, 165 (1970) (citation omitted)). We find plaintiffs' allegation that the contract "was based on a mistake of fact ... based on the representations of L.R. Gore and his agents, the land was not in a flood zone" is sufficient to state a claim for mistake. We find no merit in defendant Gore's argument. Accordingly, Gore failed to establish a lack of a genuine issue of material fact, or that the claim was barred by precedent, or insufficient pleading, and therefore the trial court improperly granted Gore's motion for summary judgment. We reverse.

In sum, we affirm the order of the trial court granting summary judgment on the misrepresentation claims, but reverse the order of the trial court granting summary judgment for defendant Gore on the claim of mistake.

Affirmed in part, reversed in part.

Judges McGEE and HUNTER concur.

Chapter Summary

A contract is a legally binding agreement between two or more parties. A contract is a result of negotiations between these parties that consist of an offer, which is one party's stated intention to enter into a binding contract and the acceptance by the other party of all the terms stated in the offer. When an offer has been accepted, a contract is created. In addition to a valid offer and acceptance, there are some additional contract law requirements. For instance, both parties to the contract must have legal capacity. Legal capacity refers to a party's competence to know and understand the consequences of entering into a contractual obligation. Some parties lack capacity either because of mental or physical defects or because of other reasons, such as being under age. Consideration is another contractual element that requires a bargained-for exchange between the parties. This is a contract requirement that necessitates both parties surrendering something of value in exchange for something of value before an enforceable contract will be found under the law.

Contract law is of vital importance in real estate transactions because so many real estate conveyances involve contract principles. In this chapter, we have explored brokerage agreements, which are contracts between home sellers and the agent to represent them, as well as offers of purchase, which consist of the binding contract between the seller and buyer. We have also explored various contract clauses, including "Time is of the essence." This is a contract clause that requires that the closing must occur on a specific date, otherwise the contract will be null and void.

Review Questions

1. What are the elements of a legally enforceable offer?
2. How does North Carolina law define the "power of acceptance?"
3. What is consideration and why is it a necessary component for contract?
4. What is legal capacity to contract? Provide some examples of individuals who lack such capacity.
5. Explain how a contract may be unenforceable when it does not have a legal subject.
6. What is mutual assent?
7. What is an option?
8. Explain the significance of a "Time is of the essence" contract clause.
9. What are the basic elements of a brokerage agreement?
10. How is an offer to purchase and contract different from an option?
11. List and explain at least three important provisions of an offer to purchase and contract.
12. What is the Statute of Frauds and why is it important in real estate contracts?
13. What are some of the penalties that a seller can bring against the buyer for the buyer's wrongful refusal to perform under the offer to purchase and contract?
14. What are some of the buyer's remedies against a seller who wrongfully refuses to perform under a contract of sale?
15. How does North Carolina define contractual mistake?
16. Why does North Carolina require both the seller and the buyers to sign the offer to purchase and contract?
17. What are equitable remedies?
18. What types of damages is a buyer entitled to against a seller who refuses to abide by an Offer to Purchase and Contract?
19. Same question as #18: what remedies does a seller have against a buyer?
20. What is specific performance?

Assignment

Using the contract of sale form provided in this chapter, create a new contract of sale based on the following facts:

Information:

- ❏ Date of contract: January 11, 1998. Sal Seller and Bill Buyer. Sal's address is: 10 Sol St. Bill's address is 12 3rd Ave. The property address is 21 Robin Lane, Morgan, North Carolina.
- ❏ Included in the sale are some built-in tool storage cabinets in the basement.
- ❏ The purchase price is $121,000. Bill put down $1,000 earnest money. No additional money will be put down prior to closing. The closing is to take place on May 11, 1998, at 3 p.m. in the offices of Al Attorney, 100 Shyster Blvd., Morgan, NC.
- ❏ Bill's offer is based on being able to obtain financing at 9% or lower, in the amount of $115,000, for a 30 year loan. He doesn't want to pay more than 2 points.
- ❏ Sal wants Bill to apply for financing as soon as possible, at least within 10 days of the contract being signed. Bill wants a termite inspection within 10 days of signing the contract.
- ❏ If termites are found, Sal wants at least 30 days to fix whatever is wrong.
- ❏ Bill wants to inspect the home within 10 days of signing the contract.
- ❏ The Realtor's name is Ron Realtor.

Terms and Phrases

Offer

Acceptance

Mutual assent

Mistake

Consideration

Capacity

Legality of subject

Legal incapacity

Brokerage agreements

Offer of purchase

Contract for sale

Option

Equitable remedies

Specific performance

Liquidated damages

Chapter 9

Deeds of Trust, Mortgages and Financing Real Estate

Chapter Objectives

At the conclusion of this chapter, you should be able to:

- Explain the purpose of mortgages in financing the purchase of real estate
- Describe the function of the secondary mortgage market
- List and explain the major clauses of a deed of trust
- Explain foreclosure
- Describe the differences between mortgages and deeds of trust

I. Financing the Purchase of Real Estate

We have all heard it said that the biggest purchase a person may make in her life is the purchase of the family home. A house is always an enormous investment, not only in money but also in personal commitment. Because houses are so expensive, most people must finance the purchase of the home in order to buy it. The mechanism used to purchase a home is referred to as a **mortgage**. A mortgage is a financial arrangement between a borrower and the lender where the borrower conveys an interest to the lender that guarantees or pledges the real estate as collateral for the loan. Mortgage lending is a huge business in the United States, involving billions of dollars every year. In this chapter, we will examine not only the basic principles of mortgage lending, but also the legal requirements of mortgages and, more specifically, deeds of trust as financing instruments in North Carolina. We will begin our discussion with an exploration of various mortgage markets available to borrowers.

> **Mortgage:** the arrangement between a borrower and the lender where the borrower pledges real estate as collateral for the loan.

II. Mortgage Markets ✵

The "mortgage market" refers to the large body of banks, loan associations, insurance companies and other lenders who are in the business of lending money for the purchase of real property.

A. Primary Mortgage Market ✫

The primary mortgage market consists of banks and other lending institutions that are in the business of extending credit to purchase real property. These lending institutions acquire the money to loan from deposits made by their customers. In a typical example, Allied Bank takes in deposits from customers and pays them 4% interest on their accounts. Allied Bank then pools all of these deposits and loans that money to borrowers so that they may purchase residential real estate. The bank charges interest on the loan, which acts as profit to the bank. The bank takes part of this profit and repays the deposit accounts and uses the remainder to finance the rest of the bank's operations.

In this stripped-down example, Allied Bank would swiftly run out of money from deposit accounts to loan to borrowers. In fact, this was a common problem for banks prior to the Great Depression and the stock market crash in 1929. After that financial disaster, the United States government helped to create and improve a secondary mortgage market, primarily through U.S. government-run enterprises, such as Fannie-Mae.

B. Secondary Mortgage Market ✫

Most lenders who offer mortgages do not hold them for the length of the loan period. Instead, these loans are sold to lending institutions that comprise the secondary mortgage market. These are institutions that do not deal directly with borrowers. Instead, they are in the business of buying mortgages from local banks and lending institutions. When an organization, such as Fannie Mae, purchases mortgages from local banks, it receives the borrower's payments. The advantage to the local bank is that it gets a lump sum of money for a mortgage that will not mature for 30 years. The bank can use this lump sum to finance other mortgages and thus continue the cycle of lending money and selling mortgages to members of the secondary mortgage market.

Although many members of the secondary mortgage market, such as Fannie Mae, were originally governmental agencies, several of them have broken off to become private organizations primarily because they have been so financially successful. Buying mortgages from local banks and receiving payments for the borrowers can be very lucrative business. Essentially, it is a win-win situation. The secondary mortgage market provides funds to the primary mortgage market, which can then use those funds to provide mortgages for the purchase of local real estate. The secondary mortgage institution will receive the regular monthly payments on the original mortgages issued by the local bank. Many times, the borrower is not even aware that his payments are now being sent to a different financial institution.

The secondary mortgage market has had a huge impact on the primary mortgage market. When institutions, such as Ginnie Mae, buy mortgages, they insist on uniform practices, forms and policies to make it easier to assess the risk of the mortgages that they buy. The long-term impact of this uniformity is that almost all primary lending institutions have adopted governmental forms, and uniform practices, in order to ensure that their mortgages can be sold on the secondary mortgage market.

1. Federal Agencies in the Secondary Mortgage Market

With the passage of the National Housing Act in 1934, the United States Congress moved to create governmental agencies whose sole function was to improve the mortgage market in the United States by purchasing local mortgages and freeing up capital across the country. The first such governmental agency was the Federal National Mortgage Association, created in 1938. FNMA, commonly known as Fannie Mae, was a huge success and has spawned similar agencies, such as the Government National Mortgage Association, known as Ginnie Mae. Ginnie Mae is a government-owned corporation that operates under the jurisdiction of the Department of Housing and Urban Development (HUD). HUD plays a major role in real estate transactions, not only because of its role in the secondary mortgage market, but also for its impact on the entire real estate process. Through Ginnie Mae, HUD forms have become the most commonly used closing and settlement forms used to track the financial transactions involved in purchasing real estate.

III. Introduction to Mortgages

In its simplest form, a mortgage is a conveyance of a right from the buyer to the lender that serves as security for the loan. If the buyer should default, such as by failing to make regular, monthly payments on the loan, the lending institute has the right to foreclose on the property, seize it and auction it off for the balance of the borrowed amount. Although there is a natural tendency to compare the financing instruments in which personal property is pledged as collateral, such as in a car loan, and mortgage interest in real property, they are similar only in general terms. When a person finances the purchase of a car, the lender actually holds title. When the borrower makes the final payment on the loan, the lender transfers the title to the borrower. That is not the case with a mortgage or deed of trust. The buyer has title to the property, but conveys part of his property rights to the lender. That conveyed interest gives the lender certain rights, not the least of which is the power to foreclose on the property in the event of a loan default.

A. The Title Theory of Mortgages in North Carolina

Although in some states a mortgage or deed of trust is seen as a lien on the property that can mature into full-fledged rights, that is not the case in North Carolina. Here, the lending institute receives a title interest to the property. While the buyer possesses many of the rights normally seen in fee simple absolute title, the lender also holds a portion of those interests. North Carolina is in a minority of states that follow the title theory of mortgages. In North Carolina the most common type of financing instrument is the Deed of Trust. Under a deed of trust, the borrower conveys legal title to a third party, called a trustee, who holds that title for the benefit of the lender. When the loan is repaid, the trustee cancels the deed of trust and full title vests back to the borrower. On the other hand, if the borrower defaults on the loan payments, it is the trustee who initiates the foreclosure action.

B. Mortgages versus Deed of Trust

In most situations there is no practical difference between a mortgage and a deed of trust. Both of these terms refer to a financing instrument that pledges the property as security for the loan. Mortgages usually only have two parties, the lender and the borrower.

Deeds of trust have three parties, the lender, the borrower and the trustee. Other than these technical differences, a layperson would see very few differences between a mortgage and deed of trust and most borrowers are unaware that there is any difference.

IV. The Basic Components of a Mortgage or Deed of Trust

In this initial discussion, we will not make any distinction between mortgages and Deeds of Trust. Instead, we will discuss them as though they are interchangeable terms. Later, when we get into the specifics of the creation of a deed of trust, we will begin to draw sharp distinctions between the two forms of financing.

Regardless of whether a financing instrument is termed a mortgage or deed of trust, there are some basic components that they both share. The most basic of these provisions is the requirement that the mortgage be in writing. Just as we saw in the last chapter, the Statute of Frauds also governs mortgages. Because a mortgage in North Carolina is a conveyance of a title interest, it must be in writing under North Carolina General Statute § 22-2. Other requirements include the fact that a mortgage must also pledge the real estate as security for the loan. Closely related to this provision is a clause that allows the lender to begin foreclosure actions if the borrower fails to make payments on the loan or defaults in some other way.

A. Mortgages and Deeds of Trusts Are Recorded Like Deeds

Mortgages and deeds of trust resemble deeds. In fact, it is common to find a deed of trust filed contemporaneously with a general warranty deed when reviewing the chain of title. Because these instruments are filed in the Deed Office, they must meet all the same requirements as any other deed. Specifically, the parties must be named. Their signatures must appear on the mortgage. The property must be described with a legal description, such as a metes and bounds description or a plat reference. In addition to these requirements, which closely resemble the requirements of a general warranty deed, a mortgage or deed of trust must also set out the terms of the loan. Like a general warranty deed, a deed of trust must also contain a granting clause that conveys a title interest from the borrower to the trustee. Finally, mortgages also contain covenants, conditions and warranties similar to ones found in other types of deeds.

B. Priority of Mortgages

These days, it is quite common for the borrower to have more than one mortgage on a single piece of property. In such a situation, there is often an issue of priority. Priority refers to the order in which lenders are paid from the proceeds of a foreclosure action. Suppose that the proceeds of the auction are not sufficient to pay off both mortgages? In that event, the lender who has priority would receive the total amount owed it, and the second lender, the one with lower priority, would receive nothing. Obviously, the rules of priority are extremely important to lenders.

North Carolina recognizes the rule of instantaneous seizin, meaning that a purchase money mortgage has immediate priority over any other mortgage or encumbrance. Purchase money mortgages are commonly seen in "owner financing."

When a seller advertises his house for sale and includes a provision for "owner financing," it means that the owner is offering to finance part of the sale himself. Owners typically offer some percentage of the total sale price under owner financing terms, meaning that the buyer would make a payment for part of the mortgage to the seller and also make a mortgage payment to a bank. Here is a typical example:

Jill offers her home for sale for $100,000, $20,000 "owner financed." This means that Jill will take a 'credit' from the buyer for the amount of $20,000. The buyer must still come up with $80,000 from some other source.

In this scenario, Jill's purchase money mortgage immediately vests title interest in Jill, thus giving her priority over any other mortgage, because, by its very nature, the purchase money mortgage immediately follows on the heels of the transfer of title interest from the previous seller to the new buyer. However, the rule of priority can be altered by a subordination agreement.

1. Subordination Agreement

Under a subordination agreement, a lender who has priority over another lender agrees to subordinate its claim to that of the second lender. Consider this next scenario.

Scenario #1.

Melissa is advertising her house for sale for $50,000. Part of her ad includes the provision "owner financing possible." Barbara sees the ad and contacts Melissa. Here are Melissa's terms: she will "take back" $10,000 on owner-finance mortgage if Barbara can secure the balance of the purchase price from a lender. The advantage of this arrangement is that when Barbara approaches a local bank to seek a mortgage, she will only be requesting to borrow $40,000 on a $50,000 house. This should help Barbara qualify for a mortgage more easily. However, the bank has some concerns, specifically priority of the mortgages. Because Melissa is providing a purchase money mortgage in the amount of $10,000, her mortgage will take priority over the bank's loan, even though the bank is loaning the lion's share of the purchase price. Before the bank will issue a mortgage to Barbara, it insists on a subordination agreement from Melissa placing her mortgage second in priority to the banks. Melissa agrees and the sale goes through.

V. Deeds of Trust

Unlike mortgages, which usually only have two parties, the lender and the borrower, a deed of trust has three parties: the lender, the borrower and the trustee. In this arrangement, the trustee acts as a representative of both the lender and the borrower. The borrower transfers title to the trustee who holds it for the lender and the trustee is also the person responsible for initiating a foreclosure action in the event that the lender reports that the borrower has defaulted on the loan. Although this arrangement is followed in a minority of states, it has several distinct advantages over mortgages. For instance, in order to bring a foreclosure action on a mortgage, the lender is normally required to file a civil action and seek judicial declaration that allows the foreclosure sale to occur. This can delay a foreclosure action for several months. On the other hand, in a deed of trust arrangement, there is no necessity of a civil action. Instead, the trustee may initiate a foreclosure on the basis of the borrower's default and apply the power of sale provision found in the deed of trust. The only requirement is a notice of sale and a brief hearing before the local Clerk of Court.

A. Typical Deed of Trust Clauses

In the next few sections, we will explore the typical clauses found in deeds of trust that not only establish the borrower's obligations to pay, but also when the borrower is in default and the lender's power to foreclose on the property.

1. Acceleration Clause

The acceleration clause is a provision in a mortgage that allows the lender to request payment in full of the entire balance of the loan in the event of the borrower's default. Often, this demand is a prelude to foreclosure. North Carolina appellate courts have specifically approved the use of acceleration clauses in deeds of trust.[1]

2. Due on Sale Clause

The due on sale provision is a clause found in most mortgages that requires payment in full of the loan balance before title to the property changes hands. Without such a provision, borrowers might be tempted to transfer title to the property as a way of avoiding their responsibilities under the deed of trust. The due on sale provision prohibits this transfer unless the borrower pays the loan balance in full or seeks the lender's permission to transfer title.

3. Default Provisions

In addition to making regular monthly payments on the mortgage, the borrower also has other obligations imposed by the mortgage or deed of trust. These duties include the obligation to pay taxes on the property and to insure the property. The obligation to pay taxes arises directly out of the government's power to seize the property for back taxes and auction it off. Because this would have a severe impact on the lender's rights to property, most lenders insist on payment of taxes as one of the obligations under the deed of trust. If the borrower fails to pay taxes, this would technically be a breach of the terms and would allow the lender to foreclose. Another obligation imposed on the borrower is to obtain insurance on the property. Insurance obviously not only protects the borrower's interest in the property, but also the lender's. Because each has an insurable interest in the property, if the borrower fails to obtain adequate insurance, or his insurance policy lapses, the lender is authorized to seek insurance on its own and then bill the borrower for the premium it must pay to protect its own interest.

---

1. *Shaw v. Lanotte, Inc.* 92 N.C.App. 198, 373 S.E.2d 882 (1988).

Figure 9-1. Three Common Causes for a Deed of Trust Default

- Failure to pay on the loan
- Failure to pay taxes
- Failure to obtain Insurance

---

4. The Promissory Note Clause

The promissory note provision found in a deed of trust is similar to any other type of promissory note. This is where the borrower pledges to repay the loan. Promissory note clauses generally have three elements:

- The borrower's promise to pay a specific sum
- The terms of the indebtedness
- The borrower's signature

The deed of trust will contain a borrower's promise to repay the specific amount borrowed to finance the purchase of the real estate. This clause will also contain the terms that have been negotiated between the borrower and the lender, including the interest rate, the total sum borrowed and the length of time that the mortgage will run, typically 30 years.

5. Power of Sale Clause

The power of sale clause specifically authorizes the lender to institute foreclosure action and to auction off the property for the total debt owed by the borrower. Without this provision, a lender would be unable to institute foreclosure proceedings.

VI. Foreclosure

There are two types of foreclosures available in North Carolina, foreclosure by action and foreclosure under power of sale. Foreclosure by action is relatively rare and consists of a civil action brought by the lender to foreclose the property. Foreclosure under power of sale is the more common proceeding and is authorized by the terms of the deed of trust itself.

> Sidebar: Foreclosure is a special proceeding and will not be found under the general Index to Judgments, Liens and Lis Pendens. Instead, foreclosures will be found in the special proceedings index.

A. Foreclosure under Power of Sale ⚹

Most modern deeds of trust contain a "power of sale" clause that authorizes the lender to auction off the real property if the borrower defaults on the loan. The reason why foreclosure under power of sale is the most common type of foreclosure is that it does not require a judicial proceeding. In order to conduct a foreclosure under power of sale, the deed of trust must specifically authorize the process. This language is normally found in a power of sale clause contained in the recorded deed of trust.

1. Procedure to Institute a Foreclosure under Power of Sale

Foreclosure under power of sale is regulated under North Carolina General Statutes §45-21. The statutes require specific steps that must be complied with before a foreclosure auction is authorized.

B. The Right to Foreclose

Although we discussed foreclosure in Chapter 5, we will address the topic in much greater detail here. Foreclosure is a right granted by the mortgage or the deed of trust. Foreclosure is the penalty that a lender can impose on a borrower who fails to make payments on the debt. Although we referred to foreclosure of mortgages and deeds of trust as though they follow the same procedures, this is one of the areas where there is a stark contrast between the two different financing instruments. Because North Carolina is a deed of trust state, we will outline the foreclosure process from that viewpoint.

1. The First Step in a Foreclosure: The Borrower's Default

The lender's right to foreclose only arises after the borrower has defaulted on one of the conditions in the deed of trust. The most common reason for a default is the borrower's failure to pay the monthly mortgage payments, although a lender is authorized to foreclose on the borrower's failure to insure the property or to pay real estate taxes.

2. The Second Step in a Foreclosure: The Acceleration Clause

In the event of a borrower's default on a deed of trust, the lender is authorized to accelerate the terms of the loan. Specifically, the lender can request payment of the entire balance on the loan within a specified period of time, such as 30 days. When the borrower fails to meet that condition, the foreclosure process begins.

3. Notice of Hearing

The next step in a foreclosure action is to file notice that there is a pending foreclosure action. All parties who have a financial interest in the property must receive notice of the pending foreclosure hearing.

4. Hearing before the Clerk of Court ✗ Due process

The hearing is conducted before the Clerk of Court. The actual hearing is usually a brief affair where the Clerk considers the evidence submitted by the parties. If the lender can show that a valid debt exists, that the borrower is in default, that the deed of trust contains the right of foreclosure and that proper notice has been given, the Clerk has little choice but to authorize a foreclosure auction. There is also no right to a jury trial in a foreclosure proceeding.[2]

---

2. *United Carolina Bank v. Tucker*, 99 N.C.App. 95, 392 S.E.2d 410(1990).

5. Advertising the Foreclosure Sale

Before the actual auction occurs, the trustee must also publish a notice of sale in the legal classifieds section of local newspaper. A notice of sale must also be mailed to interested parties. The notice must be published for at least two successive weeks in a county newspaper when the property is located.

6. The Foreclosure Auction ✫

Foreclosure sales must be held in the county where the property is located.[3] When the day for the auction arrives, the trustee will read out the foreclosure notice, usually on the courthouse steps and then open up the property for bids. The lender has an automatic bid for the total amount owed on the deed of trust. However, other people can, and often do, make higher bids on the property. Some people attend foreclosure auctions with the idea of buying property below fair market value. They believe that by purchasing the house at a foreclosure auction, they can make a minimal investment in the property and either rent it out to others or resell it. However, in today's highly-competitive real estate markets, purchasing choice real estate for pennies on the dollar is almost unheard of.

When a person bids at a foreclosure auction, he or she must present cash or certified funds for a minimum of 5% of the bid price. When a person is a successful bidder at the foreclosure sale, he or she will receive title to the property subject to any upset bids.

Figure 9-2. § 45-21.10. Requirement of Cash Deposit at Sale

(a) If a mortgage or deed of trust contains provisions with respect to a cash deposit at the sale, the terms of the instrument shall be complied with.

(b) If the instrument contains no provision with respect to a cash deposit at the sale, the mortgagee or trustee may require the highest bidder immediately to make a cash deposit not to exceed the greater of five percent (5%) of the amount of the bid or seven hundred fifty dollars ($750.00).

(c) If the highest bidder fails to make the required deposit, the person holding the sale may at the same time and place immediately reoffer the property for sale.

---

7. Upset Bid ✫

At any time within 10 days of the foreclosure auction, a person is authorized to file an "upset bid" with the Clerk of Superior Court outbidding the successful bidder at the foreclosure sale. When the upset bid is filed, the original bidder is relieved of all obligations on the property.

C. The Equity of Redemption ✫

Equity of redemption is a legal principle that allows the borrower to recover full title to the property once all the conditions of the mortgage have been satisfied. The equity of redemption allows the borrower, even one facing foreclosure, to regain title to the property by paying the outstanding loan balance, plus any late fees and interest prior to the

---

3. NCGS § 45-21.4.

actual auction. When payment is made, all conditions of the mortgage have been met and full title vests back to the borrower.

VII. Types of Mortgages

These days, there is such a wide variety of mortgages that it would be nearly impossible to list and explain them all. Instead, we will focus on the two basic types of mortgages: fixed rate and adjustable rate mortgages.

A. Fixed Rate Mortgages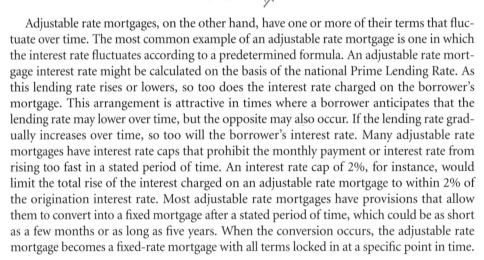

A fixed-rate mortgage is the more traditional of the two. In a fixed-rate mortgage, all terms remain the same throughout the loan repayment. The length of the loan, normally 30 years, is set as well as the monthly payment and the interest rate. Fixed-rate mortgages have the benefit of predictability because both the lender and the borrower know full well what is expected of each.

B. Adjustable Rate Mortgages

Adjustable rate mortgages, on the other hand, have one or more of their terms that fluctuate over time. The most common example of an adjustable rate mortgage is one in which the interest rate fluctuates according to a predetermined formula. An adjustable rate mortgage interest rate might be calculated on the basis of the national Prime Lending Rate. As this lending rate rises or lowers, so too does the interest rate charged on the borrower's mortgage. This arrangement is attractive in times where a borrower anticipates that the lending rate may lower over time, but the opposite may also occur. If the lending rate gradually increases over time, so too will the borrower's interest rate. Many adjustable rate mortgages have interest rate caps that prohibit the monthly payment or interest rate from rising too fast in a stated period of time. An interest rate cap of 2%, for instance, would limit the total rise of the interest charged on an adjustable rate mortgage to within 2% of the origination interest rate. Most adjustable rate mortgages have provisions that allow them to convert into a fixed mortgage after a stated period of time, which could be as short as a few months or as long as five years. When the conversion occurs, the adjustable rate mortgage becomes a fixed-rate mortgage with all terms locked in at a specific point in time.

Relevant Case

Beneficial Mortg. Co. of North Carolina v. Hamidpour[4]

HUDSON, Judge.

Beneficial Mortgage Company ("Beneficial") held a deed of trust on a parcel of real property in Rockingham County that was sold at a foreclosure sale. Beneficial did not know

---

4. 155 N.C.App. 641, 574 S.E.2d 163 (2002).

of the sale and, therefore, did not bid on the property. Beneficial then sued to quiet title and to collaterally attack the sale. All parties moved for summary judgment. The superior court granted summary judgment in favor of the appellees, and Beneficial now appeals.

BACKGROUND

On April 26, 1986, Larry Taylor acquired by deed a parcel of property located in Rockingham County, North Carolina, On April 30, 1986, Taylor executed a deed of trust ("Citizens Deed of Trust") in favor of Citizens Savings Mortgage Company ("Citizens") in the amount of $48,450.00, which was recorded in the office of the register of deeds in Rockingham County on May 2, 1986. Citizens subsequently assigned the deed of trust to Atlantic Mortgage and Investment Corporation ("Atlantic").

On September 10, 1998, Taylor and his wife executed a promissory note in the amount of $50,000.00 in favor of Beneficial. The note was secured by a deed of trust on the property ("Beneficial Deed of Trust"). The Beneficial Deed of Trust was recorded on September 16, 1998, second in priority to the Citizens Deed of Trust.

David Craig ("Craig") was appointed substitute trustee of the Citizens Deed of Trust on May 3, 1999. On July 2, 1999, at Atlantic's request, Craig instituted a special proceeding in Rockingham County to foreclose upon the Citizens Deed of Trust. The clerk of court entered an order that Atlantic was entitled to foreclose on the property and, after giving notice, Craig proceeded to sell the property at public sale on October 13, 1999. Atlantic was the high bidder at that sale, with a bid of $16,461.99. However, on October 25, 1999, Household Finance Corporation ("Household") filed an upset bid, raising Atlantic's bid by five percent.

On the same day that the upset bid was filed, the Taylors filed a voluntary petition in bankruptcy under Chapter 13 of the Bankruptcy Code. The proceedings relating to the foreclosure of the Citizens Deed of Trust were placed on inactive status in accordance with the automatic stay provisions of the Bankruptcy Code pending the outcome of the Taylors' bankruptcy case.

The Taylors' bankruptcy case was later dismissed, and Craig obtained an order reopening the foreclosure proceedings. A new notice of sale was posted at the Rockingham County courthouse on October 18, 2000, setting the date of the sale for November 7, 2000. Beneficial did not receive notice of the sale. As set forth in Craig's brief, Craig was not aware that Household, who had filed an upset bid at the first sale, was the parent company of Beneficial, nor did Household provide an address on the notice of upset bid filed with the court. Had Beneficial been notified of the sale, it would have been ready, willing, and able to bid $68,979.69 for the property.

At the November 7, 2000 sale, Atlantic again was the high bidder. Third parties, however, filed four upset bids on November 9, November 13, November 15, and November 27. Nader Hamidpour was the highest bidder, with a final bid of $22,918.90. The period for upset bids closed on December 7, 2000. On December 13, 2000, a trustee's deed conveying the property to Hamidpour was recorded in the Rockingham County register of deeds, and the final report of the trustee was filed January 10, 2001.

Beneficial filed suit in January 2001 to quiet title and to collaterally attack the foreclosure. All parties moved for summary judgment. On September 24, 2001, the superior court granted summary judgment in favor of the appellees. Beneficial now appeals.

ANALYSIS

Beneficial argues on appeal that the trial court erred in granting summary judgment for the appellees. In Beneficial's view, the November 7, 2000 foreclosure sale was improper because (1) the notice of foreclosure sale was not posted for 20 days as required by N.C. Gen.Stat. § 45-21.17(1)(a) and (2) the sale was conducted on a legal holiday in contravention of N.C. Gen.Stat. § 45-21.23. Further, Beneficial argues that these material irregularities resulted in the property being sold for a grossly inadequate price.

Before we address these issues, however, we must determine whether Beneficial, as holder of a second mortgage, has standing to challenge a foreclosure sale once it is completed. Appellee Craig has argued that Beneficial does not have standing to challenge the sale under Chapter 45 since Beneficial is not a mortgagor. Standing is a necessary prerequisite to a court's proper exercise of subject matter jurisdiction. Aubin v. Susi, 149 N.C.App. 320, 324, 560 S.E.2d 875, 878 (2002). Thus, if Beneficial does not have standing, we must dismiss this appeal. Id. at 326, 560 S.E.2d at 880.

In Gore v. Hill, the purchaser of property sold at a foreclosure proceeding argued that the foreclosure was invalid because the trustee had failed to satisfy the notice requirements set forth in N.C. Gen.Stat. § 45-21.21 governing the postponement of foreclosure sales. 52 N.C.App. 620, 620, 279 S.E.2d 102, 103 disc. review denied, 303 N.C. 710 (1981). The Court rejected this claim. In the Court's view, section 45-21.21 provided procedural protections only for the mortgagor; the "procedural requirements of notice and hearing are designed to assure mortgagors that property which they have used to secure an indebtedness will not be foreclosed without due process of law." Id. at 622, 279 S.E.2d at 104. Therefore, the "plaintiff herein, purchaser of the property, was not a party protected by G.S. § 45-21.21 and ... has no basis on which to assert that the sale was invalid because the sale was postponed in a manner not consistent with the statute." Id.

Likewise, here, Beneficial, as junior mortgagee, is not a party protected by the notice requirements in Chapter 45 of our General Statutes. Section § 45-21.17(4) provides that only those persons listed in N.C. Gen.Stat. § 45-21.16 and those who have filed a request for notice under § 45-21.17A are entitled to notice of sale. Section § 45-21.16(b)(3) specifically excludes holders of deeds of trust—Beneficial—from those entitled to notice. Thus, Beneficial was entitled **166 to notice only if it had filed a request for notice, which it did not. Because Beneficial is not entitled to notice of sale, as set forth in section 45-21.16, Beneficial has no standing to dispute the adequacy of that notice on appeal. Moreover, our logical conclusion must be that because Beneficial does not have standing to contest the adequacy of notice given in this case, it does not have standing to argue that the sale was held on a holiday in contravention of § 45-21.23.

Beneficial also argues that it has standing to bring an action to quiet title pursuant to N.C. Gen.Stat. § 41-10 because it claims a competing current interest in the property via the Beneficial Deed of Trust and that the improperly conducted foreclosure sale had not extinguished its interest. We disagree. Section 41-10 allows a person with a claim or interest in real property to bring an action to resolve that claim against others who assert rights or interest in the same real estate. Here, however, Beneficial is not attempting to resolve a situation where both it and Hamidpour have title to the same property. Rather, Beneficial is using § 42-10 to make the same claim that it has been making all along, and we conclude that it does not have standing to do so.

CONCLUSION

For the reasons set forth above, we dismiss this appeal.
Dismissed.

Chapter Summary

Purchasing real estate is an expensive proposition. Most people do not have the ready cash available to buy a house outright and therefore they must apply to a lender to borrow the funds necessary to do so. When the lender loans money to a borrower, the lender secures the loan by using the property as collateral. The mortgage or deed of trust is the legal arrangement that secures the collateral for the lender and also allows the lender to foreclose on the property in the event of the borrower's default. Mortgages and deeds of trust resemble each other very closely, but they do have several important differences. In a mortgage, there are usually only two parties, the lender and the borrower. In the deed of trust, on the other hand, there are usually three parties, the lender, the borrower and a trustee. The trustee acts as a middleman between the lender and the borrower. The borrower conveys a title interest to the trustee who holds that title until the borrower makes the final payment on the mortgage. If the borrower defaults, the trustee will bring a foreclosure action to secure the lender's interests.

Foreclosure is the process through which a lender seizes the property that has been pledged as collateral for a loan. The power to foreclose on the property arises from specific causes found in the deed of trust, specifically the power of sale provision. The advantage of a deed of trust arrangement is that foreclosure does not require a civil action. Instead, foreclosure may proceed after a brief hearing before the clerk of court.

There are various types of mortgages, from fixed-rate mortgages to adjustable rate mortgages. A fixed-rate mortgage has stable terms, such as interest rate and monthly payment as well as a fixed loan period. Adjustable rate mortgages have flexible terms, the most common of which is the interest rate charged on the loan. As the prime lending rate fluctuates, the interest rate that the borrower must pay on the mortgage also fluctuates. Many adjustable rate mortgages have provisions that allow the borrower to lock in an interest rate and convert the adjustable rate mortgage to a fixed rate.

Review Questions

1. Explain the necessity of the mortgage in financing the purchase of residential real estate.
2. Describe how a mortgage or deed of trust is created.
3. What is the secondary mortgage market?
4. What impact have government-owned corporations such as Ginnie Mae and Fannie Mae had on the mortgage market?
5. When a borrower applies for and receives a mortgage, what does the lender receive in exchange for the money it lends to the borrower?
6. What is the purpose of organizations such as Fannie Mae and Ginnie Mae?
7. What is the difference between a "lien theory" on mortgages and a "title theory" on mortgages? Which theory does North Carolina follow?
8. What are the minimum requirements of a mortgage or deed of trust?
9. Explain the significance of the acceleration clause.
10. What is a due on sale provision found in deeds of trust?
11. Explain the significance of the power of sale clause found in a deed of trust.
12. What is meant by the term "default" as that term is applied to mortgages?
13. What is the most common reason for a default on a mortgage or deed of trust?
14. What is foreclosure?
15. List and explain the basic steps involved in foreclosing real estate.
16. The chapter explains that there are actually two types of foreclosure in North Carolina. What are they? Explain.
17. What is the "equity of redemption?"
18. What is the function of a trustee in a deed of trust arrangement?
19. What is the difference between a fixed rate mortgage and an adjustable rate mortgage?
20. What is the purpose of a foreclosure hearing before the clerk of court?

Assignment

Go to your local courthouse and locate a deed of trust that has been filed to secure a lender's rights in real property. Go through the deed of trust and locate provisions and clauses that have been discussed in this chapter. What are the terms of this deed of trust? What is the interest rate? What is the total amount borrowed? Can you locate the power of sale provision? Can you locate the promissory note provisions?

Terms and Phrases

Mortgage

Primary mortgage market

Secondary mortgage market

Fannie Mae

Ginnie Mae

Department of Housing and Urban
  Development

Deed of Trust

Priority of mortgages

Subordination agreement

Acceleration clause

Due on sale clause

Default

Promissory note clause

Power of sale

Foreclosure

Upset bid

Equity of redemption

Fixed rate mortgage

Adjustable rate mortgage

Chapter 10

Public and Private Limitations on Real Estate

Chapter Objectives

At the conclusion of this chapter, you should be able to:

- Explain the role of zoning in restricting the way the property may be used
- Provide examples of typical zoning classifications
- Define restrictive covenants and how they apply to real estate
- Describe other public methods used to restrict use of real estate
- Explain the law of easements

I. Introduction to Public and Private Limitations on Real Estate

In this chapter, we will explore the various public and private restrictions that limit the ways that an individual may use his or her own property. Public restrictions are usually reflected in zoning regulations, while private restrictions are usually enforced through means of restrictive covenants. We will examine the similarities and contrasts between these two different approaches to controlling land use. We will also explore how liens restrict the use and conveyance of property.

II. Public Restrictions on Land Use

Local, state and federal governments have the right to impose restrictions on the way that private individuals may use their property. On a local level, the most common method of control is through zoning regulations.

A. Zoning

Zoning is the power of a local government to restrict private and business owners in the way that they use their property. Zoning regulations are enforced by a local Zoning Board that has the power to pass zoning ordinances, hear requests to alter zoning classifications and to enforce zoning regulations against violators. The primary purpose of zoning is to:

- Promote health and morals
- Reduce traffic congestion and improve traffic flow
- Emphasize safety from fire and other potential hazards
- Provide adequate heat, light and air flow for residents

Figure 10-1. Zoning § 153A-340. Grant of Power

(a) For the purpose of promoting health, safety, morals, or the general welfare, a county may regulate and restrict the height, number of stories and size of buildings and other structures, the percentage of lots that may be occupied, the size of yards, courts and other open spaces, the density of population, and the location and use of buildings, structures, and land for trade, industry, residence, or other purposes, and to provide density credits or severable development rights for dedicated rights-of-way.

Zoning rules and regulations are also used as an effective planning tool for local governments. By enforcing zoning regulations, local government officials can concentrate industry and commercial development in specific areas, while keeping other areas set aside for residential development.

1. The Government's Authority to Impose Zoning Regulations

Cities and towns get their authority to create zoning regulations from North Carolina general statutes and also from the state and federal constitutions.[1] Zoning is a function of the police powers granted to local, state and federal governments that allow them to take specific actions to promote health and safety and to protect citizens. Zoning regulations are usually enforced on a local level, by city or town ordinances.

2. Zoning Ordinances

A zoning ordinance is usually enacted as some form of protective zoning. In this case, a zoning regulation attempts to protect property value and the health and safety of local residents by enacting ordinances that limit individual property owners' rights to use their property in specific ways. For instance, a zoning ordinance will specify that structures must have a minimum setback distance from the road or that buildings may only be created from specific types of materials. The most common example of a zoning ordinance is a limitation on the use of the property, such as limiting properties in a designated area for residential use only, while other areas are zoned as commercial use only.

---

1. *Zopfi v. Wilmington*, 273 NC 430, 160 SE2d 325 (1968).

Zoning regulations are supposed to be limited in their focus to specific issues, such as traffic-flow patterns, safety issues, health and general welfare. When a zoning ordinance exceeds one of these limited issues, courts may strike down the regulation as excessive or over-broad.[2]

Figure 10-2. Examples of Zoning Ordinances

- Limits on the maximum height of a building
- Maximum/minimum set backs from the road
- Type of business allowed in the area
- Limitations to residential use only
- Maximum/minimum lot sizes

Some communities are also concerned about the overall appearance of their city and sometimes pass zoning ordinances that require a certain architectural style for any structure built in a specified zone. This is commonly referred to as "aesthetic zoning."

3. Typical Zoning Districts and Classifications

The first zoning ordinances in North Carolina divided towns and cities into three different districts: residential, commercial and industrial. In each of these zones, use was limited to the specific classification. These days, however, there are numerous zoning classifications and sub-classifications that can make zoning regulations rather difficult to understand. There may, for instance, be several different levels of residential zoning classifications, from single-family homes, to apartments and multi-family zones.

Figure 10-3. § 153A-342. Districts; Zoning Less than Entire Jurisdiction

A county may divide its territorial jurisdiction into districts of any number, shape, and area that it may consider best suited to carry out the purposes of this Part. Within these districts a county may regulate and restrict the erection, construction, reconstruction, alteration, repair, or use of buildings, structures, or land.

---

4. Zoning Violations and Exceptions

There are many areas of North Carolina where zoning ordinances have never been enacted. As a result, there are huge tracts of the state over which zoning boards have no authority. Even in areas where zoning ordinances exist, there are numerous structures that do not conform to the applicable zoning regulations. They may not conform because the structure existed prior to the enactment of this zoning regulation, or they may have special permission from the zoning board. There are three categories of zoning exceptions:

- Nonconforming use
- Variance
- Conditional use permit

---

2. N.C. Gen. Stat. § 153A-341.

a. Nonconforming Use

Whenever a zoning regulation is enacted, any existing structures that do not comply with the new zoning ordinance are allowed to remain as they were. A zoning regulation cannot force the closure of a pre-existing business, or force an individual out of his home. When the structure is already in existence at the time the zoning ordinances are created, it is allowed to continue to exist even though its use violates the new zoning ordinance. This is referred to as "nonconforming use."

b. Variance

The zoning board is empowered to make alterations in the overall zoning classifications. For instance, in an area that has been classified as residential, an owner might decide to turn his 100-year-old Victorian home into a Bed-and-Breakfast. In such a situation, the owner must apply to the Zoning Board for a variance that would allow him to conduct a commercial enterprise in an area zoned for residences only. The zoning board's power to issue variances allows for a certain degree of flexibility in zoning regulations. When the board issues a variance, it allows use of property that does not conform to the over-all zoning pattern in a particular area.

c. Conditional Use Permit

When the local city or town wishes to encourage business development or other types of uses, it may create a special condition in its zoning regulations referred to as conditional use permits. A conditional use permit allows the property to be used in a way that is not in strict compliance with the zoning classification, such as placing a commercial business in an area that has been zoned for residences. Zoning boards recognize that there are times when it is convenient for members of the community to have immediate access to shops and stores close to their homes. In such a situation, the Zoning Board might issue a conditional use permit to allow a commercial use in a residential area or vice versa.[3] A zoning board's power to create conditional use permit situations must not be used in an arbitrary or capricious way or in violation of public policy.[4]

5. Unconstitutional Zoning Ordinances

In the past, some zoning boards have occasionally abused zoning ordinances as a means to discriminate against members of a particular group. One example of an unconstitutional zoning ordinance is the so-called "spot zoning" regulation

a. Spot Zoning

Under Spot Zoning, the Zoning Board singles out a particular residence or area and changes the zoning for that property but not the rest of the area. Spot zoning plans were originally designed as a way of forcing out criminal activity and other undesirable elements in neighborhoods. Although North Carolina takes the minority view that spot zon-

---

3. *Vulcan Materials Co. v. Guilford County Bd. of Comm'rs,* 115 N.C.App. 319, 444 S.E.2d 639 (1994).
4. *Westminster Homes, Inc. v. Town of Cary Zoning Bd. of Adjustment,* 354 N.C. 298, 554 S.E.2d 634 (2001).

ing may not be invalid per se, the North Carolina Supreme Court is specific that certain types of spot zoning are not permissible. The North Carolina Supreme Court has defined spot zoning as: "A zoning ordinance, or amendment, which singles out and reclassifies a relatively small tract owned by a single person and surrounded by a much larger area uniformly zoned, so as to impose upon the small tract greater restrictions than those imposed upon the larger area."[5]

B. Designating Subdivisions

Many cities and towns in North Carolina have been given the power to adopt subdivision regulations to regulate neighborhoods in their areas. One method is to dedicate rights-of-way or easements for streets and utilities. Towns are also free to adopt ordinances that require a real estate developer to create a plat designating the streets, easements, rights-of-way and boundary lines for all tracts contained in a particular subdivision.

Figure 10-4. Subdivision Regulation. § 160A-372. Contents and Requirements of Ordinance

A subdivision control ordinance may provide for the orderly growth and development of the city; for the coordination of streets and highways within proposed subdivisions with existing or planned streets and highways and with other public facilities; for the dedication or reservation of recreation areas serving residents of the immediate neighborhood within the subdivision or, alternatively, for provision of funds to be used to acquire recreation areas serving residents of the development or subdivision or more than one subdivision or development within the immediate area, and rights-of-way or easements for street and utility purposes including the dedication of rights-of-way pursuant to G.S. 136-66.10 or G.S. 136-66.11; and for the distribution of population and traffic in a manner that will avoid congestion and overcrowding and will create conditions essential to public health, safety, and the general welfare. The ordinance may include requirements that the final plat show sufficient data to determine readily and reproduce accurately on the ground the location, bearing, and length of every street and alley line, lot line, easement boundary line, and other property boundaries, including the radius and other data for curved property lines, to an appropriate accuracy and in conformance with good surveying practice.

C. Building Codes

Building codes are local and state enactments that regulate construction, heating/air conditioning, plumbing and electrical work, among others. They are designed to protect the safety, health, and general welfare of citizens. In addition to building codes, many towns and cities have also passed performance standards that specify the strength, durability, or other performance characteristics of materials used in construction.

D. North Carolina Coastal Area Management Act

In addition to zoning and building codes, North Carolina also has several statutes specifically aimed at maintaining state areas. One such statute is the North Carolina

---

5. *Chrismon v. Guilford County*, 322 N.C. 611, 370 S.E.2d 579 (1988).

Coastal Area Management Act. This Act provides for local and state governments to work together to preserve natural ecological systems, such as the coastal zones.

Figure 10-5. North Carolina Coast Area Management Act*

(b) Goals. — The goals of the coastal area management system to be created pursuant to this Article are as follows:

(1) To provide a management system capable of preserving and managing the natural ecological conditions of the estuarine system, the barrier dune system, and the beaches, so as to safeguard and perpetuate their natural productivity and their biological, economic and esthetic values;

(2) To insure that the development or preservation of the land and water resources of the coastal area proceeds in a manner consistent with the capability of the land and water for development, use, or preservation based on ecological considerations;

(3) To insure the orderly and balanced use and preservation of our coastal resources on behalf of the people of North Carolina and the nation;

(4) To establish policies, guidelines and standards for:

    a. Protection, preservation, and conservation of natural resources including but not limited to water use, scenic vistas, and fish and wildlife; and management of transitional or intensely developed areas and areas especially suited to intensive use or development, as well as areas of significant natural value;

    b. The economic development of the coastal area, including but not limited to construction, location and design of industries, port facilities, commercial establishments and other developments;

    c. Recreation and tourist facilities and parklands;

    d. Transportation and circulation patterns for the coastal area including major thoroughfares, transportation routes, navigation channels and harbors, and other public utilities and facilities;

    e. Preservation and enhancement of the historic, cultural, and scientific aspects of the coastal area;

    f. Protection of present common-law and statutory public rights in the lands and waters of the coastal area;

    g. Any other purposes deemed necessary or appropriate to effectuate the policy of this Article.

* NCGS § 113A-100.

III. Private Restrictions on Land Use

In this section, we will discuss the various private restrictions on land use. The most prominent of these private restrictions is the use of restrictive covenants. In many ways, restrictive covenants resemble zoning regulations, except that they are both imposed and enforced by private individuals.

A. Restrictive Covenants

Governments are not the only entities that desire to regulate land use. Private landowners often wish to restrict the way that land is used in a particular area. Where governments use zoning or other laws, private individuals are limited to restrictive covenants.

A restrictive covenant is a condition or restriction on the way that a real estate parcel may be used that is imposed by private individuals. Typical restrictive covenants focus on the size of buildings constructed on the site, limiting the use of structures to residential units, setbacks from roads and architectural design limitations, among others. Restrictive covenants are imposed on future possessors. They are said to "run with the land" because once they are imposed, they remain with the property and are imposed on future purchasers.

Restrictive covenants are often used in planned communities. They are also used in commercial developments to help shape the manner of use and to control many different issues related to the land use. In some ways, restrictive covenants are used to maintain the overall appearance of the neighborhood and to help the individual owners retain their investment. Courts in this state have long recognized the rights of owners to impose any conditions on the future of the property that they see fit, subject to certain limitations.[6]

1. Defining Restrictive Covenants

The North Carolina Court of Appeals defines a restrictive covenant as a "private agreement, usually in a deed or lease, that restricts the use or occupancy of real property, especially by specifying lot sizes, building lines, architectural styles, and the uses to which the property may be put."[7]

The owner cannot impose restrictions that prevent future sale of the property, discriminate on the basis of race or religion or violate public policy.[8] Restrictive covenants have been described as a negative easement that instead of granting rights to others prevents the owner from carrying out certain actions.[9]

2. Types of Restrictive Covenants

Although we have so far discussed restrictive covenants as though they are a single, legal principle, there are actually three different types of restrictive covenants. They include:

- Personal covenants
- Real covenants
- Equitable servitudes

a. Personal Covenants

Personal covenants create personal obligations only between the two parties in the transaction. As a result, personal covenants are rare. Most restrictive covenants are imposed on the land, not the parties. As a result, the most common type of restrictive covenants is the real covenant. When ambiguous language is used to create a restrictive covenant, courts may interpret real covenants as personal covenants that bind only the grantor and grantee.

---

6. *Sheets v. Dillon*, 221 N.C. 426, 431, 20 S.E.2d 344, 347 (1942).
7. *Wal-Mart Stores, Inc. v. Ingles Markets, Inc.*, 158 N.C.App. 414, 581 S.E.2d 111 (2003).
8. *Runyon v. Paley*, 331 N.C. 293, 416 S.E.2d 177 (1992).
9. *Cummings v. Dosam, Inc.*, 273 N.C. 28, 159 S.E.2d 513 (1968).

b. Real Covenants

Real covenants are the most common type of restrictive covenant. They are imposed on the land, and obligate all future purchasers (until the restrictive covenant expires or is terminated). Because courts take the general view that all restrictive covenants must be strictly construed, the language used to create any restrictive covenant will be closely reviewed on appeal. We will examine the way that courts interpret restrictive covenants later in this chapter. However, it is important to note that in order to qualify as a real covenant, the provisions of the restrictive covenant must "touch and concern" the land.

i. Touch and Concern the Land

In order to be enforceable against future purchasers, the restrictive covenant must "touch and concern" the land. This term has been defined as anything that creates an economic impact on the property or the rights of the current owner.[10]

Sidebar: Real covenants must "touch and concern" the land.

c. Equitable Servitude

An equitable servitude is a type of restrictive covenant that is rarely used. Essentially, it is an equity action that seeks to enforce the provisions of a restrictive covenant.

3. Creating a Restrictive Covenant

Restrictive covenants can be created in one of three ways. They include:

- Inclusion in the deed from the grantor to the grantee
- Recording a declaration of restrictive covenants at the Registrar of Deeds office
- Recording a plat containing the restrictive covenants

a. Including Restrictive Covenants in a Deed

A grantor can include restrictive covenants in the actual deed from grantor to grantee. In this situation, the deed would contain, in addition to the normal provisions found in any general warranty deed, additional restrictions.

b. Recording a Declaration of Restrictive Covenants

The most common way to record restrictive covenants is to record a declaration of restrictive covenants as a separate document and then refer to the declaration in future deeds.

c. Recording a Plat with Restrictive Covenants

Another method used to create restrictive covenants is by reference to a plat. This is a process similar to the method used to reference legal descriptions in a plat.

---

10. *Runyon v. Paley,* 331 N.C. 293, 416 S.E.2d 177 (1992).

4. Common Features Found in Restrictive Covenants

Although restrictive covenants can contain nearly an infinite variety of restrictions, there are some that are more common than others. Restrictive covenants are often created for the following:

- Minimum lot sizes
- Limiting use to specific categories, such as residential only
- Restricting the use to residential or commercial purposes only
- Limiting the number of outbuildings
- Restricting the types of animals that can live on the premises, such as forbidding farm animals

When these provisions are included, they run with the land and will bind future owners, but only when the restrictive covenants satisfy three elements. Restrictive covenants run with the land when:

- They are intended to do so
- There is a close connection between the covenant and the property
- There is a contractual relationship between the parties

a. Interpreting Restrictive Covenants

North Carolina courts strictly construe the language used to create restrictive covenants. Restrictive covenants must be specific and drafted in a way that is unambiguous. Although courts will attempt to give effect to the party's intention, vague or uncertain terms are construed against the drafter.

5. Recording Restrictive Covenants

There is no requirement that the restrictive covenants actually appear in the deed transferring title from one individual to another. However, in order to be binding on future owners, they must be both recorded and correctly indexed. Restrictive covenants are often recorded as a separate document and then later referred to in subsequent deeds. Once recorded, restrictive covenants become part of the chain of title.

6. Enforcing Restrictive Covenants

When it comes to enforcing restrictive covenants, the responsibility lies with the originating parties or with their successors. Homeowners associations also have standing to enforce restrictive covenants on all lots contained in the subdivision.

7. Unconstitutional or Illegal Restrictive Covenant Provisions

Restrictive covenants may not be used to prevent people of a certain race, color, religion or national origin from owning property in specific neighborhoods. Restrictive covenants were used as a means to achieve discriminatory practices in the past. However, the United States Supreme Court abolished racial restrictions in restrictive covenants in the case of *Shelly v. Kraemer*.[11] Similar restrictions apply to any restrictive covenant that attempts to limit an owner's ability to transfer his interest in real estate.[12]

> Sidebar: "A covenant in a deed or contract purporting to restrict occupancy and use of property solely on the basis of race is not enforceable in equity by injunction."[13]

8. Removing Restrictive Covenants

Restrictive covenants may expire by their own terms, such as when the restrictive covenant contains language setting a termination date. They also terminate when they have been abandoned by the people they were designed to protect. When it has become obvious that the restrictive covenants no longer have any legal significance, North Carolina courts will not enforce them. "Restrictive covenants will not be enforced merely to harass and annoy some particular person, when it is clear to the court that the objective for which the restrictive covenants were originally entered into have already failed."[14]

B. Easements

An easement is one person's right to use a portion of someone else's land. The most common example of an easement is a driveway that crosses over one parcel to give a person access to another parcel. The person who possesses the easement has a right to use a portion of someone else's property in order to access his own property. Other examples of easements include rights-of-way, utility access, ditches, and water and sewer lines. Like restrictive covenants, easements run with the land. When the owner of a parcel has acquired an easement across another parcel, this easement will be imposed on future owners of both parcels.

Easements can be broken down into two broad categories: appurtenant easements and easements in gross.

1. Appurtenant Easements

An appurtenant easement is the right of an owner of one parcel to use a portion of another parcel, such as for a driveway. There are always at least two parcels of real estate involved in appurtenant easements. For instance, if one tract is developed that effectively blocks another tract's access to a public highway, then the court may award an appurtenant easement driveway across the first parcel so that the person who owns the second parcel can have access to the public roads. The legal terminology used to describe these two tracts can be somewhat confusing. For instance, the land that benefits from the easement is referred to as the dominant estate while the land that has the easement across it is referred to as the servient estate.

2. Easements in Gross

An easement in gross is the right of a person or entity to enter on or use the land for a limited purpose. The most common example of an easement in gross is the easement

---

11. 334 U.S. 1, 68 S.Ct. 836, 92 L.Ed. 1161 (1948).
12. *Smith v. Mitchell*, 44 N.C.App. 474 (1980).
13. *Philbrook v. Chapel Hill Housing Authority*, 269 N.C. 598, 153 S.E.2d 153 (1967).
14. *Logan v. Sprinkle*, 256 N.C. 41, 123 S.E.2d 209 (1961).

granted to a utility company that allows its employees to come onto the land to service their telephone poles, gas lines or telephone lines. In this case, there is no second parcel of land that benefits from the use. Instead, the easement is granted to a person or entity. An easement in gross gives the easement holder the right to enter on the property without first seeking permission from the owner.

3. Creating Easements

Easements can be created in a wide variety of ways, such as:

- Express grant
- Reservation in a deed
- By implication
- By necessity
- By dedication
- By prescription
- By Cartway proceeding
- By Condemnation (Eminent Domain)

a. Express Grant

When an easement is created by express grant, a document, similar to a deed, is filed with the Registrar of Deeds that specifically states the right of one landowner to use a portion of another landowner's property as a driveway or for some other easement purpose. In this case, the grant would be in writing, as required under the Statute of Frauds, because this would be a title interest in real estate. North Carolina law also requires that, in addition to being in writing, both the dominant and servient estates should be described with an adequate legal description, such as a metes and bounds description and the location of the easement should be identified with specificity.

b. Reservation in a Deed

When a person sells a tract of land to another, such as subdividing a larger tract into smaller parcels, the previous owner might simply reserve an easement for himself in the deed that conveys the property. In this case, the owner would reserve an easement for himself by including the reservation as a clause in the deed.

c. By Implication

Courts will often find that an easement has been created from the simple fact that without one, a person would have no access to his own property. In such a situation, the courts will interpret the transaction between the parties as implicitly stating an easement so that the new owner may cross the boundary lines of the other tract to access her property.

d. By Necessity

North Carolina courts are sometimes called upon to litigate the issue of easements. When a court awards an easement to a party it is usually in the context of an easement by necessity. In such a case, courts would make findings that it is necessary for the grantee to have an easement over the grantor's land in order to have access to the public roads or highways.

e. By Prescription

Acquiring an easement by prescription is similar to acquiring title by adverse possession. In this case, a party who owns an adjoining tract of land begins using a driveway or cartway across another's property without permission. After a period of time has elapsed, the owner of the second tract loses his right to complain about the easement. The theory underlying easement by prescription is that when an owner has the right to complain and fails to exercise it, he is impliedly waiving it. When a party wishes to establish easement by prescription, he must prove the following elements:

(1) the use is adverse, hostile or under claim of right

(2) the use has been open and notorious such that the true owner had notice of the claim;

(3) the use has been continuous and uninterrupted for a period of at least twenty years; and

(4) there is substantial identity of an easement claimed throughout the twenty year period.[15]

Figure 10-6. Cities' Rights to Grant of Easements*

A city shall have authority to grant easements over, through, under, or across any city property or the right-of-way of any public street or alley that is not a part of the State highway system. Easements in a street or alley right-of-way shall not be granted if the easement would substantially impair or hinder the use of the street or alley as a way of passage. A grant of air rights over a street right-of-way or other property owned by the city for the purpose of erecting a building or other permanent structure (other than utility wires or pipes) shall be treated as a sale of real property, except that a grant of air rights over a street right-of-way for the purpose of constructing a bridge or passageway between existing buildings on opposite sides of the street shall be treated as a grant of an easement.

* NCGS § 160A-273.

---

f. By Cartway Proceeding

In some situations, a property owner may bring a cartway proceeding to establish an easement. This proceeding is limited to situations where a person is seeking an easement to access farms, forests, quarries or mines. See Figure 10-7 for the statute that authorizes cartway proceedings.

---

15. *Potts v. Burnette,* 301 N.C. 663, 273 S.E.2d 285 (1981); *Mitchell v. Golden,* 107 N.C.App. 413, 420 S.E.2d 482 (1992).

Figure 10-7. § 136-68. Special Proceeding for Establishment, Alteration or Discontinuance of Cartways, etc.; Petition; Appeal

The establishment, alteration, or discontinuance of any cartway, church road, mill road, or like easement, for the benefit of any person, firm, association, or corporation, over the lands of another, shall be determined by a special proceeding instituted before the clerk of the superior court in the county where the property affected is situated. Such special proceeding shall be commenced by a petition filed with said clerk and the service of a copy thereof on the person or persons whose property will be affected thereby. From any final order or judgment in said special proceeding, any interested party may appeal to the superior court for a jury trial de novo on all issues including the right to relief, the location of a cartway, tramway or railway, and the assessment of damages. The procedure established under Chapter 40A, entitled "Eminent Domain," shall be followed in the conduct of such special proceeding insofar as the same is applicable and in harmony with the provisions of this section.

* N.C.G.S.A. § 136-68.

---

g. By Condemnation (Eminent Domain)

Finally, an easement can be obtained by the local government in much the same way that the government condemns entire tracts of property for use. Local, state or federal governments may seize portions of a real estate parcel as an easement through their powers of Eminent Domain granted in the state and federal constitutions.

4. Terminating Easements

Easements may be terminated by a wide variety of means, including:

- Loss of purpose
- Merger
- Expiration of the stated time period
- Release
- Abandonment

a. Loss of Purpose

An easement may be terminated when there is no longer a need for the easement. If Nancy has an easement over Chuck's property to access the public highway and the highway is removed or closed, there is no longer a need for the easement. In this situation, Chuck may request a court ruling that the easement be terminated because there is no longer a purpose for it.

b. Merger

The doctrine of merger applies in many different contexts, but especially when dealing with easements. Suppose that Chuck purchases Nancy's lot and converts the two lots into a single lot. At this point, because Chuck now owns both lots, there is no longer an easement for the benefit of another parcel. The distinction between the two parcels has disappeared and the doctrine of merger extinguishes the easement.

c. Expiration of a Stated Time Period

In some limited circumstances, easements have express time periods. When the time period lapses, the easement terminates as a matter of law.

d. Release

The person who possesses the dominant estate is permitted to release the easement he possesses over the servient estate. Just as easements must be in writing, releases of easements must also be in writing.

e. Abandonment

Abandonment is the flip side of easement by prescription. In easement by prescription, a party acquires an easement through adverse use. An easement may also be terminated when a party stops using it. In this situation, the owner of the servient estate could bring a legal action requesting that the court determine that the easement has been abandoned.

Relevant Case

JWL Investments, Inc. v. Guilford County Bd. of Adjustment, 133 N.C.App. 426, 515 S.E.2d 715 (1999)

WALKER, Judge.

Petitioners own a tract of land in Guilford County, North Carolina located behind 7964 National Service Road, on County Tax Map ACL-94-6999, Block 1093, Parcel 35 in Deep River Township. The property adjoins the right-of-way of Interstate 40 (I-40). The property is zoned RS-40, a residential zoning classification and is subject to a scenic corridor ordinance.

On 22 November 1996, petitioners were served by the Guilford County Planning and Development Department with a "Notice of Violation." The cited violation on the property was "a vehicle storage yard which is not a permitted use in the RS-40 zoned district and in the scenic corridor" pursuant to Guilford County Development Ordinance § 4-3.1 (Table 4-3-1) Permitted Use Schedule. Petitioners appealed from the notice of violation and on 4 March 1997, a hearing *428 was held before the Guilford County Board of Adjustment (the Board). At the hearing, petitioners admitted using the property to store vehicles on a residential lot in a scenic corridor, but argued that such use should be allowed to continue as the property was also previously used, in part, to store commercial vehicles. Petitioners acquired an interest in the property sometime before 1987. Petitioners alleged the property was used to park operable vehicles which they either use or sell at their business in Rockingham County. Prior to petitioners' ownership of the property, it was owned by an individual with a concrete business who littered it with debris and stored both junked and operable vehicles. Petitioners presented testimony from two neighbors as to the use of the property by its previous owners. Respondents presented evidence of aerial photos of the property taken in 1970, 1986, and 1991 which showed the property to be undeveloped and not in use. The notice of violation was affirmed and the Board gave petitioners 45 days to comply before the start of any civil penalties.

The petitioners sought review by filing a writ of certiorari and on 25 May 1998 a hearing was held. The trial court then entered judgment on 9 June 1998 in which it affirmed the decision of the Board and remanded the case to the Board for imposition of civil penalties.

On appeal, petitioners contend the trial court committed prejudicial error: (1) in finding petitioners' due process rights were not violated; (2) in finding that the Board did not lack authority to support its decision; (3) in finding and concluding that the Board had authority to impose civil penalties; (4) in finding and concluding that N.C. Gen.Stat. § 153A-340 through 345 afforded adequate constitutional protections; (5) in finding that the decision of the Board was not arbitrary and capricious, oppressive, and attended with manifest abuse of authority; and (6) in finding the decision of the Board was supported by competent, material, and substantial evidence in the whole record.

In reviewing the decisions of a board of adjustment, the trial court sits in the posture of an appellate court and is responsible for the following:

(1) Reviewing the record for errors of law,

(2) Insuring that procedures specified by law in both statutes and ordinances are followed,

(3) Insuring that appropriate due process rights of a petitioner are protected including the right to offer evidence, cross-examine witnesses, and inspect documents,

(4) Insuring that decisions of town boards are supported by competent, material and substantial evidence in the whole record, and

(5) Insuring that decisions are not arbitrary and capricious. Concrete Co. v. Board of Commissioners, 299 N.C. 620, 626, 265 S.E.2d 379, 383 (1980)

First, petitioners argue that their due process rights were violated because one of the members of the Board was a former *430 employee of the County Planning Department, and in that capacity, she had been consulted by petitioners about the possibility of rezoning the property. "A party claiming bias or prejudice may move for recusal and in such event has the burden of demonstrating 'objectively that grounds for disqualification actually exist.'" In re Ezzell, 113 N.C.App. 388, 394, 438 S.E.2d 482, 485 (1994) (quoting State v. Kennedy, 110 N.C.App. 302, 305, 429 S.E.2d 449, 451 (1993)). The petitioners did not object during the hearing to this member's presence on the Board. Furthermore, petitioners have made no showing that they were prejudiced by this member's participation in the case. Thus, we find this assignment of error to be without merit.

Next, petitioners argue that the trial court erred in finding that the Board did not lack authority to support its decision. Petitioners concede that the use of their property does not conform with the ordinance; however, they contend that the use of their property to store vehicles is "grandfathered in." According to § 3-14.2(B)(4) of the County's development ordinance, a non-conforming use of property that pre-dates the enactment of an ordinance is permitted so long as the non-conforming use is not discontinued for a period of time greater than one year. At the hearing, petitioners presented testimony from Jane Wood, a resident of the area who related the uses of property in the surrounding area and the petitioners present use of the property and Ruth Cannon, the Secretary of J.W.L. Associates, who testified to the previous owner's use of the property. Petitioners presented no evidence to establish a continuous non-conforming use of the property which would entitle them to be "grandfathered in." On the contrary, respondents presented evidence consisting of aerial photographs that showed the non-conforming use had not been continuous since the imposition of the ordinances.

Property uses that are non-conforming are not favored by the law. CG & T Corp. v. Bd. of Adjustment of Wilmington, 105 N.C.App. 32, 39, 411 S.E.2d 655, 659 (1992). "Zoning ordinances are construed against indefinite continuation of a non-conforming use." Forsyth Co. v. Shelton, 74 N.C.App. 674, 676, 329 S.E.2d 730, 733 (1985). Thus, we find the Board has ample authority with which to support its decision.

Petitioners further contend the scenic corridor ordinance is unconstitutional on its face and, as applied in this case, it amounts to a taking of property without just compensation in violation of the Fifth and Fourteenth Amendments of the United States Constitution. Specifically, petitioners argue the property is unacceptable for residential purposes because it adjoins I-40. In order to determine whether an unconstitutional taking of property has occurred, it must be determined whether, under the "ends means" test, the particular exercise of police power by the government was legitimate, whether the means chosen to regulate are reasonable, and "whether the ordinance was invalid because the interference with the plaintiffs' use of the property amounted to a taking." An interference with property rights amounts to a taking where the plaintiffs are deprived of "all economically beneficial or productive use."

The legitimacy and reasonableness of enforcement of the ordinance are not contested; therefore, we need only address whether the ordinance is invalid because it constitutes a taking. See id. We conclude the scenic corridor ordinance has not deprived petitioners of "all economically beneficial or productive use" of their property. Thus, no unconstitutional taking has occurred.

Next, petitioners argue the trial court erred in finding and concluding the Board had authority to impose civil penalties. We note that the Board stayed the imposition of a civil penalty for 45 days. N.C. Gen.Stat. § 153A-345(b) (1991) provides:

> The board of adjustment may reverse or affirm, in whole or in part, or may modify the order, requirement, decision, or determination appealed from, and shall make any order, requirement, decision, that in its opinion ought to be made in the circumstances. To this end the board has all of the powers of the officer from whom the appeal is taken.

Section 8-4 of the Guilford County Development Ordinance states that an enforcement officer may impose civil penalties against any person who violates a provision of the ordinance. Therefore, since the Board possesses all of the powers of the enforcement officer for non-compliance, the trial court did not err in finding that the Board had authority to impose civil penalties.

Petitioners' last two assignments of error concern whether the decisions of the Board are supported by substantial, competent evidence or are arbitrary and capricious, thus the reviewing court looks to the "whole record" to determine whether the Board's findings are supported by substantial evidence in the whole record. See Whiteco Outdoor Advertising v. Johnston County Bd. of Adjustment, 132 N.C.App. 465, 513 S.E.2d 70 (1999). Substantial evidence is "evidence a reasonable mind might accept as adequate to support a conclusion." Hayes v. Fowler, 123 N.C.App. 400, 405, 473 S.E.2d 442, 445 (1996). Furthermore, a decision will be reversed and found to be arbitrary and capricious only when it is established by the petitioner that "the decision was whimsical, made patently in bad faith, [or] indicates a lack of fair and careful consideration." Whiteco Outdoor Advertising, ___ N.C.App. at 70, 513 S.E.2d at 73. "When the Court of Appeals applies the whole record test and reasonable but conflicting views emerge from the evidence, the Court cannot substitute its judgment for the administrative body's decision." CG & T Corporation, 105 N.C.App. at 40, 411 S.E.2d at 660. We find the trial court exercised the appropriate scope of review; thus, we look to see if "the court did so properly."

Here, the trial court properly concluded that there was substantial evidence to affirm the decision of the Board. Therefore, the decision of the Board was not arbitrary and capricious in finding that petitioners violated the ordinances and the trial court did not err.

As to petitioners' remaining assignment of error that N.C. Gen.Stat. §§ 153A-340 through 345 fail to provide adequate constitutional protections for an aggrieved party such as the petitioners, we agree with the trial court that this contention is without merit.

Affirmed.

Judges WYNN and HUNTER concur.

Chapter Summary

There are both public and private methods used to place limitations on the way that real estate can be used. Public restrictions include zoning rules and regulations. The purpose of zoning ordinances is to promote health, safety and welfare for local citizens. Typical zoning regulations include residential, commercial and industrial. When a structure pre-exists the enactment of a zoning regulation, it is said to be a nonconforming use. A landowner may request a variance from the Zoning Board that allows him to use his property in a way different from the zoning classification. When zoning is used to discriminate against individuals, it is referred to as "Spot zoning" and is generally unconstitutional.

Private restrictions on land-use generally consist of restrictive covenants. A restrictive covenant is a condition or limitation placed on the use of the land by a previous owner. Typical restrictive covenants limit lot sizes, housing setbacks or the manner in which property can be used. In many ways, they resemble zoning regulations. Restrictive covenants can be created by including them in a deed or recording a declaration of restrictive covenants at the deed office. Easements are another type of private restriction on land use, but in this case an easement creates a right for someone who does not own the land to use a portion of it. The most common example of an easement is a driveway. There are two types of easements recognized in North Carolina, appurtenant easements and easements in gross.

Review Questions

1. What is the purpose of zoning?
2. What are the three main classifications found in zoning ordinances?
3. Compare and contrast a nonconforming use with a conditional use permit.
4. What is "spot zoning?"
5. What are building codes?
6. What are restrictive covenants?
7. What does it mean when the law requires that a restrictive covenant "touch and concern the land?"
8. What are three methods used to create restrictive covenants?
9. What are some common features found in restrictive covenants?
10. How can parties remove restrictive covenants?
11. What is an easement?
12. What are the two main types of easements recognized in North Carolina?
13. List and explain at least five methods used to create an easement.
14. List and explain at least five methods used to terminate an easement.
15. Explain the holding in this chapter's *relevant case.*
16. What does the term "variants" mean in the context of zoning law?
17. Where do governments get the authority to impose zoning regulations?
18. How does North Carolina define a "subdivision?"
19. What is the difference between a personal covenant and a real covenant under a restrictive covenant?
20. How is an easement different from a restrictive covenant?

Assignment

1. Do zoning regulations exist in your town? Contact your local Zoning Board and obtain a map showing the various zoning classifications in your area.

2. Go to the local registrar of deeds office and review the grantor index to locate a declaration of restrictive covenants. Get a copy of this declaration and then review it closely. What types of restrictions does the declaration impose on real estate owners?

Terms and Phrases

Zoning

Nonconforming use

Variance

Conditional use permit

Spot zoning

Subdivision

Building codes

Restrictive covenants

"Touch and concern to land"

Easement

Appurtenant easement

Easement in gross

Easement by implication

Easement by necessity

Easement by prescription

Easement by cartway proceeding

Merger

Release

Abandonment

Chapter 11

Title Searches

Chapter Objectives

At the conclusion of this chapter, you should be able to:

- Explain why title searches are necessary
- List and explain the basic steps involved in carrying out a title search
- Explain the significance of the Marketable Title Act
- Describe the impact of legal malpractice claims on title searches
- Describe the types of information that can be located in various public offices that are critical to a successful title search

I. Introduction to Title Searches

In this chapter, we will explore the world of title examinations. A thorough and complete title examination is required in nearly every type of real estate transaction in North Carolina. As a result, both attorneys and paralegals who practice real estate law must have a firm foundation in title search techniques and the issues that arise from them.

Although not all states use the title examination process to determine the marketability of titles, North Carolina relies heavily on the system. This raises an important question: why is a title search necessary?

A. Why Is a Title Search Necessary?

Title searches are necessary in order to determine the legal status of a parcel of real estate. As we have seen throughout this book, there are many actions that a real estate owner can take which will have a significant impact on future owners. A title search is the method used in this state to determine the legal significance of any actions against the previous owners and to determine, ultimately, the marketability of the title. Here, marketability refers to the quality of the title and a buyer's interest in purchasing it. There are some parcels so encumbered by legal problems that they are impossible to sell. This is an unmarketable title. The primary purpose of a title search is to discover any legal problems and to solve them before the closing occurs.

The end product of a title examination is an attorney's legal opinion about the current state of the property. When an attorney issues an opinion stating that the title is free and clear of all encumbrances, this is an assurance that the buyer can take the property without fear of losing it to some adverse claim. It also reassures the title insurance company, which must pay the legal costs of any action filed after it grants a policy on the title. Title examinations are often required by title insurance companies in order to ensure that there are no clouds on the title.

Sidebar: Title searches are necessary in order to ensure that the title is free and clear.

B. Beginning a Title Search

The title search usually begins when the law office is contacted by a real estate broker or the lender and asked to conduct a title examination of the property in question. The borrower usually pays the legal team's fee, thus making the borrower the firm's client.

Ordinarily, the source requesting the title examination will provide the street address of the property, the deed book and page number reference for the most recent transaction involving this property and the names of the parties involved. Lenders also usually send over a loan package that provides information about the real estate parcel, as well as information that will be required to conclude the closing. (See Chapter 12).

Sidebar: Title searches are also required when the property is refinanced.

1. Attorney Approval

The attorney must be approved by the lender or title insurance company before he or she will be allowed to give an opinion about the marketability of the title. Attorneys are approved on an individual basis. They apply to the various companies, complete approval forms and their names are placed on an approved list of title examination attorneys.

2. Information Needed to Begin a Title Search

A title searcher must have some basic information before the title search process can begin. This information ensures that the title search is conducted on the correct parcel. The more information that a title searcher obtains before beginning a search, the better off he or she will be. There is nothing more frustrating than spending several hours researching the wrong parcel.

Here is a summary of information required to begin a title search:

- The names of the current property owners
- A legal description of the real property that is the subject of the transaction, as well as street address
- The time period that the title search must cover
- The tax map and tax ID numbers, if available
- Deed book and page number

Sidebar: Many title searchers have a form that they have their clients complete that includes all of this information.

a. Names of the Current Owners

It is essential to get the current owners' names in order to begin a title search. The current owners are the ones who will be transferring title to the new buyer. Getting the owners' names ensures not only that the title searcher is researching the correct parcel, but also guards against early misunderstandings: such as when the people involved own more than one parcel of real estate.

Once a title searcher has obtained the grantors' names, it is a relatively simple matter to look this name up in the Grantor Index. We will discuss the actual process of the title search later in this chapter.

Figure 11-1. Additional Information about the Parties

- What are the ages of all parties? Are they all adults?
- Have any of the parties been declared mentally incompetent?
- Are any of the parties married? If so, what are the complete legal names of their spouses?
- When did the grantor acquire the property and from whom?
- Do we have a copy of that prior deed transaction?

---

b. Description of the Property to Be Conveyed

It is of vital importance to a legal professional to properly identify the property in question before beginning the search. Sometimes, street addresses are incorrect and the parties' descriptions may not have sufficient detail to properly identify the property. It is extremely easy to confuse different real estate tracts, especially when the only information available is a poorly drafted description. Pinpointing the actual tract involved in the transaction is an absolute necessity to a successful title search.

c. Time Period

When a title searcher reviews the public records concerning property and owners, the normal search period is at least 30 years. The reason for conducting such a lengthy search through the records is to ensure that a title searcher locates any document that could potentially have a legal impact on the property today. Although many practitioners search back 40 years or more, the North Carolina Marketable Title Act provides that any civil judgment or other encumbrance on property that is older than 30 years will have no legal impact.

Some title searchers will search not only the period that each owner possessed the property, but also for a period of up to two years after the property was conveyed. This two-year "safety net" will help catch any probate matters that might have been pending at the time of the conveyance.

i. The North Carolina Marketable Title Act

The North Carolina Marketable Title Act is legislation that was specifically designed to keep as many titles free and clear as possible. When a property's title is clouded by encumbrances or other legal problems, it is virtually impossible to sell it. This keeps potentially valuable properties from entering the marketplace and keeps them from being developed for the public. As a result, the North Carolina's Marketable Title Act declares that any legal encumbrance on real estate that is thirty years old or older will have no legal impact on the title.

Figure 11-2. Marketable Title Act. N.C.G.S.A. §47B-1

It is the purpose of the General Assembly of the State of North Carolina to provide that if a person claims title to real property under a chain of record title for 30 years, and no other person has filed a notice of any claim of interest in the real property during the 30-year period, then all conflicting claims based upon any title transaction prior to the 30-year period shall be extinguished.

§47B-2. Marketable record title to estate in real property; 30-year unbroken chain of title of record; effect of marketable title (a) Any person having the legal capacity to own real property in this State, who, alone or together with his predecessors in title, shall have been vested with any estate in real property of record for 30 years or more, shall have a marketable record title to such estate in real property.

(b) A person has an estate in real property of record for 30 years or more when the public records disclose a title transaction affecting the title to the real property which has been of record for not less than 30 years purporting to create such estate either in:

(1) The person claiming such estate; or

(2) Some other person from whom, by one or more title transactions, such estate has passed to the person claiming such estate; with nothing appearing of record, in either case, purporting to divest such claimant of the estate claimed.

(c) Subject to the matters stated in G.S. 47B-3, such marketable record title shall be free and clear of all rights, estates, interests, claims or charges whatsoever, the existence of which depends upon any act, title transaction, event or omission that occurred prior to such 30-year period. All such rights, estates, interests, claims or charges, however denominated, whether such rights, estates, interests, claims or charges are or appear to be held or asserted by a person sui juris or under a disability, whether such person is natural or corporate, or is private or governmental, are hereby declared to be null and void.

(d) In every action for the recovery of real property, to quiet title, or to recover damages for trespass, the establishment of a marketable record title in any person pursuant to this statute shall be prima facie evidence that such person owns title to the real property described in his record chain of title.

---

d. Tax ID Number

The local tax office assigns tax ID numbers or other identifiers to every parcel of real estate in the county. This tax ID number can be extremely helpful to a title searcher not only in helping to identify the property, but also in taking advantage of the enormous amount of information available in the tax office.

e. Deed Book and Page Number

It is helpful if the party who requests the title search produces a copy of the last deed that transferred title interest to the current owner. However, most clients do not provide this information. In fact, most title searchers are lucky to get a deed book and page number reference for this deed. A deed book reference is usually presented in this form:

1011/234

The first number in the sequence is the volume number. This is the number found on the binding of the volume that contains deed copies. It is also the volume number that is used to refer to microfilm, microfiche or digital storage media. The second number, "234" is the page number in the volume where the deed can be found.

A copy of the prior deed is a potential goldmine of information, because it not only provides a legal description of the property in question, but often also lists the prior conveyances stretching for decades and may also point out some of the legal problems with the property and the actions taken by previous title searchers to clear these problems up.

> **Shortcut Suggestion:** Many deeds contain a "deed history" or "deed recitation" that contains a history of all the deed transactions involving this property going back for decades. Locating this provision can be a huge time saver in establishing the chain of title.

f. Additional, Helpful Information

In addition to the basic information we have discussed so far, it is also helpful if the title searcher obtains a copy of the most recent survey of the property and the previous Title Insurance Policy. Although these two items are not essential to conducting a title search, they are extremely helpful and can often cut down the time required to conduct the search.

C. Title Search Banks

For firms that have been in the title examination business for a long time, it is possible that the attorneys have conducted a previous title search on this same property. In that situation, the title searcher should conduct a brief search through the firm's records to see if this property has ever been searched before. This can be a huge time-saver later on.

II. Steps in a Title Search

Many title searchers enjoy the process of reviewing the public records, because they get the chance to use many different skills: from interpreting domestic relations documents, reviewing wills, and going through criminal and bankruptcy records. There is also a practical reason that makes title work appealing: you are assured of being paid. The same cannot be said of other legal specialties. In this section, we will outline the basic steps involved in a title examination. You should keep in mind that the steps outlined here are the most common steps used. These steps do not provide for some of the issues that often come up with "problem properties." We will discuss common problems, and the methods to solve them, later in this chapter

A. Step 1: Establishing the Chain of Title

Before a title examiner goes to the courthouse, there is usually a more practical step to take: creating a client file. Beginning a title search involves creating a client file in the law firm's physical and computer file records. This information might be as simple as the client's name, the address of the property and the loan amount.

Once the client file has been created, and the necessary basic information has been gathered, the title searcher is ready to begin the actual title search. The first step in the search is to establish the chain of title for the property going back for a specific period of time. Most title examiners search back at least 30, if not 40, years. Although you might be tempted to go to the Deed Office first, there is actually a better place to begin: the Tax Office.

1. The Tax Office

Many title searchers begin their title search in the tax office by getting a copy of the tax map and deed reference number contained in the tax records. The tax office contains a wealth of information about real estate in the county, including owners' names, total acreage, PIN and/or parcel ID numbers, tax maps, tax ID numbers and deed references. In some counties, this information is still stored on a "tax card," but in most it is available in a computer database that not only provides all of the information set out above, but also basic floor plans, square footage and even digital photos of the property in question.

> Sidebar: Sometimes it isn't even necessary to physically visit the tax office. Many tax offices have computer terminal links to local deed rooms and some have information available online through their Geographic Information Systems Computer (GIS).

The tax office is also a huge help to the title searcher because it keeps complete records about all real property located in the county, has its own set of tax maps, and also cross-references this information with the Deed office.

Another reason to visit the tax office first is not only to obtain this information, but also to save yourself a step later on. At some point, the lender, title insurer and borrower will want to know the tax status on the property. Have the taxes already been paid, or are they outstanding? A title searcher can gather this information while obtaining other basic information.

> **Shortcut Suggestion**: The tax records will often provide deed book references for all previous transactions involving this property.

a. Tax Maps

In addition to general information about the property, the tax office also keeps its own set of maps for each parcel of real estate in the county. Tax maps will indicate the type of road access to the property. Does the property have direct access to a public road? This can be an important question later on in the transaction.

> Sidebar: The county tax number is often located on the deed itself. The tax office also keeps a cross-reference of street addresses to tax ID numbers.

2. Creating the Links in the Chain of Ownership

The first step in a title search is to go to the Grantee Index and look up the name of the current owner of the property. The Grantee Index shows all conveyances where a party received an interest in real estate. Because the current owner received his title from the previous owner of this particular parcel, his name will be listed here. The Grantee

Index will give a deed book and page number. Next, a title searcher looks up the deed. This deed will provide the name of the previous owner and the title searcher will repeat the process, looking up the previous owner's name in the Grantee Index to see from whom he purchased the property and so on, going back through the records until the title searcher has covered the specified time period.

The purpose of creating a chain of title is to learn both the names of each owner and the dates of ownership. A title searcher should make sure to note the exact date that each owner acquired the property and the exact date that each sold the property. Later, we will discuss why knowing these dates so precisely will be such a huge help.

The chain of title establishes the names and terms of ownership for each owner and will also help in the next stage when the title searcher searches the records to see what, if anything, the owners did during their ownership that might affect the legal status of the property. See Figure 11-3 for a sample chain of title form.

Figure 11-3. A Basic Form to Establish Chain of Title

Grantor Name(s):
Grantee Name(s):
Date of Transaction:
Deed book Reference
(volume and page number)
Brief description of the property:

---

3. The Grantor/Grantee Index

Effective use of the Grantor and Grantee Indexes is critical for the success of any title search. In the good, old days (which weren't all that good), title searching involved pulling out rather large and surprisingly heavy cloth bound books. You would open the book to the front listing and find out where everyone with your person's last name would be listed. Say, for instance, you were looking for someone whose last name was Bevans. Because that's not exactly a common name, chances were good that you could find that listing quickly. Because each entry was made as people walked in to record deeds, the books were not really organized alphabetically. Instead, they were chronological. With an owner who had an unusual last name, that meant you could speed through the listings until you came across the name, then follow it over to get the details. A title searcher would face exactly the opposite problem for grantors with common names. In that case, you had to look through each entry, looking for the right name.

However, in the age of computers, most counties have digitized some or all of their Grantor and Grantee Indexes. (Most have done so for the past ten years' records, at least). Using a computer both simplifies and complicates the process. Because all owners are listed alphabetically, it's a relatively simple matter to punch in a person's last name and first initial and see what transactions have been recorded under that name. However, the computer did not solve all problems with title searches, and may have created a few that weren't there before computer databases entered on the scene. The computer records are stored in a database and the computer sorts the names for you automatically and only pulls up the name a title searcher types in. Unfortunately, if the previous grantor's name was misspelled when it was entered into the system, the computer won't be able to tell you that. Remember, computers are not intelligent; they just do things quickly.

Figure 11-4. Hints and Tips for Computerized Grantor and Grantee Indexes

1. If you don't find the name the first time, try again with different spellings
2. Try different first names, too. Sometimes people use a name as their first name in their day-to-day activities, when it actually isn't their first name. Men named John often go by the nickname of "Jack." If you were searching for a real estate transaction involving John, you should be prepared to also look under "Jack." Occasionally a person's nickname seems to have no rational relationship to his legal name. How would you figure out what his legal name is? Look for other places where he has signed his name: tax records, deeds, birth certificates, marriage licenses, etc.
3. When in doubt, look it up. If you have more than one person's name listed, and you aren't sure which one is the correct listing, look them both up. The deed will give you the details you need.

Figure 11-5. Another Chain of Title Form

Current Owner(s):	Ronald and Martha Brown
Grantor Name(s):	John Doe and wife, Mary Doe
Grantee Name(s):	Ronald and Martha Brown
Date of Transaction:	January 4, 2002
Date Recorded:	January 5, 2002
Deed book Reference	v. 100/ p. 73–75
Brief description of the property:	1.2 acres, Stanley Estates Subdivision
Prior Transaction:	
Grantor Name(s):	Herman Munster and wife, Lilly Munster
Grantee Name(s):	John Doe and wife, Mary Doe
Date of Transaction:	March 12, 1996
Date Recorded:	March 14, 1996
Deed book Reference	v. 92/ p. 115
Brief description of the property:	1.2 acres, Stanley Estates Subdivision
Prior Transaction:	
Grantor Name(s):	Anthony Baretta (single)
Grantee Name(s):	Herman Munster and wife, Lilly Munster
Date of Transaction:	May 2, 1985
Date Recorded:	May 4, 1985
Deed book Reference	v. 76/ p. 122
Brief description of the property:	1.2 acres, Stanley Estates Subdivision
Prior Transaction:	
Grantor Name(s):	Joe and Tina Baker
Grantee Name(s):	Anthony Baretta (single)
Date of Transaction:	October 13, 1981
Date Recorded:	October 13, 1981
Deed book Reference	v. 63/ p. 2
Brief description of the property:	1.2 acres, Stanley Estates Subdivision

---

B. Step 2: Establishing the Out Conveyances

Once the chain of time has been established, the next step in the title search is to review the out conveyances, sometimes referred to as the "outs." This is a search of the records to see what actions were taken by the individual owners during the time that they

Figure 11-6. A Sample Chain of Title

Property:	326 Smith Road, North Wearyboro, NC
Current Owner:	Jeffrey G. Parrot
Date of Purchase:	10-28-97
Deed Book Reference:	794/374
Purchased From:	Romulus J. Edison & Brenda Edison
Date of Purchase:	5-14-96
Deed Book Reference:	759/183
Purchased From:	Alan S. Derry & wife, Marla F. Derry
Date of Purchase:	6-17-94
Deed Book Reference:	732/032
Purchased From:	Terry Michael Johnson
Date of Purchase:	2-2-90
Deed Book Reference:	677/464
Purchased From:	Kathy M. & Larry Underwood
Date of Purchase:	6-7-85
Deed Book Reference:	632/891
Purchased From:	Ray Vaughn Combs & Anne P. Combs
Date of Purchase:	4-23-85
Deed Book Reference:	631/359
Purchased From:	Roger Dale Normal, Julia Parks Normal, Ruby Parks Kermit, Kermit Kermit
Date of Purchase:	9-10-82
Deed Book Reference:	607/429
Purchased From:	Julius Parks, Virginia Parks, Jack Parks, Barbara Parks Sparks
Date of Purchase:	7-18-68
Deed Book Reference:	487/499

owned the property and to determine if any of these actions have an affect on the property's legal status today. A previous owner may have agreed to an easement across the property and now the new owner will be bound by that prior agreement. A previous owner may have failed to pay real estate taxes or incurred some special assessment, or done any of a hundred things that could put the new owner into trouble.

The Grantor Index lists any type of interest that is transferred away from the grantor, whether it is done voluntarily or involuntarily. Examples of voluntary transfers include the grantor's conveyance of part of the interest in his property to someone else, such as a new spouse. Examples of involuntary transfers include liens, judgments and special assessments. Because all of these actions must be recorded in order to be effective, the title searcher can feel confident that the Grantor Index will show entries for such actions.

When a title examiner finds any listing in the Grantor Index, the best practice is to look up the actual document and to review its provisions to make sure that it has no legal impact on the property. It is very common to find owners' names listed in the Grantor Index, especially if they are in the habit of buying and selling real estate. For instance, there should be at least one entry in the Grantor Index for every owner who financed his purchase. The Grantor Index should show a deed of trust recorded to finance the purchase. (It should also show that the deed of trust was later cancelled as part of the previous sale). We will discuss title search implications of deeds of trust later in this chapter.

1. Reviewing Title Documents

Each document that contains an owner's name should be reviewed to ensure that the listing does not involve the property for which the title examiner is searching or, if it does, that it causes no legal problems for the current title. Any questionable document should be copied and discussed with the real estate attorney in order to determine its legal significance.

Among the items that a title searcher will look for in the Grantor Index are:

- Deeds of trust
- Assignments
- Easements for utility companies
- Rights of way
- Restrictive covenants
- Leases
- Water rights declarations
- Subordination agreements

a. Deed of Trust Issues in Title Searches

One of the most important items to track down is the deed of trust that financed each of the purchases. A title searcher must be able not only to locate a copy of the deed of trust, but also to prove that each deed of trust was paid in full. In some cases, the deed of trust may actually be stamped "Satisfied," while in other situations a separate document will be filed indicating that the deed of trust was paid in full. In every situation, the title searcher must show that the deed of trust for prior transactions was cancelled or satisfied. Any outstanding deeds of trust should be noted prominently on the title search forms.

b. Liens

One important aspect that a title searcher must always be aware of concerns liens. Although we will discuss liens in Chapter 13, a word about them here is also required. A lien is an encumbrance that is filed on property in order to satisfy an outstanding judgment or debt. When a lien is outstanding, it essentially prevents any closing until the lien is satisfied. For instance, when a taxpayer fails to pay her taxes, the Internal Revenue Service has the right to file a federal tax lien against the property. When this occurs, this lien automatically takes priority over any others and must be paid off before the transaction can be concluded.

Any liens located in checking the out conveyances should be noted prominently on the title search forms and brought to the real estate attorney's attention immediately.

Figure 11-8. A Different "Out Conveyance" Form

Name of Owner(s): Timothy Cranmer and Louise Cranmer
Period checked
From: 9/14/01 To: 2/20/04

Entries in Grantor Index:

Deed Book Ref:	Description	Relate to Title Search property? Y/N?
2585/618	Rec. 9/14/01 Deed of Trust to Cling Savings Bank Amount: $116,000	Y
2585/627	Rec 9/14/01 Deed of Trust to Bruce Leopold and wife Marsha Leopold Amount: $18,600	Y
2585/630	Assignment of DOT(1258) recorded 9/14/01 Assigned from Cling Savings Bank to Moonbeam Mortgage Inc.	Y

Figure 11-7. Sample Out Conveyances

<u>Out Conveyances</u>

Current Owner:
<u>Jeffrey G. Parrot</u>
Period Checked: 10-28-97 to present
a. Out Conveyances: None
b. Lawsuits: None
c. Taxes paid: Yes; 2002—$199.92; Current
d. UCC listings: Yes; for J.G. Parrot Trucking, business; dollar amount not listed

Previous Owner:
<u>Romulus J. Edison</u>
Period checked: 6-17-94 through 5-14-96
a. Out Conveyances: None
b. Lawsuits: None
c. Taxes Paid: Yes; 1997—$125.30
d. UCC listings: None

Previous Owner:
<u>Alan S. Derry</u>
2-2-90 through 6-17-94
a. Out Conveyances: None
b. Lawsuits: Yes; 4-17-01, Equity One $3062.89
                        2-02-01, Weary Regional Medical Center $1188.25
                        *Lawsuits still open
c. Taxes Paid: Yes; 1996—$55.41
d. UCC listings: None

2. UCC Listings

The Uniform Commercial Code listings are required whenever a borrower gives personal property as collateral for a loan. The most common example would be a car loan. In a typical car loan scenario, a borrower finances the purchase of the car through a lender who keeps possession of the car title until the borrower has made his final payment. Such transactions must be recorded in the UCC listings in order for the lender to perfect its interest in the collateral (and to repossess it if the borrower fails to make payments). Although these listings are primarily for personal property, it is important for title searchers to review them for situations in which personal property has been converted to real property. An example of this situation would be the financing of a new garage door. A garage door, sitting on a store shelf, is clearly personal property. However, purchase and installation can be quite expensive, and it is common for companies that install garage doors to finance them. When the garage door is installed, it becomes a permanent part of the real estate. Its classification changes from personal property to real property. In this situation, a default on the garage door loan could have consequences for the real property. As a result, title examiners always review the Uniform Commercial Code listings. These listings only remain operative for five years before they must be renewed. Therefore, the title searcher is only required to search these records for a five-year period.

3. Index of Vital Statistics (Birth and Death Records)

The Index of Vital Statistics can provide information not only about marriages and deaths, but also provide a good picture of the family relationships. This can be very important when trying to determine whether or not a man is a "junior" or a "senior." Men have a tendency to drop the "junior" designation after their names upon the deaths of their fathers. This can cause a great deal of confusion in the records that can be cleared up by reference to birth certificates.

C. Step 3: Checking for Judgments

Establishing out conveyances not only involves the Deed Room, but also other government records. A title searcher will spend a great deal of time in the Clerk of Courts office in order to make sure that there are no pending civil actions, or judgments that have been assessed against the owners or the property.

1. The Clerk of Courts Office

Title searchers go the Clerk of Court's office to look for any liens, judgments, delinquencies, assessments, foreclosures, bankruptcies and any and all domestic or civil actions. Any of these actions could have a potential impact on the property. This information is provided in the Index to Judgments, Liens and Lis Pendens, as well as the Index of Special Proceedings, the Index to Beneficiaries and other sources.

Title examiners go to the Clerk's office primarily to locate civil judgments that have a direct impact on the property, as well as any probate matters, foreclosure actions, or divorce actions that could also have consequences for a future buyer. Most of the judgments filed in the Clerk of Court's office have a 10-year lifespan. As a result, a civil judgment must be renewed every 10 years to be legally effective, and if it isn't, it cannot be enforced. Because of this, the title examiner is only required to search back for 10 years in these records. Like the Deed Office, most Clerks' offices are computerized, making a search of the available records far more efficient, but also raising the same potential problems we outlined when discussing computer real estate records.

a. The Index to Special Proceedings

The Index to Special Proceedings is the index where all court records relating to divorce, competency and foreclosure actions are stored. A title searcher must consult both this index and the Index to Judgments, Liens and Lis Pendens in order to thoroughly check all records. In most counties, both indexes are listed in the computer databases, making the search process go much more quickly and efficiently.

A title searcher should also check for any special assessments on the property, which would include state, county and city taxes and assessments. This information is found in the Clerk of Court's office, and may also be located in the Tax office.

D. Step 4: Putting All the Information Together

The end result of a title search is to gather all of the information that the title searcher has located and present it to the real estate attorney. The information must be complete and provide answers to obvious questions. If there are taxes outstanding for the year, how much are they? Have all deeds of trust been cancelled? If so, where is the proof? A title searcher must always have a hard-boiled, practical approach to the job: What are the problems? Where is the proof that they have been resolved? When in doubt, the safest course is to assume that an entry is a problem until it can be shown otherwise.

Throughout this chapter, you will find various types of title search forms and abstracts. Different firms use different forms and if you go to work as a title searcher, your firm will use its own forms. The important aspect of a title search is not what form you use, but how thorough you are in your research.

Title searchers must often multi-task, searching the public records while also arranging for an appraisal of the property, a survey of the land and inspections. Title searchers must be efficient in the way that they allocate their time.

1. Preparing Abstract Title Forms

When a title searcher has more than one pending title exam, he or she will often prioritize the title searching time by doing all of the research work on a county-by-county basis. For instance, if the title searcher has three title searches pending in Wilkes County and two in Burke County, the title searcher might take care of all three Wilkes' County searches on one day before proceeding to the next county.

Like any skill, the more practice you have doing title searches, the better you will get at performing them.

Figure 11-9. Chain of Title: Burke Property

From 1979–2004
Property Address: 133 Robinhood Ave, Asheville, NC 28655
See Notes regarding address and name discrepancies

Date of Search: June 12, 2004 **Name of Title Examiner:** Paula Paralegal

Grantee: William R. Burke and wife, Deborah L. Burke
Grantor: Alyson Perkins Johnson
133 Robinhood Ave, Asheville, NC
Date Recorded: 4/28/97
Deed Book Reference: 1961/37

––––––

Previous Grantee: Alyson Perkins Johnson
Grantor: Clawston E. Reid and Dorothy J. Reid, husband and wife
133 Robinwood Ave
Date Recorded: 7/08/96
Deed Book Reference: 1914/292

––––––

Previous Grantee: Clawston E. Reid & Dorothy L. Reid,
Grantor: Charles Bailey & wife, husband & wife Alice N. Bailey
133 Robinhood Ave
Date Recorded: 8/09/61
Deed Book Reference: 848/484

––––––

NOTES: the current deed is listed as **Robinhood Avenue.** The previous deed lists the address as **Robinwood** and the Deed for Reid lists it as **Robinhood.** The plat shows the street as **Robinwood.** NAME-Db 1914/292 lists a grantor as **Dorothy J. Reid** while Db 848/484 lists her as **Dorothy L. Reid.**

E. Step 5: The Preliminary and Final Title Certificates

The purpose of all title search investigations is to produce a legal opinion about the current status of the property. The lender, title insurance company and borrower all want to know that there are no problems that could affect the closing and transfer of title. In North Carolina, real estate attorneys offer their legal opinions through Preliminary and Final Title Opinions. Most practitioners use the Preliminary and Final Opinion on Title approved by the North Carolina Bar Association. These forms offer the attorney's preliminary review of the legal status of the property (and any actions taken to clear up outstanding issues) and a final title opinion that details the exact nature of the interest conveyed—and a final report on any actions taken to clear up potential legal problems.

It is the attorney's preliminary and final title opinions that open the attorney up to a claim of legal malpractice when this research is not complete. Consider this chapter's "Relevant case" for an example of a legal malpractice case arising directly from an error in a title examination.

III. Legal Malpractice Issues in Title Searches

When an attorney offers a Final Opinion on Title, the attorney is certifying that there are no title problems with the property, other than those detailed in his or her letter. If the opinion is wrong because the legal team has missed an important entry, or failed to notice an outstanding legal claim against the property, the borrower, lender and title insurance company may all have causes of action against the attorney for legal malpractice.

There are also some practices used by legal professionals that may put the attorney in danger of a legal malpractice action, including "tacking."

A. Tacking

Tacking refers to the process of relying on a previous title search and simply conducting a review of the public records since the last title search was conducted. For instance, if the title search was conducted in 1999 and the property is now up for sale again, the title examiner might simply examine the last few years' of public records, assuming that the title search done in 1999 was sufficient to catch any errors or problems that occurred prior to that time. Although tacking is a common practice, there are many legal professionals who question the ethics of the practice, especially when it is based on the assumption that the previous title examination was sufficient. In many cases, a title examiner will request permission from the lender or the title insurance company before engaging in the practice.

Tacking is often used as a short cut in completing a title search. When there is a preexisting title insurance policy, and the property is being re-financed, a title insurance company might not wish to have a complete title search done. Instead, the title insurance company might simply authorize a check of the records from the date of the last title search. This is usually referred to as "bringing the title forward."

B. The Paralegal's Role in Title Searches

Although some attorneys believe that having paralegals carry out title examinations is an ethical issue, the vast majority of real estate attorneys in North Carolina use paralegals to carry out the routine tasks of searching the real estate records. Paralegals conduct title searches every day in this state and their role in the process will only grow in the next few years. The North Carolina Bar Association has issued some ethical opinions on the topic of paralegals and real estate practices. The Bar has specifically addressed the issue of attorneys engaging in the practice of "rubber stamping," where an attorney simply signs off a paralegal's title search without actually reviewing the materials. This practice is considered unethical.

In the next chapter we will also encounter other ethical dilemmas concerning paralegals and real estate closings.

IV. Common Problems in Title Searches

In this final section of the chapter, we will detail some of the most common problems encountered by title searchers, and suggest some methods to deal with them.

A. Sub-Divided Properties

One common problem in searching real estate records occurs when a large tract of land has been subdivided into many smaller tracts. Sometimes, a contractor or real estate development company will purchase large tracts of land and then subdivide them into neighborhoods. In this situation, it can be very difficult to sift through all of the previous transactions involving the real estate developing company to find the specific one that the title searcher is looking for. This is when reading the deed can pay huge dividends. Many deeds have a section detailing the previous transactions in the chain, including deed book reference. This can save an enormous amount of time, especially when dealing with a huge volume of transactions.

B. "Missing" Transactions

Here is another common problem: you have a deed showing that Mr. Smith acquired the property from Joan Brown. But when you look up Joan Brown's name in the Grantee Index (showing when and from whom she bought the property), you don't find anything. As far as the Grantee index is concerned, Joan Brown doesn't exist. Without being able to find that previous deed, you can't continue on with your search. Why has this happened? There are a couple of possibilities:

Joan has changed her name. If Joan bought the property under the name of Joan Able (her maiden name) but then sold the property under the name Joan Brown (married name), there won't be any entry in the Grantee Index for Joan Brown. (She wasn't called that when she bought the property). How do you deal with this problem? Fortunately enough, it's not that hard. Take a look at the marriage certificates under Joan Brown. You'll probably find an entry showing that an unmarried lady named Joan Able got married to a man named Bobby Brown and now she is known as Joan Brown. In more modern deeds, this specific problem is often addressed by the attorney, who spells out exactly what happened. This is another example where reading the deed closely can solve many potential problems.

The other possibility here is that the deed was filed correctly, but indexed incorrectly. In this situation, you should look up Joan's deed using variations on the spelling of her name.

V. Payment for Title Searches

Finally, there is the issue of payment. Attorneys who routinely handle title searches usually represent the buyer in a transaction. As a result, they are normally paid at the closing, when all of the other proceeds are disbursed. Most attorneys are paid a percentage of the closing price for conducting the title search. This fee is often one half of 1% of the total purchase price.

Relevant Case

Title Ins. Co. of Minnesota v. Smith, Debnam, Hibbert and Pahl[1]

LEWIS, Judge.

This appeal arises out of plaintiff's action for legal malpractice. The jury returned a verdict of $60,000 for plaintiff. The trial court then entered judgment notwithstanding the verdict in the amount of $171,860.35 for plaintiff. From the judgment, defendants appeal.

On 5 October 1988 plaintiff issued a title insurance policy, effective as of 17 August 1988, to First Federal Savings and Loan Association of Raleigh (hereinafter "First Federal"). The policy insured that a First Federal deed of trust, dated 17 August 1988 and securing a loan to Regency Residential, Inc. (hereinafter "Regency"), was a first lien on four tracts of land on Millbrook Road in Raleigh. Plaintiff issued the title insurance policy based on defendant Debnam's certifying that all of the requirements in plaintiff's commitment for title insurance had been met. The requirements included the cancellation of all superior deeds of trust on the property. In fact, two superior deeds of trust, one to Fred and Carolyn Deer (hereinafter "the Deers") and one to First Wachovia Mortgage Company (hereinafter "Wachovia"), were not cancelled. Thus, as to the portion of the property covered by the Deer and Wachovia deeds of trust, First Federal's lien was not superior.

The property described in the Deer and Wachovia deeds of trust was previously owned by the Deers and was sold by them to Regency. At the time of the sale, there was a deed of trust on the property to Wachovia. The Deers agreed to finance the sale and take as security for the debt a deed of trust on the property. The note to the Deers was referred to at trial as a "wraparound loan." That is, it included within its total the balance owed on the Wachovia note.

In December 1990, First Federal was taken over by the Resolution Trust Corporation (hereinafter "RTC") pursuant to a purchase and assumption agreement. In response to a claim on the title insurance policy by First Federal, plaintiff paid, in April 1991, $164,109.96 to the Deers and $7,341.79 to Wachovia. The Wachovia deed of trust was then cancelled. The Deers assigned their rights under their deed of trust to plaintiff, and the Deer deed of trust was not cancelled. Plaintiff instituted this action against defendants for Debnam's negligent certification of title and sought as part of this action a judicial determination that it was, in fact, liable to its insured under the policy. After the close of evidence, the court so ruled, and while the jury was in deliberation, plaintiff cancelled the Deer deed of trust. The jury returned a verdict for plaintiff in the amount of $60,000. The trial court then granted judgment notwithstanding the verdict for plaintiff in the amount of $171,860.35.

Defendants' first contention on appeal is that plaintiff had no damages at the time it filed suit, and therefore its claim was not actionable. Defendants point to the fact that plaintiff received an assignment of rights under the Deer deed of trust in exchange for the payment made to the Deers. Thus, until the Deer deed of trust was cancelled, plaintiff had

---

1. 119 N.C.App. 608, 459 S.E.2d 801 (1995).

suffered no damages. Defendants moved for a directed verdict based on this argument, and the court denied the motion. We agree that plaintiff suffered no actual damages until it cancelled the deed of trust, which it did while the jury deliberated. However, we do not agree that defendants were entitled to a directed verdict.

In North Carolina, a plaintiff may recover nominal damages in a negligence action. The Asheville School v. D.V. Ward Constr., Inc., 78 N.C.App. 594, 599, 337 S.E.2d 659, 662 (1985), disc. review denied, 316 N.C. 385, 342 S.E.2d 890 (1986). Nominal damages are recoverable where some legal right has been invaded but no actual loss or substantial injury has been sustained. Potts v. Howser, 274 N.C. 49, 61, 161 S.E.2d 737, 747 (1968). Nominal damages are awarded in recognition of the right and of the technical injury resulting from its violation. Id. The idea of the redress of grievances in court by an orderly process has been favored in our law from the beginning. Especially in a case involving the negligence of a professional person, the redress of the wrong may be no more than the showing, in court, that the attorney did not do his job. Even where the plaintiff has no evidence of actual damages, if he is entitled to nominal damages, it is error to grant a directed verdict for the defendant on the basis of the plaintiff's lack of damages. See Robbins v. C.W. Myers Trading Post, Inc., 251 N.C. 663, 666, 111 S.E.2d 884, 886–87 (1960) (holding denial of nonsuit proper even though plaintiff in breach of contract action had produced no competent evidence of damages, since plaintiff was entitled to nominal damages for breach of contract). Further, proof of actual damage may extend to facts that occur and grow out of the injury, even up to the day of the verdict. Jewell v. Price, 264 N.C. 459, 461–62, 142 S.E.2d 1, 3 (1965).

In this case, we believe that the evidence before the court at the time of defendants' motion for directed verdict entitled plaintiff to nominal damages. Plaintiff's legal right to a correct certification of title (see section II.) was denied by Debnam's negligence. The resulting technical injury to plaintiff's rights entitled plaintiff to nominal damages. Thus, the trial court properly denied defendants' motion for directed verdict.

Defendants' next contention is that they cannot be held liable to plaintiff because Debnam, who was Regency's attorney, had no duty to plaintiff regarding the certification of title. Defendants argue that the trial court therefore erred in not granting their motion for directed verdict on this ground. Defendants cite Chicago Title Insurance Co. v. Holt, 36 N.C.App. 284, 244 S.E.2d 177 (1978), in support of their position. That case held that claims for attorney malpractice "may properly be brought only by those who are in privity of contract with such attorneys by virtue of a contract providing for their employment." Id. at 288, 244 S.E.2d at 180. In Chicago Title, a non-client general contractor sued an attorney for the attorney's alleged negligent certification of title. This Court upheld the dismissal of the plaintiff's complaint on the ground that the plaintiff was not in privity of contract with the attorney.

However, in United Leasing Corp. v. Miller, 45 N.C.App. 400, 406, 263 S.E.2d 313, 317, disc. review denied, 300 N.C. 374, 267 S.E.2d 685 (1980), this Court stated:

> In the line of cases since our decision in [Chicago Title], we have re-examined the rule prohibiting recovery in tort by a third person not in privity of contract with a professional person for negligence in the performance of his employment contract with his client, even though such negligence was the proximate cause of a foreseeable injury to the third person.

In Miller, this Court held that a non-client could sue an attorney for negligently certifying title to property. In the case at hand, there is substantial evidence in the record that Debnam furnished the title certificate to plaintiff, a non-client, for the purpose of inducing plaintiff to issue a title policy for the benefit of his client and that it was foreseeable that plaintiff would be harmed by any failure to accurately certify the title. See id. at 406–08, 263 S.E.2d at 318 (discussing the factors to be considered in determining whether there is a duty to a non-client). We therefore conclude that Debnam had a duty to plaintiff and that denial of directed verdict for defendants on this basis was correct.

For the reasons stated, the judgment is reversed as to the award of damages and the case is remanded for a new trial on the issue of damages alone. In light of our holding, we will not address defendants' remaining argument concerning damages, as the alleged error may not recur at retrial.

Affirmed in part, reversed in part, and remanded for new trial on damages.

Chapter Summary

Title examinations are required in nearly every real property transaction in the state. The purpose of a title examination is to ensure that the title to a particular parcel is marketable, as that term is defined under the North Carolina law. A title search involves a review of the public records in order to ensure that there are no adverse claims or outstanding interests on the property that might affect the purchaser's legal rights. A title search begins when the office is contacted by a purchaser, title insurance company or lender and requested to examine a title for a particular piece of property. The title examiner begins by establishing the chain of title, which consists of a list of the owners of the property going back for a specified time period, usually 30 or 40 years. Once the chain of title has been established, the title searcher checks the out conveyances by examining the actions of each owner during the time that he or she owned the property in order to discover any actions by or against an owner that might affect future interest in the property. Typical examples of items that a title searcher would look for include unsatisfied deeds of trust, liens, conveyances by an owner to a third-party and any transaction that could affect the current purchaser's interest in the property, including civil judgments on the property. Once the chain of title and the out conveyances have been established, the next step is to review documents in the Clerk of Courts office for any civil judgments or other actions against an owner of the property during the time that he possessed it. Finally, the title searcher will also review probate materials in order to determine whether or not a portion of the property has been conveyed to another person by will or intestate proceeding.

The end result of a title search is a certification by an attorney who offers a legal opinion about the marketability of the title. The lawyer's opinion that the property is marketable allows the real estate transaction to proceed, but it also opens up the attorney to a claim of legal malpractice if the title search fails to locate important documents in the public record. Paralegals play a large role in title searches, not only because they carry out much of the work of the title search, but also because they work under the direct supervision of an attorney who must offer a legal opinion on the title based on the paralegal's work.

Review Questions

1. Why is a title search necessary?

2. How does a title search normally begin?

3. How does a title examiner establish the chain of title?

4. How long a period is usually involved in a title search?

5. What is the significance of the North Carolina Marketable Title Act?

6. What are out conveyances or "outs?"

7. What is the purpose of a preliminary title opinion?

8. What are some ways that an attorney can commit legal malpractice in title examinations?

9. How far back in the public records must a normal title search go?

10. Maria is working on a title search in which a single woman owned the property for a period of time. Unfortunately, she cannot locate the conveyances showing where this woman acquired the property. What is the likely cause of this apparent hole in the records?

11. What is "tacking" as that term is applied to title searches?

12. Why is it important to determine whether or not a previous deed of trust has been canceled?

13. How can title searchers use the Grantor and Grantee Indexes to double-check their own work?

14. Why is it only necessary to check for civil judgments for a 10-year period?

15. What types of information can be learned about property in the tax office?

16. What are the Uniform Commercial Code listings and why must they be checked by a title searcher?

17. Why would a title searcher refer to the Index of Vital Statistics?

18. What are some examples of out conveyances that could affect interest or title to property?

19. What does it mean when an attorney is on an "approved list" with a title insurance company or lender?

20. What is the significance of this chapter's "relevant case" as it relates to title searches?

Assignment

Using the forms provided in the figures throughout this chapter, prepare a complete title search on a piece of property, beginning with a chain of title going back for 40 years, out conveyances for each owner in the chain, Uniform Commercial Code listings back for five years, all civil judgments back for 10 years.

Terms and Phrases

Title Search	Liens
Out Conveyances	UCC Listings
Tax ID Number	Index of Vital Statistics
Deed book reference	Index to Judgments, Liens and Lis Pendens
North Carolina Marketable Title Act	Index of Special Proceedings
Title Search Banks	Preliminary Title Opinion
Chain of Title	Final Title Opinion
Grantor/Grantee Index	Tacking

Chapter 12

The Closing

Chapter Objectives

At the conclusion of this chapter, you should be able to:
- Explain the legal significance of a real estate closing
- List and explain the various participants and their function at the closing
- Detail the basic steps involved in a closing procedure
- Explain "escrow" closings
- Explain the disbursement procedure at a closing

I. Introduction to Loan Closings

Because interest rates in recent years have been at all-time lows, real estate closings have been at an all-time high. This has put a great deal of pressure on real estate professionals to streamline the closing process, to make it more efficient, while still meeting the clients' needs and providing quality service.

A. Loan Closings Require Close Attention to Detail

Nowhere in real estate is attention to detail more important than during the closing. Closings can be both complicated and time-consuming while at the same time facing scheduling deadlines. Mistakes are easy and the consequences can be disastrous. In most law offices, the legal assistant does most of the work setting up the closing, usually under the supervision of the real estate attorney.

II. Preparing for the Closing

In order to prepare for the financing, the borrowers must first contact a mortgage lender and arrange for financing to purchase the real estate. While they are arranging a mortgage, the borrowers must also retain an attorney to represent them in the closing itself. The legal team will then be responsible for gathering all of the information necessary to successfully complete the closing process.

A. Financing

Obviously, before the closing can proceed, the client-buyer must arrange for financing. Usually, the offer to purchase and contract has an express clause that requires a loan commitment from the lender within 10 days of the contract date. Without this financing, there can be no closing because the funds used and dispersed at the closing come from the lender.

B. Contacting the Attorney

The first step in a closing occurs when the clients hire a law firm to handle it for them. Like any legal representation, the clients retain the attorney to represent them in a legal action and will pay for this service. In this scenario, the attorney represents the buyer. Later, we will investigate dual representation issues that arise when the attorney handles the closing for both the buyer and the seller.

C. Setting a Closing Date

Setting the closing date is not a simple matter. Usually the legal assistant in charge of setting the closing date and time must coordinate this meeting with the various attorneys, clients, the lender and the real estate agents.

1. The Fine Art of Scheduling Closings

Scheduling a closing can be one of the most challenging parts of real estate title work. Some professionals believe that the only thing more challenging than scheduling the closing is actually conducting it. Scheduling must take into account the needs of several different parties, including the client, the closing attorney, the real estate agents, and the lender. It is of no help to anyone to schedule a closing too soon, because the lender will not have had time to prepare its loan package and the real estate team will not have had time to conduct a title examination. On the other hand, waiting too long to set the closing can cause a whole host of other problems. The parties may become disgruntled at having to wait so long, and if the contract contains a "time is of the essence" clause, waiting beyond the specified date can result in a void agreement.

D. Gathering Information Necessary to Complete the Closing

The first and most important job in organizing a closing is gathering information. Many attorneys use an intake form in order to make sure that they obtain as much information as possible. When real estate agents and lenders are familiar with the law firm's form, they can anticipate the questions asked and also help improve the overall efficiency of the process. These days, it is always important to obtain e-mail addresses in addition to street addresses and telephone numbers of the people involved. Many of the transactions that were formally handled by couriers and faxes are now done by e-mail. In order to successfully complete the closing, it is necessary for the real estate paralegal or the attorney to gather information from a wide variety of sources. The typical information needed to complete the closing includes:

1. Loan Payoff Amounts

2. Title Search

3. Tax Information

4. Legal Description of Property

5. Termite Inspection Report

1. Loan Payoff Amounts

Prior to the closing, is absolutely essential that the legal team discover the total payoff amount for any outstanding mortgages or other fees, including late fees, and make sure that the payoff amounts are current as of the date and time of the closing.

a. The Seller's Attorney

The seller should provide complete information about outstanding mortgages, including the lender's name, address, account numbers and estimated payoff amounts. The legal team will pin down the actual payoff amounts, but it is always helpful to have a baseline to compare estimated payoffs with actual payoffs. When the seller's estimate is wildly divergent from the actual estimate, this can be a tip-off that there may be more than one mortgage on the property. One way of determining payoff amounts is by creating a standardized form that is sent to all lenders requesting this information. This letter may be followed up with a phone call shortly before the closing to determine the most up-to-the-minute payoff amount.

2. The Title Search

The title search must also be completed prior to closing. For a complete summary of title searches, see Chapter 11.

a. Encroachments

When a neighbor has built a structure or a fence over the seller's property boundary line, this is an **encroachment**. A property that has an encroachment has a title defect that must be remedied before the closing can occur. In some cases, the seller may request that the neighbor remove the offending structure or the seller may be required to institute legal action against the neighbor to force the removal of the fence or structure that is encroaching on the boundary line. The law on encroachments is similar to the law of adverse possession. As we saw with adverse possession, when a party holds title against the interests of the owner for a specified period of time, the party may actually acquire title. Similarly, a neighbor who encroaches on the boundary line of another for a specified period of time may petition the court to readjust the boundary lines to reflect the change. A proper title search and survey will usually discover any encroachments.

Encroachment: A structure that crosses another property owners' boundary line.

b. Repairing Title Defects

When a title search has discovered potential title defects, such as encroachments, liens on the property, or any other issue that clouds title, it is up to the seller and the seller's attorney to make all efforts to clear up these title defects prior to the closing. One of the conditions that the buyer included in the Offer to Purchase and Contract was a provision requiring free and clear title to the property prior to closing. If that condition is not met, the transaction may be void.

c. The Preliminary Opinion on Title

As we saw in the previous chapter, the preliminary opinion on title is the attorney's legal opinion whether the title is free and clear of legal encumbrances, including easements, liens, rights-of-way, restrictive covenants, special assessments or any other action that could have a potential legal impact on the property. The preliminary title opinion goes to the lender and is the basis of the lender's decision to continue with the financial arrangements and the closing.

The preliminary title opinion will also go to the title insurance company. Based on this opinion, the title insurance company will issue a binder that covers the real estate title. We will discuss title insurance in greater detail later in this chapter.

3. Tax Information

Before the closing can occur, the legal team must know whether or not the current tax assessment on the property has been paid. If it has not, the seller must bring the taxes current before the transaction can proceed. The title searcher will discover this information during the title examination.

4. The Legal Description

It usually falls to the legal assistant or paralegal to create a legal description of the property that will be inserted in the deed that is delivered during the closing. The legal description usually comes from prior deeds or recent surveys. In most situations, it will be a metes and bounds description as outlined in chapter 7.

5. Termite and Other Inspections

There are several different types of inspections that must occur prior to the actual closing. One of the conditions in the Offer to Purchase Contract was a buyer's inspection of the property shortly before the closing. The purpose of this inspection is to make sure that there are no last minute issues that should be addressed before the closing can proceed. The buyer will also arrange for a termite pest inspection.

A termite inspection is a requirement for a closing and must be carried out by a certified professional. This inspector will examine the entire physical structure of the house, searching for any type of wood boring insect. The inspector's final certification that the house is free of termites or other infestations is one of the documents that is required in order to conclude the closing.

Figure 12-1. Information Needed for Closing

❑ Loan Payoff Amounts
❑ Property survey
❑ Tax Information
❑ Termite inspection and report
❑ House inspection
❑ Buyer's inspection, shortly before the actual closing
❑ Last-minute title search
❑ Title insurance Binder
❑ Clearing up any title problems
❑ Applying for and receiving a Binder for property insurance
❑ Sewage certification or percolation test for unimproved property

---

E. Loan Closing Software

Although loan closings were always completed by hand, including all of the financial calculations, modern real estate practice uses software. Closing software was developed with the needs of the legal team in mind. By entering data into the software program, such as purchase price, real estate agent's commission, tax information and other information, the software can calculate many of the amounts needed to create the disbursement checks as well as prepare the settlement closing statement. Such software can be an enormous timesaver over the old-fashioned method of preparing all of the settlement documents by hand. Examples of loan closing software include "Display Soft" and "Soft Pro."

III. The Closing Procedure

Immediately before the closing, the real estate paralegal is usually responsible for putting all the documents together to ensure that the closing proceeds smoothly. During the closing, the attorney will meet with the parties, explain the purpose of the various documents and make sure that they are all signed and forwarded back to the proper parties. When the clients sign the documents, they are immediately notarized. This is one of the many times where having a legal assistant who is also a Notary Public can be extremely useful.

A. Preparing the Loan Package

Several days prior to the actual closing, the lender should send the legal team a loan package that includes all the documents that must be completed during the closing. Many lenders have specific instructions and requirements for the way that their loan documents must be prepared and finalized. Unfortunately, some lenders wait until the last minute, sometimes the actual day of the closing, before they send the loan package to the real estate paralegal.

Sidebar: It is usually the paralegal's role to ensure that all loan package forms are filled out correctly.

B. Verifying Hazard Insurance

The legal team must also verify that hazard insurance is in place for the property prior to closing. Hazard insurance (or homeowner's insurance) is a requirement imposed by the lender to protect its financial interest in the real estate.

C. Documents Required at the Closing

The attorney is also responsible for generating several documents that are used at the closing. These include:

1. The General warranty deed
2. Deed of trust
3. Subordination agreements (if needed)
4. Lien waiver affidavits (if required)
5. IRS Forms
6. HUD-1 Settlement Closing Form
7. Bill of sale for any personal property
8. Compliance Agreement
9. Credit Insurance Documents
10. Loan Application
11. US Patriot Act Requirements
12. PMI Disclosures
13. Trust disbursement records
14. Truth In Lending Documentation
15. Termite Inspection Letter
16. Survey

1. The General Warranty Deed

It is the sellers' responsibility to hire an attorney to prepare the deed that conveys their interest to the buyers. In many situations, the sellers may retain the buyer's attorney to carry out this function. There are some important ethical concerns that arise in this arrangement that we will discuss in the last part of the chapter when we address the issue of dual representation.

a. Preparing the Deed

The closing attorney may prepare the deed or it may be prepared by the seller's attorney. In either situation, the deed must be prepared prior to closing and must meet all the legal requirements we have discussed in previous chapters.

2. Deed of Trust

As we have already seen, the deed of trust is the financing document that sets out the arrangement between the buyer and the lender and that finalizes the lender's right to foreclose on the property in the event of the borrower's default. An important feature of the deed of trust is the promissory note that creates the legal obligation on the part of the borrower to repay the loan.

a. Promissory Note

The promissory note shows the terms of the loan, including the total loan amount, interest payment, annual percentage rate, loan dates, dates when payments are due, and the lender's address.

3. Subordination Agreements

Subordination agreements are required in situations where there is more than one deed of trust on the property and there is an issue about priority. When an owner "gives back" a mortgage on the property, this mortgage automatically takes priority over any others. The lending institution may require a subordination agreement in order to place its loan at a higher priority than the owner-financed mortgage.

4. Lien Waiver Affidavits

This is an affidavit often required by title insurance companies showing that there have been no liens or other encumbrances filed on the property prior to the closing and that no one who has provided materials or services to the property is legally entitled to file a lien on the property. The essence of a lien waiver affidavit is that the seller knows of no judgments, encumbrances, liens or other pending matters that could act as a bar to the transaction being completed. Lien waiver affidavits are often attached to the Final Opinion on Title submitted by the attorney to the title insurance company.

5. IRS Forms

There are various Internal Revenue Service forms that may be required as part of the closing. One of the most important of these is form 1099. This is a form that has been required by the IRS since 1987 and it shows the total proceeds received by the seller at the conclusion of the closing. This document is important because it shows any profit that the seller has taken from the sale.

a. IRS Form 4506

In addition to form 1099, other IRS forms may also be required. Another common form used is form 4506.This form allows the lender to request a copy of the borrower's income tax from the Internal Revenue Service.

b. W-9 Form

This form verifies the borrower's Social Security number.

6. HUD-1 Settlement Closing Form

Almost all lenders and attorneys use the Housing and Urban Development Administration's form for the settlement closing statement. Most closing software programs have this form available as part of their menus. In some cases, the lender may require the real estate paralegal to fax a copy of the proposed settlement statement to it prior to the closing so that it may approve the transaction. You will find a blank HUD-1 settlement closing form in the Appendix.

7. Bill of Sale for Personal Property

In some situations, the seller and buyer may have negotiated the purchase of items of personal property in addition to the real property. If, for instance, the seller has agreed to sell curtains, appliances or other personal property, this sale must be set out in a separate bill of sale that is included with the closing materials. A bill of sale is not required for the real property or anything that technically qualifies as real property because this has already been negotiated through the other documents.

8. Compliance Agreement

This is a provision that allows the lender to request additional documents and other information from the buyer to correct clerical errors in the paperwork within 30 days of the closing

9. Credit Insurance or Protection Plan Addendum

This is a form of disability insurance that will make mortgage payments on behalf of the borrower in the event of total disability or death.

10. Loan Application

Although the borrowers completed a loan application form at the time that they first met with the lender, it is common practice for the lender to type up the handwritten notes and present this form to the borrower at the closing so that the borrowers may sign a new form.

11. U.S. Patriot Act Requirements

The Patriot Act was passed after the terrible events of September 11, 2001. One of the requirements of the Patriot Act is that the attorney presiding at the loan closing must verify the identity of the borrowers. The borrowers must produce at least two different forms of identification, such as driver's license or United States passport.

12. PMI Disclosure

Private Mortgage Insurance is insurance that protects the lender when the borrower has put down less than 20% of the loan purchase price. In the event that the borrower defaults on the mortgage, Private Mortgage Insurance will reimburse the lender for money lost.

The PMI disclosure is a document that explains to the borrower what PMI is. The PMI disclosure form also informs the borrower how he or she can remove the PMI premium from the loan and when the PMI is scheduled to terminate.

Sidebar: PMI is a form of insurance that insures the lender for that portion of the mortgage that is above 80% of the loan-to-value ratio. It protects the lender in the event the borrower defaults on the loan.

13. Trust Disbursement Records

The trust disbursement record is a way for the attorneys to keep track of the collection and disbursement of funds paid by the parties prior to closing. When the attorney receives funds, he or she deposits them into the firm's trust account. Disbursement checks are then written on the trust account for all the parties who receive payment at the closing.

Figure 12-2. Trust Disbursement Record

Client: John Doe
Re: Purchase of residence
          Closing date: October 1, 2004
          Disbursement date: October 5, 2004
          Amount received: $133,000, September 24, 2004

Disbursement Date	Payee	Amount
October 5, 2004	Bank of America	$508.50
October 5, 2004	Bank of America "Escrow and taxes, other"	$1123.65
October 5, 2004	Burke County Registry	$61
October 5, 2004	Burke County tax collector (2004)	$624.22
October 5, 2004	First Citizens' Bank mortgage payoff, loan number 456789	$89,004
October 5, 2004	Attorney's fee	$824
October 5, 2004	Title insurance premium	$203.50
October 5, 2004	Cash out to seller	$8,457.20
October 5, 2004	Total disbursed amount	$133,000
October 5, 2004	Balance	$0

---

14. Federal Truth-in-Lending

The Federal Truth-in-Lending disclosure statement shows the annual percentage rate of the loan, the finance charges, the amount financed, the total number of payments, and the total amount the borrower will pay if he makes all payments for the full term of the loan.

15. Termite Inspection Letter

If the termite report shows that the house is currently infested with termites, the seller must have the property treated for the infestation. Many lenders will require an additional inspection after a treatment in order to ensure that all of the pests have been killed.

16. Survey

Given the fact that a survey of the property can reveal a host of problems, from encroachments to unrecorded easements, most lenders require a new survey as part of the lending process. The new survey will help reveal any encroachments or boundary line issues that may have arisen since the last survey was completed. In some situations, a lender may be satisfied by a seller's affidavit.

a. Seller's Affidavit

A seller's affidavit is a sworn statement that there have been no changes, improvements or boundary line changes since the last survey. A seller's affidavit is sometimes used in place of a new survey. The problem is that the sellers may, in good faith, believe that there have been no changes, while forgetting something that has occurred recently or not being aware of actions taken by their neighbors that affect boundary lines or other real estate issues.

When the buyers refuse a new survey, the best practice is to get a survey waiver in writing with the client's signatures attached. Many attorneys have a pre-printed form stating the benefits of a new survey and the risks involved in not obtaining one and use this as a basis for a client waiver (and to protect themselves in the event of a future legal malpractice claim).

IV. Conducting the Closing

Although closings generally follow a set procedure, no two closings will ever be exactly the same. The simple reason for this disparity is that there are always unique issues in closings that can result in different types of problems. In the next section, we will outline the steps that occur in most closings. However, you should keep in mind that there are frequently issues that arise in closings that can dramatically complicate the issues.

In preparing for the closing, the paralegal usually provides the closing packet to the attorney so that the attorney may review it prior to the meeting. During the closing, the attorney explains the function and significance of the various documents and makes sure that they are all signed correctly. The attorney also answers any questions raised by the parties.

A. People Normally Present at a Closing

There are several people who are normally present at the closing. They include the attorney, the paralegal, the buyers and the sellers. Others may also be present.

1. Attorney

The attorney is responsible for conducting the closing, answering any questions that arise and making sure that all legal documents are prepared correctly. In order to successfully complete the closing, most attorneys rely on a paralegal.

2. Paralegal

The paralegal has done much of the preparation work to get the closing ready. The paralegal has probably been responsible for scheduling the closing by coordinating the date and time among many different parties. In addition, the paralegal has also prepared the loan closing paperwork, including the deed, the deed of trust, and prepared many of the other documents in order to make sure the closing is a success. In addition to these duties, the paralegal is often also a Notary Public who will notarize various documents as the closing proceeds. The paralegal may also be the person who takes the deed and deed of trust to the courthouse to record them when the closing is concluded.

3. The Buyers

The buyers are normally present at the closing. The buyers will be present in order to receive the deed once it has been signed by the sellers, but they are also present in order to sign the loan paperwork and to present certified funds for any fees and other deposits required to complete the closing.

4. The Sellers

The sellers are usually present at the closing as well. The sellers will sign the deed and deliver it to the buyers. In addition, the sellers will normally receive a disbursement check for their profit from the sale.

5. Real Estate Agent

There is no requirement that the real estate agent must be present at the closing. The agent's check is one of many that the legal team will prepare as part of the closing disbursements, and this check can be sent to the real estate agent just as easily as presenting it to the agent in person. In fact, because the agent may actually be splitting this check with another agent and the agents' respective companies, several checks may be cut and distributed as part of the real estate commission.

B. Disbursing the Funds

The lender deposits the mortgage money into the law firm's trust account prior to the closing. The attorney then writes checks on that account, distributing the funds to various parties at the closing. In this section, we will detail some of the disbursements that occur at a typical real estate closing. Among the items that will be paid at the closing include:

- The previous mortgage
- The lender's fees
- The attorney's fees
- The recording fees
- The seller's profit
- The real estate commission
- The real property taxes

Sidebar: It is common practice for real estate attorneys to keep copies of all checks in the file in order to verify exactly what was paid out at the closing.

Practice pointer: Always make copies of all documents signed by the buyers and sellers at the closing and keep them in the settlement closing file in case there is a question about them later. Also keep copies of the forms of identification produced by the parties to avoid any claims of forgery (and to satisfy the U.S. Patriot Act).

1. Lender's Fees

Among the fees that must be accounted for at the closing include the lender's fees. These include any fees associated with giving the loan, such as "points" (a fee based on a percentage of the total amount financed), and other fees assessed by the lender. The lender may also require payment of interim mortgage interest on the loan and additional monthly payments for hazard or homeowner's insurance and taxes. These are commonly referred to as "escrow accounts."

a. Escrow Accounts for Insurance and Taxes

In most mortgage situations, the lenders require a monthly payment that includes not only the monthly loan repayment, but also an additional amount that is set aside to pay the annual hazard insurance premiums and tax assessment.

Not all lenders set up escrow accounts for their borrowers. Some lenders leave it to the borrower to pay the homeowners insurance and annual tax assessments.

2. Attorney's Fees

Other fees paid at the closing include the attorney's fee for handling the closing and carrying out the title search. This fee is usually a percentage of the total loan amount, such as half of 1% of the total purchase price. The attorney may also simply charge a flat rate for the service.

3. Recording Fees

Recording fees are what the Deed Office charges to place deeds and other documents into its record. Deed offices charge on a sliding scale, with a higher fee for the first page ($14) and lower charges for subsequent pages ($3 for each subsequent page).

4. Seller's Profit on the Transaction

The seller's profit on the transaction will come in the form of a check from the attorney's trust account. This profit is the amount that is left over after paying off the seller's mortgage, real estate agent's commission and other charges.

5. Certified Funds from the Buyer

The check for certified funds from the buyer is one of the few checks that is not written on the attorney's trust account during the closing. This is a check presented by the buyer and reflects additional amounts that the buyer must pay in order to conclude the transaction. This check could cover additional lender fees, attorney fees or any other amount that the buyer's initial earnest money and down payment were insufficient to cover.

6. Real Estate Agent's Commission

Earlier in this chapter, when we discussed the parties present at the closing, we mentioned that the real estate agent may or may not be present. Although in this chapter we have simplified the issues surrounding the real estate agent's commission, we know from chapter 2 that commission sharing can be complicated. The listing agent will receive a portion of the commission, as will the agent's company. The real estate broker who furnishes the buyer is also due a commission, as is that broker's company. Some or all of these checks may be written at the closing, or handled by the real estate agents subsequent to disbursement.

7. Tax Payments

If there are any outstanding real property taxes from prior years, those must be paid prior to the closing. Such payments would be the seller's responsibility. However, a different issue arises when the tax payment is for the current year's assessment. In that case, if the sellers have paid the taxes for the entire year, they would be due a partial refund from the buyers. After all, without such a refund, the buyers would be taking advantage of the sellers pre-payment. The same question would arise when the taxes have not yet been paid for the year. In that situation, the buyers' payment would reflect an entire year's residence, when they only occupied it for part of the year. In both situations, taxes must be pro-rated.

a. Pro-Rated Taxes

Pro-ration is the process of assessing payments based on the amount paid and the quantity of time that a party resides in the premises. We will take a simple example to illustrate the point.

Scenario #1.

On January 2nd of this year, Joan paid her county real property taxes for the entire year. The amount that she paid was $1000. On June 30th, Joan closed on her house, transferring title to Frida. Because Joan lived in her house for only half of the year, she wants a refund of the balance of the year that has already been paid for, but which she will not enjoy because she no longer lives in the home. How much will Frida pay to reimburse her?

Answer: If we assume that the closing date was exactly half the tax year, then Frida must refund Joan half of her tax payment, or $500.

Obviously pro-ration can become much more complicated, especially when you consider that there are other payments that the parties make in advance, including heating oil, utilities, city taxes, etc.

V. Other Closing Issues

A. "Escrow" Closings

We have already used the term "escrow" to describe an account that the buyer pays extra money into every month that will eventually be used by the lender to pay insurance premiums and taxes, but escrow also refers to a closing process.

Although the face-to-face closing method is the most common type of closing in North Carolina, there are provisions that allow an escrow style of closing as well. Escrow closings are very common in other states, but they have not reached the same level of popularity in this state. In an escrow closing, some or all of the parties are absent from the actual closing. Instead, the parties sign an agreement, usually referred to as an "Escrow Agreement" and complete all of the necessary paperwork to complete the closing prior to the actual event. The law then applies a legal fiction to the agreement that states that although the paperwork was signed prior to the actual closing, it will not have legal effect until the closing occurs. This legal fiction is referred to as the "Doctrine of Relation Back."

1. The Doctrine of Relation Back

The Doctrine of Relation Back is used in escrow closings in order to satisfy certain elements. We know that a deed is not effective until the seller has delivered it and the buyer has accepted it. However, when both parties are not actually present at the closing, without some doctrine that allows the seller to place the signed deed into escrow, no closing could occur. The Doctrine of Relation Back also settles some tricky legal questions that arise when the seller has signed a deed, placed it into escrow, and then dies prior to the actual closing. Under most situations, because the seller has failed to carry out the actions required to conclude the closing, there can be no transaction. However, when the seller has signed the deed and placed it into escrow, the closing may continue as though the seller was physically present at the closing.

When the sellers and buyers place signed documents into escrow, it is usually on express conditions that certain things must occur before the closing can continue. For the seller, these conditions will include presentation of the funds to conclude the transaction. For the buyer, these conditions will include a signed and delivered copy of the deed and any other pre-conditions that were negotiated in the Offer to Purchase and Contract.

B. Dual Representation

In the typical real estate transaction, it is very common for both the buyer and seller to request that the same attorney handle the transaction for both. This can put an attorney in a potential ethical dilemma. After all, the buyers and sellers interests are, by definition, adverse to one another. In certain situations, the attorney is allowed to represent both parties, but only after full disclosure and agreement from both sides. Consider Figure 12-3.

Figure 12-3. RPC 210

A lawyer may reasonably believe that the common representation of multiple parties to residential real estate closing will not be adverse to the interests of any one client if the parties have agreed to the basic terms of the transaction and the lawyer's role is limited to rendering an opinion on title, memorializing the transaction, and disbursing the proceeds. Before reaching this conclusion, however the lawyer must determine whether there is any obstacle to the loyal representation of both parties.

Having one lawyer represent both sides in a transaction raises a host of potential problems when the parties come into conflict later on. This is one reason why full disclosure is so important to the legal team.

C. Disclosures

One way of avoiding an ethics complaint is for the legal team to disclose dual representation in writing to all parties. Some firms use their initial representation letter to advise the parties about dual representation and to disclose any other information so that both the buyer and seller will understand the nature of the legal service being provided.

D. Refinances

In situations where the closing involves refinancing an existing mortgage, there is a three-day waiting period before the checks can be disbursed.

E. Title Insurance

Once the closing has been completed, the title insurance company will issue a final owner's policy conveying title to the property. It is common practice to mail the title insurance policy to the client's attorney who then forwards it to the lender and the client.

Title insurance is a form of insurance that protects the buyer and the lender against any loss caused by a defective title to the property. For instance, if the title examination gives the title a clean bill of health, and there is a later boundary line dispute that the owner loses because of documents that were clearly a part of the public record, the title insurance company will not only pay to defend this suit, but also any damages that are assessed as a result. Because most lenders require title insurance before they will issue a mortgage on property, title insurance has become not only a multi-million-dollar industry, but also an important factor in the transaction itself. Title insurance companies demand proper title examinations and certifications of titles before the transaction can proceed. If the title insurance company refuses to issue a policy on a parcel, this effectively renders the parcel incapable of being sold. Title insurance companies have also brought legal malpractice actions against real estate attorneys who have incorrectly certified title after missing public records that clearly place a cloud on the title.

VI. After the Closing

After the closing, the general warranty deed and deed of trust must be filed at the courthouse. It is common practice to make copies of all signed documents, sending the originals back to the lender and providing copies both for the attorney file and the client. In particularly-efficient attorneys' offices, the legal assistant will often go to the courthouse during the closing, record the deed and deed of trust, and return with stamped copies to give to the client before the clients leave.

Figure 12-4. Closing Checklist

- ❑ Offer to purchase and contract
  - ○ Copy of tax record
  - ○ Taxes outstanding? Amount?
- ❑ Client file created?
- ❑ Names of parties
  - ○ Complete legal name of buyer
  - ○ Realtor(s) names
- ❑ Lender
- ❑ Seller's name
  - ○ Seller's address:
- ❑ Title insurance binder (policy number)
- ❑ Seller's deed of trust prepared?
- ❑ Termite letter completed?
- ❑ Survey completed by:
  - ○ Survey fee:
- ❑ Lien waiver
- ❑ W-9 form
- ❑ General warranty deed
- ❑ Restrictive covenants?
- ❑ Loan package (provided by lender)
- ❑ HUD-1 form completed
- ❑ Checks typed up and ready?
- ❑ Federal Express or United Parcel Service fees
- ❑ Final title opinion
- ❑ Title insurance policy mailed client and lender
- ❑ Certified copies of the General Warranty Deed and Deed of Trust provided to clients and lender
- ❑ File closed out? Date:

A. Filing Issues

When filing the general warranty deed and deed of trust, it is important to get the sequence correct. The deed must be filed first, followed by the deed of trust immediately thereafter. The deed must be filed first in order to officially transfer the seller's interest to the borrower and the deed of trust must be filed immediately afterwards in order to protect the lender's interest in the property (and to give it priority over any other claim).

Relevant Case

Brumley v. Mallard, L.L.C.[1]

EAGLES, Chief Judge.

Mallard, L.L.C., and Bonn A. Gilbert, Jr., ("defendants") appeal from the trial court's granting of summary judgment in favor of A. Neal Brumley ("plaintiff") and award of

---

1. 154 N.C.App. 563, 575 S.E.2d 35 (2002).

$150,000 plus interest and attorneys' fees. On appeal, defendants have two assignments of error: (1) that the trial court erred in granting plaintiff's motion for summary judgment; and (2) that the trial court erred in denying defendants' motion for summary judgment. We discern no error and affirm.

The evidence tends to show the following. Plaintiff is the executor of the estate of William Dellinger. The estate owned two tracts of land. As executor, plaintiff contracted on 6 May 1996 with Bonn Gilbert ("Gilbert") to sell the two parcels of land. The total purchase price was $532,000; $354,666 of the purchase price was to be a promissory note secured by a purchase money deed of trust.

At the property closing on 31 December 1996, plaintiff was informed that Gilbert intended for plaintiff to convey the land to Mallard, L.L.C. ("Mallard") instead of conveying it to Gilbert personally. Mallard's articles of incorporation were filed in the North Carolina Secretary of State's office on 31 December 1996 as well. Plaintiff refused to convey land to Mallard unless the security instruments were amended to show they were "for consideration" instead of "purchase money" and unless Gilbert personally guaranteed the obligations. Gilbert's attorney, Jameson Wells, prepared the documents according to those specifications.

This action only involves the sale of Parcel II. The purchase price was financed by a promissory note in the amount of $150,000. Mallard defaulted on payment of the note. Plaintiff began this action on 7 July 2000 against Mallard as the maker and Gilbert as the guarantor of the note. Defendants allege that the note is a purchase money note and plaintiff's action is barred by the anti-deficiency statute. Defendants alternatively allege that they are entitled to indemnification, if the note is not a purchase money note. Defendants also allege there is a lack of consideration.

On appeal, defendants argue that the trial court erred by granting plaintiff's motion for summary judgment. Defendants' argument is based on its contention that the promissory note here was a purchase money note. We disagree.

Here, the only issues contested are questions of law, namely the applicability of the anti-deficiency statute. The anti-deficiency statute reads:

> In all sales of real property by mortgagees and/or trustees under powers of sale contained in any mortgage or deed of trust executed after February 6, 1933, or where judgment or decree is given for the foreclosure of any mortgage executed after February 6, 1933, to secure to the seller the payment of the balance of the purchase price of real property, the mortgagee or trustee or holder of the notes secured by such mortgage or deed of trust shall not be entitled to a deficiency judgment on account of such mortgage, deed of trust, or obligation secured by the same: Provided, said evidence of indebtedness shows upon the face that it is for balance of purchase money for real estate. G.S. § 45-21.38 (2001).

This section of the anti-deficiency statute is only applicable if the "evidence of indebtedness" indicates on its face that it is a purchase-money transaction.

Here, the promissory note states that it was "given for consideration," while the offer to purchase and contract state that the note was to be "secured by purchase money deed of trust." Defendants allege that the phrase "evidence of indebtedness" includes all documents surrounding the sale of the property. We disagree. Here, neither the deed of trust nor the promissory note contain any language indicating that they are purchase money instruments. Accordingly, the anti-deficiency statute cannot be applied to bar plaintiff's suit against defendants.

The phrase "evidence of the indebtedness" in G.S. § 45-21.38 refers only to the promissory note and the deed of trust. If there is no indication on the face of the promissory note or deed of trust that "the indebtedness is for the balance of purchase money," the anti-deficiency statute cannot be applied by implication. If there is language in the promissory note that denominates the transaction which does not appear in the deed of trust, the deed of trust is deemed to include the same language as the note.

In Green Park Inn, Inc. v. Moore, 149 N.C.App. 531, 562 S.E.2d 53 (2002), this Court did not apply the anti-deficiency statute to a long-term lease followed by an option to purchase. "We hold that the Anti-Deficiency Statute does not apply to this transaction, in which there is neither an instrument of debt nor a securing instrument stating on its face that the transaction is a purchase money mortgage." Moore, 149 N.C.App. at 537, 562 S.E.2d at 57–58. Accordingly, this assignment of error fails.

Defendants alternatively allege that plaintiff must indemnify them for any loss as a result of the transaction because the promissory note was prepared under the supervision of plaintiff as seller. Defendants argue plaintiff's insistence that the words "purchase money" be removed from the promissory note before the sale, coupled with the addition of Gilbert as guarantor, created a responsibility to indemnify them according to G.S. § 45-21.38. We disagree.

Defendants rely on a portion of the anti-deficiency statute that reads, in pertinent part:

> Provided, further, that when said note or notes are prepared under the direction and supervision of the seller or sellers, he, it, or they shall cause a provision to be inserted in said note disclosing that it is for purchase money of real estate; in default of which the seller or sellers shall be liable to purchaser for any loss which he might sustain by reason of the failure to insert said provisions as herein set out. G.S. § 45-21.38 (2001).

This portion of the anti-deficiency statute has never been judicially interpreted. Plaintiff, the seller here, took no part in the preparation of the promissory note or deed of trust. His only involvement was his refusal to sign the original documents as purchase money instruments. Defendant Gilbert's attorney prepared the documents according to the agreement of the parties at the property closing. The above portion of the statute upon which the defendants rely anticipates a situation where the seller prepares security documents without the buyer's participation and consent, unlike the instant case. Here, defendants were present and represented by counsel when the security documents were amended. In fact, defendants' attorney prepared the amended documents. Accordingly, the provision of the anti-deficiency statute relied upon by defendants does not require plaintiff here to indemnify defendants for actions taken by their own attorney.

Finally, defendants allege that the agreement to amend the security documents at closing was not supported by consideration. Plaintiff was under a contractual obligation to sell to defendant Gilbert or his designee as a result of the offer to purchase. Defendants contend that Gilbert's agreement to personally guarantee the loan and the changing of the words "purchase money" to "for consideration" in the promissory note were not supported by additional consideration and are unenforceable. We disagree.

It is well-settled law that a contract must be supported by consideration in order to be enforceable. A modification to a contract occurs if there is mutual assent to the terms of the modification and consideration supporting the modification. Here, both parties were present and agreed to change the language of the security documents and make defendant Gilbert guarantor of the note. Defendants' lack of protest at the time of closing precludes them from raising this defense after they have already accepted partial performance of the obligation and have performed partially in return.

In addition, there was ample consideration to support the modification of the contract at the property closing. Plaintiff accepted a different buyer (Defendant Mallard, L.L.C.), with different potential for liability than the original buyer (Defendant Gilbert). The new buyer Mallard had not even been created as a legal entity when the original contract was formed between plaintiff and Gilbert. In return, the language of the security instruments was amended and Gilbert agreed to guarantee the transactions. This exchange represents sufficient consideration to support the contract as modified.

For the foregoing reasons, we conclude that the trial court did not err in granting plaintiff's motion for summary judgment and denying defendants' motion for summary judgment. Accordingly, we dissolve the temporary stay preventing execution of summary judgment entered in plaintiff's favor on 30 May 2001.

Affirmed.

Chapter Summary

The loan closing brings together many different elements of a real estate transaction. At its simplest, the closing is where the title is transferred from the seller to the buyer, and also where loan documents, deeds and other documents are signed and notarized. Loan closings are handled by a real estate attorney who advises clients about the legal impact of various documents, makes sure that they are all signed in the appropriate places and disburses the checks. Prior to the closing, the attorney will have received a check from the lending company that the attorney will deposit into the law firm's trust account. The attorney then disburses checks from that trust account, paying off outstanding mortgages, the realtor's commissions, attorney's fees, and any other payout amounts. When all of the disbursements have been made, the total funds deposited into the trust account by the lender should be completely divested.

The people who are normally present at the closing include the closing attorney, who is responsible for conducting the closing, the buyers and the sellers. Sometimes, the real estate agent is also present. There is usually one other legal professional present at the closing, a person without whom the closing would probably not occur: the paralegal. Paralegals play a large role in organizing and coordinating the closing so that it runs smoothly and efficiently for all concerned. Paralegals often use closing checklists in order to ensure that all activities have been done correctly. Closings require precision and accuracy. An error during the closing can have disastrous consequences for the parties involved.

Once the closing has been completed, the new general warranty deed and deed of trust will be recorded at the Registrar of Deeds office and the title insurance company will issue a binder covering the property.

Title insurance is an insurance policy that is designed to do one thing: to reimburse the policyholder for any claims made on the property based on liens, encumbrances or other adverse claims. The purpose of a title search is to ensure that there are no such claims. The title insurance company usually insists on a title examination and an attorney's certificate that the property is free and clear of any encumbrances before it will issue a policy to the buyer.

Review Questions

1. What is the significance of the termite inspection letter?

2. What are the ethical concerns surrounding dual representation at a closing?

3. What is the "loan package?"

4. What are the names of some of the closing software products currently available?

5. Is the arranging of financing to purchase a home a prerequisite for the closing? Why or why not?

6. What are some of the concerns that go into scheduling a loan closing?

7. What are "loan payoff amounts" and why are they important?

8. Why is it important to know the tax payment status on a parcel of real estate prior to closing?

9. Explain the role that title insurance plays in the closing.

10. List and explain the basic steps involved in conducting a closing.

11. List the people who are typically present at the closing and what roles they play?

12. What documents are usually required at the closing?

13. What is a trust disbursement record?

14. What effect has the Patriot Act had on real estate closings?

15. What is the Federal Truth-in-Lending statement and what purpose does it serve?

16. What is a survey and why is it important to the closing? What is a seller's affidavit concerning the survey and what dangers does it pose?

17. In this chapter the term "escrow" is used in two different contexts. In one, the text refers to the payment of insurance and taxes into an escrow account and in the other, the text refers to an escrow closing. Compare and contrast these two different types of escrows.

18. What are some examples of title defects that could affect the closing?

19. What is disbursement?

20. What is the importance of Title Insurance?

Assignment

Using the blank form provided in the appendix, and the example provided in this chapter, complete a basic HUD-1 settlement closing form using the following information:

It was a gloomy, dreadful, August day when Lisa and Carl Paralegal finally found the house of their dreams. It was a huge, rambling, one hundred-year-old Victorian, badly in need of a paint job and with a suspicious amount of bunny cages next door. They put in an offer for $120,000, which was promptly accepted by the owner, Randy Dandy.

The Paralegals didn't have much money for a deposit, so they only came up with $750 earnest money.

Randy Dandy agreed to pay $2,000 towards closing costs.

Since it is an FHA loan, the Paralegals only have to come up with 3% for a down payment.

Other terms from the contract:

1. 1.5% loan origination fee
2. 1 point
3. Appraisal fee: $220.00
4. Mortgage Insurance Application fee of $966.00
5. Pest Inspection: $60
6. Reserves of 2 months of Hazard Insurance
7. Daily interest due from closing to first of next month: $18.23
8. Title Insurance is required.

Hazard Insurance premium: $230.00

Survey: $350.00

The deed will cost $8 to record; deed of trust will cost $1 to record. Attorney's fee is 1/2 of 1% of the selling price, and Dandy has attorney's fees of $120.00

Real property taxes are $415.00, and they have not been paid for this calendar year, putting them in arrears, since Randy Dandy should have paid them.

Dandy has a mortgage balance of is $42,233.00. The closing date is on August 25th.

The commission check is being split between Madge Realtor and Sal Salesman on a fifty-fifty basis.

Terms and Phrases

Loan Closing
Loan Payoff
Encroachment
Title Defects
Termite Inspection
Loan Closing Software
Loan Package
Promissory Note
Subordination Agreement
Lien Waiver Affidavit
HUD-1
Compliance Agreement

U.S. Patriot Act
PMI Disclosure
Trust Disbursement Record
Truth-in-Lending
Survey
Disbursement
Escrow accounts
Escrow closing
Doctrine of Relation Back
Dual Representation
Disclosures
Title Insurance

Chapter 13

Taxes, Liens and Assessments

Chapter Objectives

At the conclusion of this chapter, you should be able to:
- Explain how tax rates are calculated
- Describe the process of assessing taxes
- Define ad valorem taxes
- Explain assessments
- Describe the importance of liens in real estate transactions

I. Real Property Taxes

We have already discussed the topic of real property taxes in prior chapters, but always in the context of title searches or real estate closings. The topic of taxation could easily consume an entire volume by itself. There are several important statutes on the topic that govern the assessment and appraisal of property for taxation purposes as well as what property can be taxed, what property excluded, and the methods that the government may use to impose its tax regulations. We will discuss the topic of taxes as it touches on real estate conveyances. Taxes are based on the assessed value of the property, otherwise known as **ad valorem taxation**.

Ad valorem taxes: taxing according to the value of the property.

A. The Power to Levy Taxes

North Carolina statutes authorize cities to impose taxes on real and personal property located within their geographic limits. Taxes can be assessed to pay for service government debt, pay for government deficits and meet law enforcement costs.

B. The Types of Property That Can Be Taxed

North Carolina's State Constitution authorizes State and local governments to assess taxes against real and personal property. Courts have determined the definition of "real and

---

Figure 13-1. NCGS § 160A-209. Property Taxes

(a) Pursuant to Article V, Sec. 2(5) of the Constitution of North Carolina, the General Assembly confers upon each city in this State the power to levy, within the limitations set out in this section, taxes on property having a situs within the city under the rules and according to the procedures prescribed in the Machinery Act (Chapter 105, Subchapter II).

(b) Each city may levy property taxes without restriction as to rate or amount for the following purposes:

(1) Debt Service. — To pay the principal of and interest on all general obligation bonds and notes of the city.

(2) Deficits. — To supply an unforeseen deficiency in the revenue (other than revenues of any of the enterprises listed in G.S. 160A-311), when revenues actually collected or received fall below revenue estimates made in good faith in accordance with the Local Government Budget and Fiscal Control Act.

(3) Civil Disorders. — To meet the cost of additional law-enforcement personnel and equipment that may be required to suppress riots or other civil disorders involving an extraordinary breach of law and order within the jurisdiction of the city.

---

personal property" to encompass all types of property.[1]

Under this ruling, all property found in the jurisdiction of the state is subject to taxation unless it has been specifically exempted by statute.

1. Homestead Exclusion

Under North Carolina General Statute § 105-277.1, permanent residences can qualify for homestead exclusion under the tax code. This means that a taxpayer can exempt up to 50% of the appraised value of the residence or $20,000, whichever is greater. In order to qualify for the homestead exclusion, a taxpayer must be at least 65 years of age and meet other income eligibility requirements.

2. Property Excluded from Tax Calculations

Certain types of property are excluded from taxation under North Carolina General Statute § 105-275. They include real property owned by a nonprofit water or sewer association, nonprofit corporations, real estate owned by the federal government, real estate owned by nonprofit corporations and property that is used for recycling purposes.

C. Determining the Value of Real Property for Tax Purposes

Real property value is determined as of January 1 of each year. The tax assessor's office is responsible for determining real property value. When a property is "listed" it simply means that it is being inventoried for tax purposes. Appraisal, on the other hand, is the actual determination of the property's value. When the tax office determines the appraised value for real estate, it uses the market value as determined by North Carolina General Statutes § 105-283.

---

1. *Redmond v. Town of Tarboro*, 106 N.C. 122, 10 S.E. 845 (1890).

Among the factors that the tax office may consider in its appraisal of real property includes zoning, access, past income, crop value and a host of other considerations that affect the overall value of the property. A taxpayer may challenge the appraised value by showing that it was reached through arbitrary means or through an illegal method of valuation.

1. Calculating the Tax Rate

When local governments create their annual tax rates, they begin with the assessed value of all real property located within the geographic limits. They then take that estimated value and divide by the budgetary needs for the upcoming year to arrive at the tax rate. If the total value of the property in the county is $100 million and the government needs $10 million for its operating budget, the tax rate would be $10 million divided by $100 million, or a tax rate of .1 or $.10 on every dollar of value. That would be an extremely high rate. Most rates are closer to one or two cents per dollar of value.

This rate is then applied per $100 of value. Therefore, the tax rate using the numbers in the preceding paragraph would result in a calculation of 100 x .1, or $10.

Using the numbers above, if Joan's property is worth $100,000 and the tax rate is .1, what is her annual tax?

Answer: divide $100,000 x 100 for the total amount of assessed value per 100. That is $1000. $1000 multiplied by a $10 tax rate equals a tax bill of $10,000 per year. Again, these numbers are used purely for demonstrative purposes. Local voters would never stand for such a high tax rate.

In the real world, governments are limited to a combined rate of $1.50 per $100 in value in their tax rates.[2]

D. Reassessment

The tax office is empowered to reassess the value of all property every eight years and to adjust the assessment on each property after that reassessment.

E. Enforcing Tax Regulations

North Carolina statutes give governments the power to enforce their tax regulations through a wide assortment of remedies, including levies, garnishment and attachments. Governments are also authorized to issue liens on property and to enforce those liens with tax auctions of the property in question.[3]

1. Tax Liens

A tax lien has important consequences. When the tax is unpaid, local government has a right to file a lien against the property. The lien remains on the property and is trans-

---

2. NCGS § 160A-209(d).
3. NCGS § 160A-207.

ferred when title is transferred. This means that a tax that was not paid by a previous owner can be assessed against the current owner.

a. Tax Lien Priorities

Tax liens have special priority status under the law. Regardless of when they are filed, they will take precedence over any other claim, meaning that when the property is foreclosed or auctioned off, the taxes must be paid before any other judgment against the property.

2. Foreclosing a Tax Lien

North Carolina statutes authorize local government to foreclose tax liens and auction off property for outstanding taxes. See Figure 13-2.

Figure 13-2. § 43-48. Foreclosure of Tax Lien

The lien for ad valorem taxes may be foreclosed and the property sold pursuant to G.S. 105-375. A note of the sale under this section shall be duly registered, and a certificate shall be entered and an owner's certificate issued in favor of the purchaser in whom title shall be thereby vested as registered owner, in accordance with the provisions of this Chapter. Nothing in this section shall be so construed as to affect or divert the title of a tenant in reversion or remainder to any real estate which has been returned delinquent and sold on account of the default of the tenant for life in paying the taxes or assessments thereon.

II. Assessments

When taxes are applied to all qualifying real property within the county, an assessment is an individual charge placed against a particular parcel. The most common example of a special assessment arises when local government installs sidewalks or streets. Adjoining parcels can be assessed for the costs associated with installing these improvements. See Figure 13-3.

III. Liens

A lien is an encumbrance on property that is either transferred with the title or prevents title transfer in the first place. We have already discussed liens, at least in part, in our discussion of deeds of trust. For instance, we saw that in some states, a mortgage operates as a lien on property. Under certain circumstances, the lien may be perfected into a foreclosure action, such as when the borrower fails to make regular monthly payments. Earlier in this chapter, we saw references to liens in regard to the enforcement of real estate taxes imposed by county or city governments. However, this still begs the question, what is a lien?

Figure 13-3. § 153A-185. Authority to Make Special Assessments

A county may make special assessments against benefited property within the county for all or part of the costs of:

(1) Constructing, reconstructing, extending, or otherwise building or improving water systems;

(2) Constructing, reconstructing, extending, or otherwise building or improving sewage collection and disposal systems of all types, including septic tank systems or other on-site collection or disposal facilities or systems;

(3) Acquiring, constructing, reconstructing, extending, renovating, enlarging, maintaining, operating, or otherwise building or improving

    a. Beach erosion control or flood and hurricane protection works; and

    b. Watershed improvement projects, drainage projects and water resources development projects (as those projects are defined in G.S. 153A-301).(4) Constructing, reconstructing, paving, widening, installing curbs and gutters, and otherwise building and improving streets, as provided in G.S. 153A-205.

(5) Providing street lights and street lighting in a residential subdivision, as provided in G.S. 153A-206.

A county may not assess property within a city pursuant to subdivision (1) or (2) of this section unless the governing board of the city has by resolution approved the project.

A. What Is a Lien?

A lien is an encumbrance on real estate imposed by a creditor who may enforce the lien as a way of receiving payment. When the government is owed taxes, for instance, it may impose a lien on the taxpayer's real property in order to secure payment. In some cases, the lien simply acts as an encumbrance on the real estate, which can be perfected into a judgment that could force the sale of the property to satisfy the outstanding debt. It is important to draw a distinction, however, between liens and judgments. Liens are a mechanism used to protect a creditor's rights, but a lien does not give a creditor an automatic right to seize property or to have it auctioned off. Instead, a lien is the first step in obtaining a judgment against the debtor that could be enforced by other action.

B. Types of Liens under North Carolina Law

North Carolina recognizes several different types of liens, from the previously-discussed tax liens to statutory liens and judgment liens. We will begin our discussion with statutory liens.

1. Statutory Liens (Mechanics and Materialmen's Liens)

A mechanic's lien is a right given to a person who provides service to file a lien on real property in order to receive payment for that service. Under common law, there was a distinction made between mechanics (those who provided a service) and materialmen (those who provided supplies for materials). These days, the distinctions have all but disappeared in North Carolina General Statute 44A-8 in 1996. See Figure 13-4.

> **Figure 13-4. §44A-8. Mechanics', Laborers' and Materialmen's Lien; Persons Entitled to Lien**
>
> Any person who performs or furnishes labor or professional design or surveying services or furnishes materials or furnishes rental equipment pursuant to a contract, either express or implied, with the owner of real property for the making of an improvement thereon shall, upon complying with the provisions of this Article, have a lien on such real property to secure payment of all debts owing for labor done or professional design or surveying services or material furnished or equipment rented pursuant to such contract.

a. Statutory Liens

When a person has contracted to provide services or materials to improve real property, and does not receive payment, the party is entitled to file a lien against the property. Under North Carolina General Statutes 44A-12, the claimant has up to 120 days from the last date of service to file the lien. See Figure 13-5.

> Sidebar: A person can acquire a valid lien against real property if the person provides labor or materials and follows the statutory steps to perfect the lien.[4]

C. The Importance of Liens

Liens are important not only because they have a substantial impact on the real estate transaction, but also because they act as an encumbrance on the property. Most lenders will refuse to finance property that has a lien against it. Any prudent buyer should also have the same reservations about purchasing such a property for cash. Searching for liens is one of the main functions of the title examination. Lenders and title insurers dealing with newly constructed property typically require affidavits from the general contractors and sub-contractors that they have all been paid in order to avoid a lien being placed on the property at a later time.

> Sidebar: Statutory liens are only available when there is an express or implied contract.[5]

D. Judgment Liens

When a person loses a civil lawsuit, there are provisions of law that allow the winning party to file a judgment lien on all real or personal property owned by the loser as a means of collecting the monetary judgment. This judgment can be enforced by a judicially ordered sale of the property to satisfy the judgment.

E. Perfecting and Enforcing a Lien

When a creditor wishes to perfect and enforce a lien against real property, the creditor must follow the dictates of Chapter 44A of the North Carolina General Statutes. When

---

4. *Lynch v. Price Homes, Inc.*, 156 N.C.App. 83, 575 S.E.2d 543 (2003).
5. *Embree Const. Group, Inc. v. Rafcor, Inc.*, 330 N.C. 487, 411 S.E.2d 916 (1992).

Figure 13-5. §44A-12. Filing Claim of Lien

(a) Place of Filing. — All claims of lien against any real property must be filed in the office of the clerk of superior court in each county wherein the real property subject to the claim of lien is located. The clerk of superior court shall note the claim of lien on the judgment docket and index the same under the name of the record owner of the real property at the time the claim of lien is filed. An additional copy of the claim of lien may also be filed with any receiver, referee in bankruptcy or assignee for benefit of creditors who obtains legal authority over the real property.

(b) Time of Filing. — Claims of lien may be filed at any time after the maturity of the obligation secured thereby but not later than 120 days after the last furnishing of labor or materials at the site of the improvement by the person claiming the lien.

(c) Contents of Claim of Lien to Be Filed. — All claims of lien must be filed using a form substantially as follows:

CLAIM OF LIEN

(1) Name and address of the person claiming the lien:

(2) Name and address of the record owner of the real property claimed to be subject to the lien at the time the claim of lien is filed:

(3) Description of the real property upon which the lien is claimed: (Street address, tax lot and block number, reference to recorded instrument, or any other description of real property is sufficient, whether or not it is specific, if it reasonably identifies what is described.)

(4) Name and address of the person with whom the claimant contracted for the furnishing of labor or materials:

(5) Date upon which labor or materials were first furnished upon said property by the claimant:

    (5a) Date upon which labor or materials were last furnished upon said property by the claimant:

(6) General description of the labor performed or materials furnished and the amount claimed therefor: ....

Lien Claimant

Filed this ...... day of ....

....

Clerk of Superior Court

A general description of the labor performed or materials furnished is sufficient. It is not necessary for lien claimant to file an itemized list of materials or a detailed statement of labor performed.

---

a lien has been duly filed and perfected, a court can order a judicial sale of the property to satisfy the debt. Any extra money left over after the auction would go to the real property owner.

Relevant Case

Southeastern Sav. & Loan Ass'n v. Rentenbach Constructors, Inc.[6]

BRITT, Chief Judge.

This matter is before the court on cross appeals from an order of the Bankruptcy Court for the Eastern District of North Carolina, pursuant to Title 28, United States Code, Sec-

---

6. 114 B.R. 441 (E.D.N.C., 1989).

Figure 13-6. §44A-13. Action to Enforce Lien

(a) Where and When Action Instituted.—An action to enforce the lien created by this Article may be instituted in any county in which the lien is filed. No such action may be commenced later than 180 days after the last furnishing of labor or materials at the site of the improvement by the person claiming the lien. If the title to the real property against which the lien is asserted is by law vested in a receiver or trustee in bankruptcy, the lien shall be enforced in accordance with the orders of the court having jurisdiction over said real property.

(b) Judgment.—Judgment enforcing a lien under this Article may be entered for the principal amount shown to be due, not exceeding the principal amount stated in the claim of lien enforced thereby. The judgment shall direct a sale of the real property subject to the lien thereby enforced.

(c) Notice of Action.—Unless the action enforcing the lien created by this Article is instituted in the county in which the lien is filed, in order for the sale under the provisions of G.S. 44A-14(a) to pass all title and interest of the owner to the purchaser good against all claims or interests recorded, filed or arising after the first furnishing of labor or materials at the site of the improvement by the person claiming the lien, a notice of lis pendens shall be filed in each county in which the real property subject to the lien is located within 180 days after the last furnishing of labor or materials at the site of the improvement by the person claiming the lien. It shall not be necessary to file a notice of lis pendens in the county in which the action enforcing the lien is commenced in order for the judgment entered therein and the sale declared thereby to carry with it the priorities set forth in G.S. 44A-14(a). If neither an action nor a notice of lis pendens is filed in each county in which the real property subject to the lien is located within 180 days after the last furnishing of labor or materials at the site of the improvement by the person claiming the lien, as to real property claimed to be subject to the lien in such counties where the action was neither commenced nor a notice of lis pendens filed, the judgment entered in the action enforcing the lien shall not direct a sale of the real property subject to the lien enforced thereby nor be entitled to any priority under the provisions of G.S. 44A-14(a), but shall be entitled only to those priorities accorded by law to money judgments.

---

tion 158. The issues have been thoroughly briefed, a hearing held, and the matter is now ripe for disposition.

On 27 October 1988 a trial in an adversary proceeding was held before Judge Thomas Small. The principal issue before that court was whether plaintiff Rentenbach's (hereinafter appellee) materialmen's lien is superior to defendant Southeastern's (hereinafter appellant) deed of trust covering the same property. On 15 March 1989 the court issued an opinion finding in favor of appellee.

The findings of fact of the bankruptcy court were prepared by appellee and agreed to by the parties. Briefly summarized, appellee entered into a contract with the debtor to furnish renovation services for the Capital Club Building located in Raleigh, North Carolina. Appellant loaned the debtor money to accomplish same.

The events that led to this dispute are as follows: On 31 December 1984 Capital Club Associates, Ltd. (CCA-F), a Florida limited partnership acquired title to the Capital Club Building. On 26 July 1985 CCA-F changed its name to Urban Properties IV, Ltd. (its original name). During July 1985 appellee negotiated with the soon-to-be-formed limited partnership, CCA-NC, to furnish the renovation services. At the same time Urban Properties, as the owner of the property and general partner on the proposed project, obtained financing from appellant. On 5 August 1985 CCA-NC executed a deed of trust in favor of appellant. The deed of trust was signed as follows: "CAPITAL CLUB ASSOCIATES, LTD., a North Carolina limited partnership By its Sole General Partner: URBAN PROPERTIES, IV, LTD., a Florida limited partnership." Allen J. Koch actually signed the deed of trust. At that time, CCA-NC was not the owner of the property. On 14 August 1985 the property was deeded by Urban Properties to CCA-NC [the deed was back dated to 1 August 1985]. The deed of trust in favor of appellant was not rerecorded until 20 May 1987. Appellee commenced work in August 1985 and, following completion of its services, filed a lien in March 1987.

Appellee successfully argued before the bankruptcy court that the original filing was ineffective and outside of CCA-NC's chain of title. The court was persuaded that appellee's lien preceded the effective deed of trust of May 1987 and is therefore superior.

The bankruptcy court determined the amount of appellee's lien to be $334,377 plus interest pursuant to the terms of the construction contract. The court arrived at this figure by adding the final actual costs, a base fee as called for in the contract and an additional fee provided for in the event of changes in work and then deducting an amount of retainage which the court determined appellee had waived.

On appeal, Southeastern contends first, that appellee Rentenbach failed to establish a valid laborer's and materialmen's lien on the debtor's property; second, that the bankruptcy court erred in finding appellee's *443 lien superior; and third, that the court erred in its determination of the amount of the lien in favor of appellee. Rentenbach's cross-appeal alleges that the bankruptcy court erred when it concluded that Rentenbach waived $91,662 in retainage funds.

DISCUSSION

Appellant's first contention is that the bankruptcy court erred in concluding that appellee established a valid laborer's and materialmen's lien on the debtor property.

Under N.C.Gen.Stat. §44A-8:

> Any person who performs or furnishes labor or professional design or survey-ing services or furnishes materials pursuant to a contract, either express or im-plied, with the owner of real property for the making of an improvement thereon shall, upon complying with the provisions of this Article, have a lien on such real property to secure payment of all debts owing ... pursuant to such contract.

According to appellant, in order to establish a valid lien, appellee must prove:

(1) that it performed pursuant to a contract;

(2) that its contract was with the owner of the property (or a successor in interest); and

(3) the date it first furnished labor or materials at the Capital Club Building.

The court is persuaded that appellee has established these elements. It is undisputed that appellee performed pursuant to a contract. It is also undisputed when appellee first furnished labor and/or materials at the Capital Club Building. What is disputed by appellant is whether appellee can establish that its contract was with the owner of the property without simultaneously defeating the priority of its lien. Appellant contends that in order to establish this element appellee would be required to rely on the same evidence of record which Rentenbach contends Southeastern cannot rely, namely, the Deed recorded August 14, 1985, conveying the property from Urban Properties to CCA-NC. This deed recites that Urban Properties is the successor in interest to CCA-F, information which is an essential link in both Rentenbach's and Southeastern's chain of title and thus establishes the validity and priority of their respective liens.

Appellant is mistaken. There is no question as to the validity of the deed of 14 August 1985. As of that date, CCA-NC became the legal owner of the Capital Club Building. The fact that the deed refers to Urban Properties as successor in interest to CCA-F does not save appellant from the consequences of its failure to rerecord a valid deed of trust in a timely fashion. The reference to Urban Properties and CCA-F does not bring the deed of trust filed 5 August 1985 into CCA-NC's chain of title. Even absent an explicit finding by the bankruptcy court, this court is persuaded that all of the elements necessary to establish a valid lien under N.C.Gen.Stat. Chap. 44A were met.

Appellant next contends that the bankruptcy court erred when it concluded that appellee's lien is superior to appellant's. Judge Small recognized that since appellee had actual notice of appellant's deed of trust the equities seem to favor appellant. However, relying principally on Schuman v. Roger Baker & Associates, 70 N.C.App. 313, 319 S.E.2d 308 (1984), he also recognized that North Carolina law favors appellee. Judge Small was not convinced that the Capital Club Building was the property of CCA-NC prior to the time that the property was deeded to it by Urban Properties on 14 August 1985. Further, Judge Small was not persuaded that appellee had constructive notice of the deed of trust held by appellant. While the deed recorded 14 August 1985 and the deed of trust recorded 5 August 1985 were listed in the grantor index under the names of both Urban Properties and CCA, Ltd., Judge Small noted that there was no mention in the index of whether the reference to CCA was to the North Carolina limited partnership ("CCA-NC") or to the Florida limited partnership ("CCA-F"). The 14 August deed conveying the property from Urban Properties to CCA-NC does not make any reference to the earlier deed of trust in favor of appellant. As such, Judge Small held that the deed of trust recorded on 5 August did not provide appellee with constructive notice.

As of 5 August 1985 Urban Properties owned the Capital Club Building but, as stated by Judge Small, "the deed of trust which was recorded did not convey Urban Properties' interest in that property, but instead purported to convey the interest of CCA-NC." Opinion at pp. 19–20. This interest, of course, was an interest which CCA-NC did not have. The deed was indexed with CCA as grantor and thus was recorded outside of CCA-NC's chain of title and "has the same effect on notice as no registration." Schuman, 70 N.C.App. at 316, 319 S.E.2d at 310.

Appellant argues that partnership law should dictate the effect of the deed of trust. Appellant contends that as of 5 August 1985 Urban Properties (as true owner of the property) actually executed the deed of trust through its general partner; thus, appellant contends this case is distinguishable from Schuman.

Appellant points out that the 5 August 1985 deed of trust, which lists CCA-NC as grantor, also reveals that Urban Properties, the actual owner of the property, executed that deed of trust as general partner. Directing the court's attention to N.C.Gen.Stat. §59-39(a) [FN4] appellant points out that the 5 August 1985 deed of trust was signed by Allen J. Koch, as the general partner of Urban Properties, and that "[b]y letter dated August 16, 1985, Mr. Koch advised [appellee] that he had authority as general partner … to sign for the partnership on any and all agreements." See Opinion at pp. 4–5; Trial Exhibit H. It is undisputed that Urban Properties was bound by the deed of trust signed by Koch. That conclusion, however, does not answer the question of the validity of the 5 August 1985 deed of trust with respect to anyone else.

Appellant urges this court to put a whole new gloss on title searches; that is, appellant would demand title searches be conducted in any number of directions depending on the existence of partnership arrangements. The overlay of partnership law is inappropriate here. Principles of partnership law do not aid in the resolution of this dispute and do not control its outcome; rather, the rules under N.C.Gen.Stat. Chapter 47 illustrate that Judge Small correctly concluded that the deed of trust filed 5 August 1985 was ineffective and therefore outside of CCA-NC's chain of title. As the courts of North Carolina have often said, "[N]o notice, however full or formal, will supply the want of registration...." Schuman, 70 N.C.App. at 316, 319 S.E.2d at 310.

Finally, appellant contends that the bankruptcy court erred in its calculation of the amount of appellee's lien. Appellant contends, inter alia, that Judge Small failed to consider the operation of Article 9.3.3. of the "General Conditions of the Contract for Construction" (supplement to the contract between appellee and the debtor). Appellant argues that this contract provision bars "most, if not all, of [appellee's] lien amounts." Article 9.3.3. provides, in part, that:

> The Contractor warrants that title to all Work, materials and equipment covered by an Application for Payment will pass to the Owner either by incorporation in construction or upon the receipt of payment by the Contractor, whichever occurs first, free and clear of all liens, claims, security interests or encumbrances....

Appellant argues that under this provision an application for payment by appellee warranted that it was free and clear of all, including its own, liens. It appears that appellant waived this argument when it failed to raise it at trial. The court has, nevertheless, considered this issue and is persuaded that Article 9.3.3., if construed as appellant urges, that is, as a complete waiver of statutory lien rights, is invalid and unenforceable under North Carolina law. Additionally, it appears to the court that this provision is intended to cover the liens of materialmen and subcontractors.

The order of the bankruptcy court is hereby AFFIRMED.

Chapter Summary

All governments have the power to impose taxes in order to pay for the services they provide to their citizens. In North Carolina, ad valorem taxes are imposed on both personal property and real property. The tax rate is based on the government's budgetary needs and the estimated value of property located within its geographic limits. Real property taxes are assessed based on the appraised value of the property. Properties are assessed every eight years. Governments have the power to enforce their tax regulations by placing liens on properties owned by delinquent taxpayers.

Assessments are similar to taxes except that they are placed against particular parcels that had benefitted from nearby improvements. When a party provides services or materials to a landowner, that party is entitled to enforce payment through a lien. Liens come in many different forms, from mechanic's liens to materialman's liens, but they share similar features. A lien is an encumbrance on property that prevents the property from changing hands. Liens can be perfected under North Carolina General Statutes and enforced through civil judgments, including auctioning off the property for the amount due.

Review Questions

1. Where do governments get the power to levy taxes?
2. What are ad valorem taxes?
3. What is the difference between a property tax assessment and an appraisal?
4. How is the tax rate calculated?
5. Are local and city governments authorized to conduct tax auctions for past due taxes?
6. How long after the last date of service can a person file a lien?
7. What is the difference between a mechanic's and a materialman's lien?
8. What is the homestead exclusion?
9. List and explain three types of properties that are exempt from tax calculations.
10. What are some of the methods that governments may use to enforce tax regulations?
11. How are the rules of priority different for tax liens as opposed to other types of encumbrances?
12. Why would a local government levy a special assessment against a property owner?
13. Can governments assess taxes against both real and personal property? Explain.
14. Under North Carolina law, who is entitled to file a lien?
15. What contents are required in a lien claim?
16. What effect do liens have on real estate transactions?
17. How long does a party have to file a lien after a service or material has been provided?
18. What is a judgment lien?
19. What is the difference between a lien and a judgment?
20. How often is a county required to reassess its property valuations?

Assignment

What is the tax rate in your county? Contact your local tax office and find out how the tax rate was arrived at. What is the county's budget for the year? Does the county anticipate receiving 100% of all taxes owed? Why or why not? What actions will the tax office take on delinquent taxes?

Terms and Phrases

Ad valorem taxes
Homestead Exclusion
Tax Rate
Reassessment
Tax Lien
Tax Lien Priorities
Assessments

Mechanic's Lien
Materialmen's Lien
Statutory Liens
Claim of Lien
Judgment Lien
Perfecting a Lien
Enforcing a Lien

Appendix

Catawba County Register of Deeds
Ruth Mackie, Registrar
www.co.catawba.nc.us

Alexander County Register of Deeds
Ben Hines, Registrar
www.co.alexander.nc.us

Cleveland County Register of Deeds
Bonnie E. Reece, Registrar
www.clevelandrod.com

Iredell County Register of Deeds
Brenda D. Bell, Registrar
www.co.iredell.nc.us

Mecklenburg County Register of Deeds
Judy Gibson, Recorder
http://meckrod.hartic.com

Caldwell County Register of Deeds
Lois Greene, Registrar
www.co.caldwell.nc.us

Lincoln County Register of Deeds
www.lincolncounty.org

Guilford County Register of Deeds
Katherine Lee Payne, Registrar
www.guilford.co.nc.us

Moore County Register of Deeds
Judy D. Martin, Registrar
www.moore.co.nc.us

Wake County Register of Deeds
Laura M. Riddick, Registrar
www.wake.co.nc.us

Watauga County Register of Deeds
Wanda C. Scott, Registrar
www.wataugacounty.org/deeds/personnel.shtml

Buncombe County Register of Deeds
Otto W. Debruhl. Registrar
www.buncombecounty.org

Orange County Register of Deeds
Joyce H. Pearson, Registrar
www.co.orange.nc.us/deeds

Chowan County Register of Deeds
Susan S. Roundtree, Registrar
www.co.chowan.nc.us/deeds.htm

Alleghany County Register of Deeds
Lizabeth Reeves Roupe, Registrar
www.alleghany.co.nc.us

Durham Co. Register of Deeds
Willie L. Covington, Registrar
www.co.durham.nc.us/rgds

Cumberland County Register of Deeds
George E. Tatum, Registrar
www.ccrod.org

Anson County Register of Deeds
Joanne S. Huntley, Registrar
www.anson.co.nc.us

Nash County Register of Deeds
www.deeds.co.nash.nc.us

Brunswick County Register of Deeds
Robert J. Robinson, Registrar
www.co.brunswick.nc.us/rod2.asp

Wilson County Register of Deeds
Celia W. Brinson. Registrar
www.wilson-co.com/rodwelcome.html

Forsyth Co. Register of Deeds
Dickie C. Wood, Registrar
www.co.forsyth.nc.us/RodD

Martin County Register of Deeds
Tina P. Manning, Registrar
www.ces.ncsu.edu/martin/departments/registerofdeeds/html

A. Settlement Statement

U.S. Department of Housing and Urban Development

OMB Approval No. 2502-0265

B. Type of Loan

1. ☐ FHA 2. ☐ FmHA 3. ☐ Conv. Unins.	6. File Number:	7. Loan Number:
4. ☐ VA 5. ☐ Conv. Ins.		8. Mortgage Insurance Case Number:

C. Note: This form is furnished to give you a statement of actual settlement costs. Amounts paid to and by the settlement agent are shown. Items marked "(p.o.c.)" were paid outside the closing; they are shown here for informational purposes and are not included in the totals.

D. Name & Address of Borrower:	E. Name & Address of Seller:	F. Name & Address of Lender:

G. Property Location:	H. Settlement Agent:	
	Place of Settlement:	I. Settlement Date:

J. Summary of Borrower's Transaction		K. Summary of Seller's Transaction	
100. Gross Amount Due From Borrower		**400. Gross Amount Due To Seller**	
101. Contract sales price		401. Contract sales price	
102. Personal property		402. Personal property	
103. Settlement charges to borrower (line 1400)		403.	
104.		404.	
105.		405.	
Adjustments for items paid by seller in advance		**Adjustments for items paid by seller in advance**	
106. City/town taxes to		406. City/town taxes to	
107. County taxes to		407. County taxes to	
108. Assessments to		408. Assessments to	
109.		409.	
110.		410.	
111.		411.	
112.		412.	
120. Gross Amount Due From Borrower		**420. Gross Amount Due To Seller**	
200. Amounts Paid By Or In Behalf Of Borrower		**500. Reductions In Amount Due To Seller**	
201. Deposit or earnest money		501. Excess deposit (see instructions)	
202. Principal amount of new loan(s)		502. Settlement charges to seller (line 1400)	
203. Existing loan(s) taken subject to		503. Existing loan(s) taken subject to	
204.		504. Payoff of first mortgage loan	
205.		505. Payoff of second mortgage loan	
206.		506.	
207.		507.	
208.		508.	
209.		509.	
Adjustments for items unpaid by seller		**Adjustments for items unpaid by seller**	
210. City/town taxes to		510. City/town taxes to	
211. County taxes to		511. County taxes to	
212. Assessments to		512. Assessments to	
213.		513.	
214.		514.	
215.		515.	
216.		516.	
217.		517.	
218.		518.	
219.		519.	
220. Total Paid By/For Borrower		**520. Total Reduction Amount Due Seller**	
300. Cash At Settlement From/To Borrower		**600. Cash At Settlement To/From Seller**	
301. Gross Amount due from borrower (line 120)		601. Gross amount due to seller (line 420)	
302. Less amounts paid by/for borrower (line 220)	( )	602. Less reductions in amt. due seller (line 520)	( )
303. Cash ☐ From ☐ To Borrower		603. Cash ☐ To ☐ From Seller	

Section 5 of the Real Estate Settlement Procedures Act (RESPA) requires the following: • HUD must develop a Special Information Booklet to help persons borrowing money to finance the purchase of residential real estate to better understand the nature and costs of real estate settlement services; • Each lender must provide the booklet to all applicants from whom it receives or for whom it prepares a written application to borrow money to finance the purchase of residential real estate; • Lenders must prepare and distribute with the Booklet a Good Faith Estimate of the settlement costs that the borrower is likely to incur in connection with the settlement. These disclosures are mandatory.

Section 4(a) of RESPA mandates that HUD develop and prescribe this standard form to be used at the time of loan settlement to provide full disclosure of all charges imposed upon the borrower and seller. These are third party disclosures that are designed to provide the borrower with pertinent information during the settlement process in order to be a better shopper.

The Public Reporting Burden for this collection of information is estimated to average one hour per response, including the time for reviewing instructions, searching existing data sources, gathering and maintaining the data needed, and completing and reviewing the collection of information.

This agency may not collect this information, and you are not required to complete this form, unless it displays a currently valid OMB control number.

The information requested does not lend itself to confidentiality.

Previous editions are obsolete

Page 1 of 2

form **HUD-1** (3/86)
ref Handbook 4305.2

L. Settlement Charges

			Paid From Borrowers Funds at Settlement	Paid From Seller's Funds at Settlement
700. Total Sales/Broker's Commission based on price $		@ % =		
Division of Commission (line 700) as follows:				
701. $	to			
702. $	to			
703. Commission paid at Settlement				
704.				
800. Items Payable In Connection With Loan				
801. Loan Origination Fee	%			
802. Loan Discount	%			
803. Appraisal Fee	to			
804. Credit Report	to			
805. Lender's Inspection Fee				
806. Mortgage Insurance Application Fee to				
807. Assumption Fee				
808.				
809.				
810.				
811.				
900. Items Required By Lender To Be Paid In Advance				
901. Interest from to	@$	/day		
902. Mortgage Insurance Premium for		months to		
903. Hazard Insurance Premium for		years to		
904.		years to		
905.				
1000. Reserves Deposited With Lender				
1001. Hazard insurance	months @$	per month		
1002. Mortgage insurance	months @$	per month		
1003. City property taxes	months @$	per month		
1004. County property taxes	months @$	per month		
1005. Annual assessments	months @$	per month		
1006.	months @$	per month		
1007.	months @$	per month		
1008.	months @$	per month		
1100. Title Charges				
1101. Settlement or closing fee	to			
1102. Abstract or title search	to			
1103. Title examination	to			
1104. Title insurance binder	to			
1105. Document preparation	to			
1106. Notary fees	to			
1107. Attorney's fees	to			
(includes above items numbers:		)		
1108. Title insurance	to			
(includes above items numbers:		)		
1109. Lender's coverage	$			
1110. Owner's coverage	$			
1111.				
1112.				
1113.				
1200. Government Recording and Transfer Charges				
1201. Recording fees: Deed $	; Mortgage $	; Releases $		
1202. City/county tax/stamps: Deed $	; Mortgage $			
1203. State tax/stamps: Deed $	; Mortgage $			
1204.				
1205.				
1300. Additional Settlement Charges				
1301. Survey to				
1302. Pest inspection to				
1303.				
1304.				
1305.				
1400. Total Settlement Charges (enter on lines 103, Section J and 502, Section K)				

Index